29.50

“... TO SET THEM IN ORDER ;”

"... TO SET THEM IN ORDER ;"

Some Influences of the Philadelphia Baptist Association Upon Baptists of America to 1814

Dr. James L. Clark

Supplemented with related historical material & edited by Terry Wolever

---

The Philadelphia Association Series

Particular Baptist Press
Springfield, Missouri

The main text of this publication
is from a dissertation presented to
The New Orleans Baptist Theological Seminary
New Orleans, Louisiana,
in 1948

Printed with the kind permission of

Mrs. Ruth Clark
Downers Grove, Illinois
&
The New Orleans Baptist Theological Seminary

Particular Baptist Press
2766 W. Weaver Road
Springfield, Missouri 65810

Typeset by Mrs. Brenda Reed
Strafford, Missouri

Clark, James L., 1908-1980

Dissertation originally entitled: *Some Influences of the Philadelphia Baptist Association Upon Baptists of America to 1814.* (1948)

ISBN 1-888514-11-6 (Acid-Free Paper)
1. Baptists—United States—History. 2. Philadelphia Baptist Association. 3. Title.

First Edition

Printed in the United States of America

Preface

The Philadelphia Baptist Association, organized on Saturday, July 27, 1707, was for 44 years the only such association in America until Oliver Hart of Pennsylvania and other Baptists from the North connected with the Philadelphia Association constituted the second Baptist association in America at Charleston, South Carolina on October 21, 1751.

These early Baptists who came over mainly from England and Wales left their mark in the decidedly Calvinistic character of the churches they established in the Middle Colonies. And, in the words of historian Henry C. Vedder,

> From 1742 the influence of the Philadelphia Association was paramount. Its missionary zeal was great; men closely connected with this body, and fully believing its confession, became preachers of the gospel in New England, New York and the Carolinas. By the close of the century, the Calvinistic party was in the ascendency everywhere.*

In many aspects of both doctrine and polity the Philadelphia Association set the standards of Baptist faith and practice in America. And there were other positive legacies left by the association, such as in the field of education, where the groundwork was laid for the formal training of Baptist ministers, through the establishment of seminaries and colleges.

In the following revised work, Dr. Clark examines some of these more enduring influences of this association on Baptist development in America, from the time

---

* Henry C. Vedder. *A History of the Baptists in the Middle States* (Philadelphia: American Baptist Publication Society, 1898). p. 93.

of its inception in 1707 until the formation of the General Missionary Convention in 1814.

If it is true that the signal mark of a good book is that of being a "thought breeder", then certainly this work by Dr. Clark would meet that qualification. Not only could the various influences presented herein be still further explored and developed, but there are other aspects of this association's influence which were not specifically treated in this study, yet also deserving of thoughtful consideration and careful investigation. One could, for example, research the influence of the Philadelphia Association on Baptist hymnody in America, beginning with Morgan Edwards' statement that the Welsh Tract church in Delaware "was the principal, if not sole, means of introducing singing...among the Baptists in the Middle States."*

Drawing on many sources, this historical and theological overview of the influences of this premier Baptist association in the New World will delight those interested in its development and the stability it provided amid the sometimes complex panorama of Baptist life in early America.

Terry Wolever

---

* Morgan Edwards. *Materials Towards a History of the Baptist in Delaware,* in *Materials Towards a History of the Baptists,* Vol. I, prepared by Eve B. Weeks and Mary B. Warren. (Danielsville, Georgia: Heritage Papers, 1984), p. 6.

Foreword

My indebtedness to many authors and sources is fully acknowledged in the footnotes throughout this presentation.

I am deeply grateful to Miss Nelle C. Davidson, Librarian of the New Orleans Baptist Theological Seminary and her staff for their friendly interest and valuable assistance. Furthermore, I am also grateful for the courteous service given me during May of 1947 at the University of Chicago Library and the Newberry Library both of Chicago, Illinois.

I am happy to acknowledge my indebtedness to the faculty of the New Orleans Baptist Theological Seminary for instruction and encouragement along the way. My chief obligation, however, is to Doctor C. Penrose St. Amant, my major professor, for the many valuable suggestions which he has offered in this study. His acute interest in the field of Christian history has been a source of inspiration and encouragement.

To my wife I am deeply indebted for the constant care she has exercised in typing and proofreading this work.

James Clark, 1948

List of Illustrations

CONTENTS

THE OLD BAPTIST CHURCH ON THE "MORRISTOWN GREEN"

Baptist meeting-house at Morristown, New Jersey. This 44' x 36' building was constructed in 1770 on a one-and-a-half acre lot purchased from Jonathan Hampton, situated about 85 miles northeast of Philadelphia. Morgan Edwards said of the congregation which met here that "it has been a nursery of ministers," in consequence of the many notable pastors in the association who had been members here.

Introduction

The purpose of this study is to find, present, and interpret the historical data concerning the influences of the Philadelphia Baptist Association[1] upon the Baptists of America.[2] These influences have been exerted in a number of ways. In this investigation the aim, however, is only to treat these influences as they had a bearing upon the education, doctrine, organization, and discipline of the Baptists of this country to 1814. These influences, of course, persisted beyond this date and some persist to this day. However, no effort is made in this study to treat the period beyond the organization of the Triennial Convention.[3]

---

[1] The term "Philadelphia Baptist Association" is the commonly used name of this body and is so used in the minutes. In historical accounts, however, the shortened form—Philadelphia Association—is used to designate it. We will follow this latter procedure. [In a formal letter to brethren in England dated May 16, 1762, the association officially designated itself as "The Association of Particular Baptist Churches annually held at Philadelphia." See A. D. Gillette, *Minutes of the Philadelphia Baptist Association*, p. 84—Editor].

[2] The term "America" will be used to denote the predominately English-speaking colonies along the Atlantic sea-board, which later became the original thirteen states of the United States, unless otherwise designated.

[3] So-called because it met once every three years. Its official name was "The General Missionary Convention of the Baptist Denomination in the United States of America for Foreign Missions." This body was organized May 18, 1814 in the First Baptist Church of Philadelphia, Pennsylvania, largely as a result of the efforts of Luther Rice.

This investigation is important because of the role played by the Philadelphia Association in the history of the Baptists of this country. This was the first Baptist association organized in the New World and it remained the only body of its kind in the colonies for forty-four years. During this period the Baptists in all parts of the country looked to it for advice and assistance. It, therefore, became the model for the other early associations and retained this distinction long after those associations began to appear in the colonies.[4]

The author has sought to use primary sources critically, allowing them in so far as possible, to speak for themselves. Several secondary sources[5] have also been used for the purpose of forming a background for this research. For the treatment at hand, however, mainly the available primary sources[6] have been relied upon.

---

[4] David Benedict, *A General History of the Baptist Denomination in America and Other Parts of the World* (New York: Lewis Colby and Company, 1848), p. 605.

[5] Albert Henry Newman, *A History of the Baptist Churches in the United States* (Philadelphia: American Baptist Publication Society, 1915), hereafter referred to as: Newman, *A History of Baptist Churches;* Thomas Armitage, *A History of the Baptists* (New York: Bryan, Taylor, & Co., 1887), hereafter referred to as: Armitage, *A History of the Baptists;* Henry C. Vedder, *A History of the Baptists in the Middle States* (Philadelphia: American Baptist Publication Society, 1898), hereafter referred to as: Vedder, *Baptists in the Middle States*; Henry C. Vedder, *A Short History of the Baptists* (The American Baptist Publication Society, 1941), hereafter referred to as: Vedder, *Short History*; John T. Christian, *A History of the Baptists of the United States* (Nashville, Tennessee: Broadman Press, 1945), hereafter referred to as: Christian, *A History of the Baptists;* Benedict, *General History, op. cit.*, (1848 ed.).

[6] See page 6 for the list of primary sources.

This is an absolute necessity for a worthy treatment of any historical subject.

The first work devoted entirely to the Philadelphia Association was published in 1851. It is not a history but a reprint of the minutes of this body for the first one hundred years, from 1707 to 1807.[7] It therefore contains an abundance of source material for the person who is content to delve into its pages. It remains a foundational work for a thorough investigation and treatment of the history of this body.

In 1944 Torbet's, *A Social History of the Philadelphia Baptist Association: 1707-1940,* was published. This was perhaps the first and only serious attempt by anyone to give a worthy historical account of any phase of the influence or activity of this body.[8] The author of the book, as the title suggests, proposed to give the social history of the Philadelphia Association and did so in an acceptable manner. The treatment of other aspects of this body's history is out of line with the main purpose of that work and, therefore, they are treated in a sketchy manner, when even referred to in his book.

---

[7] A. D. Gillette, *Minutes of the Philadelphia Baptist Association.* Hereafter referred to as: Gillette, *Minutes.*

[8] Robert G. Torbet, *A Social History of the Philadelphia Baptist Association: 1707-1940* (Philadelphia: Westbrook Publishing Company, 1944), hereafter referred to as: Torbet, *Social History of the Philadelphia Association.* [Since the time of the writing of this study, another very significant work by Francis W. Sacks, *The Philadelphia Baptist Tradition of Church and church Authority, 1707-1814* (Lewiston, N. Y.: The Edwin Mellen Press, 1989), has been published.—Editor]

An older work, Spencer's, *The Early Baptists of Philadelphia,*[9] gives a full account of the Baptists in the city and sometimes gives treatment of other churches in the vicinity of the city. It was not the intention of Spencer to give a history of the Philadelphia Association, however, in the development of his book he has given many significant quotations from valuable sources that have an important bearing upon the history of this body.

In the more general works the fullest historical treatment of this association is to be found in Vedder's, *A History of the Baptists in the Middle States.* But in this work, as the title indicates, the treatment of the Philadelphia Association is merely incidental. It is not a connected whole since it came in for treatment only as it had a bearing on the subject matter of the various chapters. There was very little effort made to relate this association to the Baptist organization or history beyond the boundaries of the Middle States,[10] as that was outside the range of Vedder's investigation.

Another work of great value to the investigator of any phase of early Baptist history in America is Benedict's *A General History of the Baptist Denomination in America and Other Parts of the World.*[11] A

---

[9] David Spencer, *The Early Baptists of Philadelphia* (Philadelphia: William Syckelmoore, 1877), hereafter referred to as: Spencer, *Early Baptists of Philadelphia*..

[10] New York, New Jersey, Pennsylvania and Delaware.

[11] Benedict, *General History* (1848 ed.). This work was first published in two volumes in 1813 under the same title (Boston: Manning & Loring, 1813), hereafter referred to as: Benedict, *General History* (1813 ed.). The later work was an abridgment of the older. It also brought the older up to date, i.e., to 1848. The two

more recent secondary work of importance to the student of Baptist history is Newman's, *A History of the Baptist Churches in the United States*. The treatment, however, in this last work merely touches the outer fringes of the activities of the Philadelphia Association.[12]

---

works taken together are indispensable to the Baptist historian.

[12] The following works treat the Philadelphia Association in a sketchy or outline manner. This is due in part, to the scope and purpose of each. Christian, *A History of the Baptists* ; Armitage, *A History of the Baptists* ; Vedder, *Short History.*

"...TO SET THEM IN ORDER :"

The most important primary sources used for this work are:

A. D. Gillette, editor. *The Minutes of the Philadelphia Baptist Association, from A. D. 1707, to A. D. 1807, Being the First One Hundred Years of Its Existence* (Philadelphia: A.B.P.S.: 1851).

Morgan Edwards, *Materials Towards a History of the Baptists in Pennsylvania,* (Philadelphia; Joseph Crukshank and Isaac Collins, 1770), hereafter referred to as: Edwards, *Baptists in Pennsylvania.*

Morgan Edwards, *Materials Towards a History of the Baptists in [New] Jersey* (Philadelphia: Thomas Dobson, 1792), hereafter referred to as: Edwards, *Baptists in [New] Jersey.*

John Rippon, editor. *The Baptist Annual Register* (London: 1790-1802), hereafter referred to as: Rippon, *Annual Register.*

Other primary sources, having an important bearing are:

A Compendium of the Minutes of the Warren Baptist Association From Its Formation in 1767 to the year 1825, Inclusive, hereafter referred to as: *Minutes of the Warren Association.*

John Asplund, *The Annual Register of the Baptist Denomination in North America* (Southhampton County, Virginia: 1791), hereafter referred to as: Asplund, *Annual Register.*

Minutes of the Warren Association-26th-71st Annual Meetings.

A Confession of Faith Put Forth by the Elders and Brethren of Many Congregations of Christians (Baptized upon Profession of Their Faith) In London and the Country. Seventh Philadelphia Edition (Philadelphia: John Dunlap, 1773).

Miss L. F. Greene, editor. *The Writings of the Late Elder John Leland, Including Some Events in His Life, Written by Himself with Additional Sketches* (New York: G. W. Wood, 1845), hereafter referred to as: *Writings of John Leland* .

Elhanan Winchester, *The Universal Restoration Exhibited in Four Dialogues Between a Minister and His Friend* (Bellows Falls, Vermont: Bill Blake & Co., 1819), hereafter referred to as: Winchester, *Universal Restoration.*

Other sources used in this study, will be given in the footnotes and the Bibliography.

Chapter One

The Background and Formation of the Philadelphia Baptist Association

The Philadelphia Baptist Association has exerted numerous influences upon the Baptists of this country. In order that one may have a proper perspective of this body and its influences, it is necessary to obtain some knowledge of the background and formation of this association, as well as the men who played a leading role in its history.

The churches which formed the Philadelphia Association were made up of members who had come over from England and Wales in the latter part of the seventeenth century. The freedom of religious opinion which had been instituted by William Penn was one of the leading factors in their settling in this area. Other determining factors, which led them to this vicinity, were cheap land and liberal terms of payment. Consequently, as early as 1683 some Baptists began to buy land and settle in and around Philadelphia.[1]

First Churches Founded

The first permanent Baptist church in Pennsylvania was the Pennepek, located on Pennepek Creek a

[1] Gillette, *Minutes,* p. 3.

This wooden structure served as the meeting-house for the incipient First Baptist Church, Philadelphia, from 1707-1731. The building had been erected by the Keithian Quakers in 1692. On March 15, 1707 the Baptists, by invitation of the Keithian Quakers "who were greatly reduced in numbers and were threatened with extinction," occupied this meeting-house "on Lagrange Place, Second Street above Market, just north of Christ Church." The building was dismantled in 1731, and a new brick structure erected in its place. The congregation would remain at the location until the removal to Broad and Arch Streets in 1856, a period of 149 years. The drawing is a copy of a sketch made toward the end of the eighteenth century and furnished by German Pietist historian Julius F. Sachse to William W. Keen who published it in his book, *The Bi-Centennial Celebration of the Founding of the First Baptist Church of the City of Philadelphia, 1698-1898* (Philadelphia: American Baptist Publication Society, 1899) p. 27. The same picture also appears in Ilsley Boone's *Elements in Baptist Development* (Backus Historical Society, 1913) p. 137, but is erroneously captioned as "the Pennepek church."

In 1707 a new 25-square-foot meeting-house was erected by the Pennepek congregation on land donated by Samuel Jones (1657-1722) one of its early pastors. The building was "repaired' in 1760. And in 1770 Morgan Edwards described it as "a neat stone building 33 feet by 30, with pews, galleries, and a stove. In one corner of it stands the pulpit, and the galleries in the opposite angles which is worth noticing, because hereby are remedied the usual inconveniences attending galleries in small places of worship." —*Materials Towards a History of the Baptists in Pennsylvania,* (Philadelphia, 1770), p. 6. In 1774 the building was "enlarged to 30 feet by 45 feet." In 1805 after further improvements, it was rebuilt as the now familiar stone structure above. The simple, graceful design of the building with its Palladian window in front is a fine example of meeting-house architecture of this period of our Early Republic. This simplicity well-suited the Baptists of the period, who for the most part disapproved of such things as stained glass and steeples. To illustrate this point, when the new First Baptist meeting-house was completed in Providence, R. I. in 1773, Congregationalist Ezra Stiles, on viewing the building with its lofty spire, commented, "It is the most costly and superb edifice of its kind in New England," to which he added concerning the Baptists, "This denomination have greatly changed their taste. Ten years ago they would not have suffered a steeple or bell to their meeting-house."—Sydney V. James. *Colonial Rhode Island, A History.* (New York: Charles Scribner's Sons, 1975) , p. 216.

few miles north of the city of Philadelphia, which later became the Lower Dublin Baptist Church.[2] Most of the members of this church came from Radnorshire, Wales, where they were baptized "upon profession of faith." Elias Keach, son of Benjamin Keach, the celebrated preacher of London, became their first preacher in 1687. Under the ministry of Keach, the church had several preaching stations in the adjacent country.[3]

The Pennepek church from its inception was fortunate in having very capable pastoral oversight. Abel Morgan became pastor of this church in 1711 and served it in an acceptable manner until his death in 1722. Other outstanding pastors of this church were, Jenkin Jones, Peter Peterson VanHorne and Samuel Jones.[4]

Three churches had been organized in nearby New Jersey by 1690, namely, Piscataqua, Middletown and Cohansie. Unfortunately very little is known about the time and circumstances which led to the organization of these churches; however, as early as 1686 Thomas Killingsworth was preaching to a group at Piscataqua. In 1687 when the church at Lower Dublin was organized they advised the group at Middletown likewise to organize. This is the first record of the Middletown

---

[2] Benedict says, "The first church of the denomination in the country was formed at a place called the Coldspring, in Buck's county, between Bristol and Trenton, by Thomas Dungan, who removed thither from Rhode-Island in 1684." On the same page, however, he adds, "The one gathered by Mr. Dungan was broken [disbanded] in 1702." Benedict, *General History* (1813 ed.), Vol. I, p. 580.

[3] Gillette, *Minutes,* p. 11. See also Benedict, *General History* (1848 ed.) p. 600.

[4] Benedict, *General History* (1813 ed.) Vol. I, pp. 583, 584.

church. The next record is of Elias Keach pastoring this church in 1690. The church at Cohansie was organized sometime before 1690.[5]

The church at Welsh Tract was organized in Pembrokeshire, South Wales in 1701, composed of sixteen persons. Thomas Griffith, one of the number, was an ordained minister and so was called to be pastor of the newly constituted church. On September 8th of the same year this congregation landed in Philadelphia and at the invitation of the Baptists of that area were settled near the Pennepek Creek church. However, in 1703 this body moved to what became known as the Welsh Tract in Delaware, where its members had purchased a tract of land totaling 30,000 acres.[6]

The Welsh Tract church, under the pastoral leadership of Griffith became one of the leading Baptist churches of the Middle Colonies. It was later instrumental in the other Baptist churches adopting the two articles of "Laying on of Hands" and "Singing Psalms." These articles were only practiced in the Welsh Baptist churches[7] at this time and the practice never became widespread in this country beyond the Philadelphia Association.

---

[5] Gillette, *Minutes,* pp. 13, 14, 15. Benedict, *General History,* (1848 ed.) p. 600.

[6] Benedict, *General History* (1813 ed.), Vol. II, pp. 4, 5.

[7] *Ibid.,* pp. 5,6. Gillette, *Minutes*, p. 15. For a good secondary account see, Newman, *A History of Baptist Churches*, pp. 202-209.

"...TO SET THEM IN ORDER :"

Formation of the Philadelphia Association

A. D. Gillette, the editor of the *Minutes of the Philadelphia Baptist Association from A. D. 1707 to A. D. 1807*, states that he found no trace in the available records of any confederation among the first churches of Pennsylvania and the Jerseys before 1707. At that time a general meeting was held at Lower Dublin in which it was decided to have messengers selected from the "most capable" men of the five Baptist churches, who would meet later that year for the purpose of consulting about the things "wanting in the churches and to set them in order."[8] Samuel Jones observed in the Associational Centennial Sermon that, "it originated in what they called general and sometimes yearly meetings."[9]

At the first annual meeting of the association the messengers from the churches decided that the business should be conducted during a period of not more than three days. The messengers at this meeting adopted and recommended to the churches a definite policy of caution concerning any unknown minister who came among them without a letter of introduction or recommendation. It further suggested that such a minister be required to prove himself before being asked to "preach among them." Another point discussed at this first meeting involved churches and members which were at variance. The decision required both the member and the individual to "acquiesce" fully to the decision of the assoc-

---

[8] Gillette, *Minutes*, p. 25. [It is from this statement that this present work derives its' title—Editor].

[9] *Ibid.*, p. 454.

iation's committee.[10] This ruling, however, seemingly was never diligently adhered to.

Valuable recruits came to the association during the years 1710 and 1711 from "South Wales and the West of England." Among these recruits were some preachers and laymen destined to play an important role in the establishment of the young association on a high level. They were experienced in the "affairs of churches and associations" in the countries from which they had come.[11] These veterans of church affairs at once became prominent leaders in the Philadelphia Association.

Growth of the Association

From its inception the Philadelphia Association was composed of churches from the colonies of Pennsylvania, New Jersey and Delaware. Great Valley in Pennsylvania was the first church to join this association after its organization.

The first record found in the minutes was that of two churches, Scotch Plains, New Jersey and Horseneck, Connecticut, admitted in 1747; however, other churches had been admitted to the association before that.[12] In

---

[10] *Ibid.*, p. 25.

[11] Gillette, *Minutes,* p. 25. The names of three men are given —Nathaniel Jenkins, John Burrows and Abel Morgan. All three were at one time or other pastors of the Pennepek church. Jenkins went to Cape May and later to Cohansie. Burrows went from Pennepek to Middletown. Morgan remained as pastor of the Pennepek church from 1711 until his death in 1722. *Ibid,* pp. 12-17.

[12] *Ibid.*, pp. 57, 93. The latter page has a Table which gives the date on which each church joined the Association.

1754 the messengers voted to receive the churches at Ketocton and Opekon in Virginia into the fellowship of the association. The following year two more churches from Virginia and one from Maryland were received into its fellowship.[13] In 1758 a church in New York was received into union with this association.[14] These facts corroborate the statement of Benedict, "At one time this association extended from Northeastown, in the State of New York, to Ketocton, in Virginia, a distance of about four hundred miles."[15] The association was gaining many churches near its center as well as extending its boundaries during this period, as can be seen by a "Table of the Churches" which was drawn up by Morgan Edwards in 1762. Edwards reveals that the Philadelphia Association contained twenty-nine churches, twenty-five of which reported a total of 1,418 members.[16]

The association had grown to fifty-three churches by 1791. That year, however, only forty-five churches reported to the association but their membership was

---

[13] *Ibid.*, pp. 71, 72. The churches received by this body in 1755 were: "the church constituted in Baltimore county, Maryland, and two churches constituted in the province of Virginia, viz., one in Fairfax county, Oketon Tract; the other at Mill Creek, Frederick county."

[14] *Ibid.*, p. 77. This church was "Bateman's Precincts, Dutchess county, in the province of New York."

[15] Benedict, *General History,* (1848 ed.), p. 607.

[16] Gillette, *Minutes,* p. 85. These churches were located in Connecticut, New York, New Jersey, Pennsylvania, Delaware, Maryland and Virginia. Only three of these churches had more than one hundred members, namely, Scotch Plains, New Jersey 134; Great Valley, Pennsylvania, 110; and Cohansie, New Jersey, 104.

3,253.[17] This year the association granted permission to four churches in New Jersey to join the New York Association.[18] The year before six churches in the New York area had been granted permission by this body to form a new association, however, some of their reports were listed in the Table of Churches for 1791.[19] In the report of the centennial year there were thirty-nine churches and all reported. The total membership listed in 1807 was 3,632.[20]

Associational Projects

During the one hundred and seven years covered by this study the Philadelphia Association promoted many projects which give some insight into the breadth of view and purpose of this body.

As early as 1731 it began the policy of soliciting financial aid from its churches in behalf of the struggling sister churches, when it asked aid for the Philadelphia church in its building program. The churches of the association in 1788 were informed that the church in Wilmington, Delaware was about to lose its building; and the church at Staten Island, New York was badly in need

---

[17] *Ibid.,* pp. 278-280.

[18] *Ibid.,* p. 271. The churches in New Jersey were: Scotch Plains, Canoe Brook, Piscataqua and Morristown.

[19] *Ibid.,* p. 256. The six churches in the vicinity of New York were: Stamford, Warwick, First and Second of New York, King Street, and Staten Island.

[20] *Ibid.,* pp. 447-449.

of a building.[21] Again in 1795 a plea was made to the churches for money to be sent to Savannah, Georgia with which to construct a church for the "blacks."[22] The following year an urgent plea was sent to all its churches to send immediate aid for the church at Shemokin, Pennsylvania, which needed to erect a building "as the winter season is coming on, and the people are entirely destitute of a suitable place to worship in."[23]

In 1750 an effort was made to establish a fund in the bank to be used for promotional activities. Again in 1766 the association voted to take offerings quarterly to be deposited by trustees; the interest only to be used for the "support of ministerial traveling on the errand of the churches." John Gano, in 1774 received the interest due on this fund "towards defraying his expenses in traveling

---

[21] *Ibid.*, pp. 32, 238.

[22] *Ibid.*, p. 307. [This is in reference to the First African Baptist church in Savannah. Under the leadership of pastor Andrew Bryan, this congregation experienced tremendous growth, building 3 successive meeting-houses in the decade of the 1790's. The actual entry in the minutes reads: "On application for assistance to build a meeting-house in Savannah, Georgia, large enough to admit some hundreds of blacks in the galleries, we recommend to the churches to make subscriptions or collections for the above purpose, and to forward the amount to Mr. Ustick by the 20th of November next; which Mr. Ustick is requested to convey by the first opportunity; together with a letter of condolence to the above-mentioned blacks, and our ardent wishes that Providence may interfere in their favor, at least so far, that their masters may be moved to allow them the free enjoyment of public and private worship."—Editor]

[23] Gillette, *Minutes*, p. 318. A financial report is given on the last two appeals: $71.89 for the church in Savannah and $60.02 for the church in Shemokin, Pennsylvania. *Ibid.*, p. 343.

the last year."[24] In these money-raising projects, however, the church members seem never to have been as liberal with their gifts as the leaders were in their plans.

The Philadelphia Association also made use of the printed page for informative as well as for doctrinal purposes. This body decided in 1738 to have a catechism printed and for its supervision appointed Jenkin Jones and John Holmes. Another printing of this pamphlet was subscribed to in 1747.[25] In 1742 this association provided for the "reprinting" of an edition of *A Confession of Faith, Put Forth by the Elders and Brethren of Many Congregations of Christians, (Baptized Upon Profession of Their Faith), In London and the Country* with a brief treatise on "Church Discipline" annexed. This edition was printed in the year 1743 on the press of Benjamin Franklin in Philadelphia.[26] A "treatise in vindication of believers baptism" was printed by subscription in 1746. Samuel Jones, David Jones and Burgiss Allison were appointed in 1788 to draw up a "collection of Psalms and Hymns for the use of the associated churches."[27] This association

---

[24] *Ibid.,* pp. 65, 97, 142. The amount received by Gano was 12 pounds.

[25] *Ibid.,* pp. 39, 57.

[26] W. J. McGlothlin, *Baptist Confessions of Faith* (Philadelphia: American Baptist Publication Society, 1911), pp. 295-296, hereafter referred to as: McGlothlin, *Confessions;* Gillette, *Minutes,* p. 46. [See Appendix A for a facsimile reprint of the 1743 sixth edition of this confession.]

[27] Gillette, *Minutes,* pp. 54, 239. [The title of this hymnal was *A Selection of Psalms and Hymns, Done Under Appointment of the Philadelphia Association* (Philadelphia: R. Aitken & Sons, 1790). It was reprinted in 1801, 1807, and 1819.—Editor]

began to print its minutes through the efforts of Morgan Edwards.[28]

Another project, which was taken seriously by this body, was that of securing supplies for the pastorless and destitute churches of its number. This business came up for consideration in most of its annual meetings.[29] The churches were encouraged to share their ministers with these destitute churches.

Missionary Outlook of This Association

The early missionary outlook of this body was concerned with domestic evangelization only. This remained true for many years after its organization. In 1770 Morgan Edwards proposed that this body appoint an evangelist to travel and preach in the colonies. He maintained this would help to bring about a colonial-wide organization of the Baptists.[30] The following year this proposal was brought before the association and it was "universally agreed that such an appointment promised much advantage to the Baptist interests."

---

[28] Jonathan Davis, *History of the Welsh Baptists, from the year Sixty-Three to the Year One Thousand Seven Hundred and Seventy* (Pittsburgh: D. M. Hogan, 1835) p. 80 cites William Rogers, "Funeral Sermon on Morgan Edwards," hereafter referred to as: Davis, *Welsh Baptists.*

[29] Gillette, *Minutes* , pp. 129, 130, 136, 141, 149, 156, 170. These pages alone are sufficient to show the importance of this business to the Philadelphia Association.

[30] Edwards, *Baptists in Pennsylvania,* Vol. I, "Preface," p. ii.

Edwards was chosen for the office, which "he accepted on the conditions then specified."[31]

John Gano was appointed to fill this office when Edwards declined it in 1773. Gano accepted the appointment and as a result of his report to the association at its next meeting the clerk concluded, "it appears he has been indefatigable in his labors, and that a minister, traveling annually, according to the plan proposed, may answer very valuable purposes."[32]

Gano was the last evangelist appointed by the Philadelphia Association. Nothing is said about the cause for the discontinuation of this project. It is possible, however, that the unrest which was prevalent at this time in the colonies may have been the cause.

In 1772 David Jones reported to the association, which met at New York, that he "intends to visit the western tribes of Indians the next Winter." At his request the association voted "to recommend his case to the respective churches" for financial aid with which to pay an interpreter.[33] An observer says that Jones, "like an apostle amongst the Gentiles, was to set out on the first of this month, at his own charges" to preach the gospel to the Indians between the Ohio and Mississippi

---

[31] Gillette, *Minutes,* p. 119. Those nominated for the office were John Gano, Benjamin Miller, Samuel Jones, David Jones, and Morgan Edwards.

[32] *Ibid.,* p. 135.

[33] *Ibid.,* p. 124.

Rivers. This undertaking of Jones was likely the first of its kind among the Baptists.[34]

The Philadelphia Baptist Mission Society, which was under the sponsorship of the Philadelphia Association, sent T. G. Jones to Ohio. He was instrumental in organizing a "new Baptist church near the town of Lisbon." This body rejoiced that its missionary had led believers "into waters where this holy ordinance was never administered before."[35]

This association seems to have had little consideration for foreign missions before 1794, when William Rogers made a report to the Philadelphia Association on information he had received from William Carey in India. Consequently the association reported to the churches that, "it desired that all donations for the propagation of the Gospel among the Hindoos" be forwarded to Rogers.[36] The following year the churches were "advised to make

---

[34] Reuben Aldridge Guild, *Life, Times, and Correspondence of James Manning and the Early History of Brown University* (Boston: Gould and Lincoln, 1864), pp. 204, 205. The author cites a letter sent by James Manning to Samuel Stennett, dated November 13, 1772. This work will hereafter be referred to as: Guild, *Life of James Manning.* [For an account of Jones' tour in Ohio, see David Jones, *A Journal of Two Visits Made to Some Nations of Indians on the West Side of the River Ohio, in the Years 1772 and 1773.* (Burlington, 1795). Facsimile reprint of the 1865 edition, *With Biographical Notice of the Author,* by Horatio Gates Jones, published by Galleon Press, Fairfield, Washington, 1973. —Editor].

[35] Gillette, *Minutes,* p. 431.

[36] *Ibid.,* p. 298.

collections for the missionaries to the East Indies, and forward the same to Dr. Rogers."[37]

In 1801 Rogers read letters to the association from Carey and from "Dr. Hawes of England respecting promising appearances among the Hottentots." As a result of these letters the "Association exults in every prospect of the success of the gospel, and wish the missionaries God speed."[38] In 1805 when Rogers gave his report on the "progress of the Bengal mission" it is recorded that it "gave peculiar satisfaction" to those present.[39] In 1808 this body expressed its regret "that vigorous and systematic opposition" had been made to the missionary cause in India.[40]

As can be seen, William Rogers took an acute interest in the cause of foreign missions. He also kept the subject before the Philadelphia Association, which in turn became keenly interested in the subject. This body did not, however, organize a foreign missionary society until 1813, when it organized The Philadelphia Baptist Society for Foreign Missions.[41]

---

[37] *Ibid.*, p. 307.

[38] *Ibid.*, p. 360.

[39] *Ibid.*, p. 412.

[40] "American Baptists," *The Baptist Magazine* (London: 1809), p. 469.

[41] *The First Annual Report of The Baptist Board of Foreign Missions For The United States* (Philadelphia: William Fry, Printer, 1815), p. 23.

Associational Leaders

A background study of this association would be incomplete without some notice being taken of its leaders. It will be necessary, however, to give only a brief consideration of its outstanding leaders, since a full consideration of these would be out of line with our present purpose and scope.

The leaders of the early period, who stood above all others were Thomas Griffith, pastor of the Welsh Tract church and Abel Morgan, pastor of the Pennepek church. The former traveled and preached to all the first churches of this association and counseled with their pastors and leaders on various issues that arose in that day.[42] The latter was also a prominent leader, both as a pastor and writer. He prepared the first Welsh Concordance of the Bible that was ever published. He was brother to Enoch Morgan who later became pastor of the Welsh Tract church. His life of service was cut short by his untimely death in 1722.[43]

These men were followed by Jenkin Jones of Pennepek (and later of Philadelphia) and Benjamin Griffith of Montgomery, Pennsylvania. Jones was a capable preacher and was eminent in the councils of this body. According to Morgan Edwards, Griffith was not considered a great preacher, although a writer and counselor of no mean rank. He prepared the treatise on

---

[42] Benedict, *General History,* (1813 ed.), Vol. II, pp. 5, 6.

[43] "Abel Morgan," in Annals of the American Pulpit, Vol. VI, *The Baptists,* edited by William B. Sprague (9 Vols.; New York: Robert Carter & Brothers, 1860), p. 33, hereafter referred to as, Sprague, *The Baptists.* Gillette, *Minutes,* pp. 25, 455.

Church Discipline, which was adopted by the Philadelphia Association in 1743.[44] He wrote an "Essay on the Powers and Duties of an Association," which was adopted by this body in 1749 and incorporated in its minutes that year.[45] He also prepared "A Brief Narrative of the Churches Holding Believer's Baptism, in Pennsylvania and the Jerseys" in 1758. This work was placed in the minute book of the association.[46] Griffith was a half brother of Abel and Enoch Morgan.[47]

During this early middle period, the outstanding leaders were Isaac Eaton, Benjamin Miller, Peter Peterson VanHorne and John Gano. Eaton was pastor of the Baptist church in Hopewell, New Jersey from 1748 to his death in 1772. He was the founder and head of the Hopewell Academy or Latin Grammar School.[48] Miller, pastor of the Baptist church in Scotch Plains, New Jersey, VanHorne, pastor of the Pennepek Baptist church and John Gano formed what might be called the missionary triumvirate of the Philadelphia Association. This group made several trips into Virginia and North Carolina in behalf of this association to assist needy

---

[44] Gillette, *Minutes,* p. 46.

[45] *Ibid.,* pp. 60-63.

[46] *Ibid.,* pp. 11-24.

[47] "Benjamin Griffiths," Sprague, *The Baptists,* p. 38. Elsewhere the "s" is left off. This book will follow the latter practice.

[48] Isaac Backus, *A History of New England with Particular Reference to the Denomination of Christians Called Baptists* (Newton, Massachusetts: Published by the Backus Historical Society, 1871), Vol. II, p. 346, hereafter referred to as: Backus, *A History of New England.*

churches.[49] Gano especially was concerned with the spiritual welfare of the people and churches of all areas of this country. He made numerous preaching tours into the South and New England. In 1788 he settled in Kentucky where he later died in 1804.[50]

Later in this same period Samuel Jones, pastor of the church at Pennepek came to the front as a leader of this group. He served in various positions of responsibility for more than fifty years.[51] Morgan Edwards came to this country in 1761 to take over the pastorate of the First Baptist Church of Philadelphia. He was also a leader of note. Among other things he caused the leaders of this body to become more concerned about preserving its history. In his efforts to find and to preserve the available sources of Baptist history Edwards rendered valuable service not only to the Philadelphia Association but to Baptists in general.[52]

---

[49] Gillette, *Minutes*, p. 72. Benedict, *General History* (1848 ed.), pp. 642, 643, 682.

[50] Backus, *A History of New England,* p. 494; *Minutes,* p. 408. For a fuller treatment of Gano see *Biographical Memoirs of the Late Rev. John Gano of Frankfort* (Kentucky) *Formerly of the City of New York Written Principally by Himself.* (New York: Printed by Southwick and Hardcastle, 1806), hereafter referred to as: *Memoirs of John Gano.* [*The Biographical Memoirs of the Late Rev. John Gano* have been published complete as the second chapter of *The Life and Ministry of John Gano,* Vol. I, by Terry Wolever, Particular Baptist Press, Springfield, Missouri, 1998.]

[51] Gillette, *Minutes,* pp. 89 ff.

[52] *Ibid.,* pp. 82 ff. In the associational meeting of 1761 he was appointed to serve on four committees and from that day forth he took a prominent part in the activities of this body. See especially p. 248; Benedict, *General History* (1848 ed.) p. 606.

Three of the prominent leaders of this association during the latter part of this period—William Rogers, Thomas Ustick, and Burgiss Allison—were graduates of Rhode Island College.[53] Rogers was for a short period of time pastor of the First Baptist Church of Philadelphia, from 1772 to 1775, after which he served as professor of English at the University of Pennsylvania. During his entire stay in Philadelphia he took an active part in the affairs of the Philadelphia Association.[54] Ustick became pastor of the same church in 1782 and served it and the association in a capable manner until his death in 1805.[55] Allison was pastor of the church in Jacob's Town, New Jersey. Here he also conducted an academy. Edwards said that Allison "approaches towards an universal genius beyond any of my acquaintance."[56]

Relations with Other Associations

Since the Philadelphia Association stood alone in the colonies for more than four decades and covered such a wide area it could easily have been jealous of the possible encroachments of new associations upon its prestige. However, it seems that no such feelings ever arose. When four churches in Virginia requested

---

[53] Guild, *Life of James Manning,* pp. 88, 194.

[54] Gillette, *Minutes,* pp. 130 ff.

[55] *Ibid.,* pp. 181 ff. Ustick in some accounts is written "Eustick," but in this work the original form is used. [The church was without a settled pastor for most of the Revolutionary War years.—Editor].

[56] Edwards, *Baptists in [New] Jersey,* Vol. II, p. 122; Gillette, *Minutes,* p. 465.

permission to organize themselves into an association this body gladly gave its approval to the request "provided they go on the same plan, and hold union with us."[57] When news came of the efforts to organize an association in New England in 1766 it sent encouragement to the messengers met in Warren, Rhode Island.[58] In 1789 it recommended that the churches in the New York area consider the advisability of forming themselves into an association, consequently two years later the Warwick and New York Associations were organized in that vicinity.[59]

The relations of this association with other associations and churches seem always to have been cordial. At least the author has been unable to find one primary source giving any instances of this body trying to exercise authority or coercion over any kindred church or body. On this point Benedict says, "I do not find that it was ever complained of for infringing on the independency of any church in its connection."[60]

---

[57] Gillette, *Minutes,* p. 95. William Fristoe, *A Concise History of the Ketocton Baptist Association* (Staunton, Virginia: William Gilman Lyford, 1808), p. 7, hereafter referred to as: Fristoe, *Ketocton Association.*

[58] Guild, *Life of James Manning,* pp. 74, 76, 77.

[59] Benedict, *General History* (1848 ed.), pp. 543, 546, 547; Gillette, *Minutes,* p. 248. The Warwick Baptist Church had joined the Philadelphia Association in 1769 under the name Goshen. *Ibid.,* p. 108.

[60] Benedict, *General History* (1813 ed.), Vol. I, p. 596. For an opposite view see G. W. Paschal, "Shubal Stearns", *The Review and Expositor,* XXXVI: 43, 44, January, 1939, hereafter referred to as, Paschal, *Shubal Stearns.*

In 1766 the subject came before the Philadelphia Association concerning relations with the new association in Virginia and the one proposed in New England. At that time it was decided that a "yearly intercourse" should be maintained between these two associations by "letters and messengers." This body in 1770 agreed, "That messengers from other associations are members of this."[61] As a result of this decision these visiting messengers were sometimes elected to places of responsibility by the host association.[62]

The messengers and others at the association in 1771 had "great joy and entertainment" from reading a letter sent hither by Samuel Harris. This letter reported on the rapid progress that had been made in Virginia and the Carolinas during the preceding year. The report of this year to the churches was "we have good news" from the associations.[63] This body took a keen interest in the

---

[61] Gillette, *Minutes,* pp. 97, 112.

[62] *Ibid.,* pp. 123, 227, 254, 369. James Manning, from the Warren Association was once elected clerk (1772) and twice elected moderator (1787, 1790) of the Philadelphia Association. Hezekiah Smith, also from the Warren Association, was elected moderator of this association in 1802.

[63] *Ibid.,* pp. 120, 121. Asplund, *Annual Register,* p. 49. Asplund stated that the Philadelphia Association corresponded with "Warren, Shaftsbury, Danbury, Charleston, Ketocton, the general committee in Virginia and England, and sometimes with Stonington and Salisbury associations both by letters and delegates." Richard B. Cook, *The Early and Later Delaware Baptists* (Philadelphia: American Baptist Publication Society, 1880), p. 92, hereafter referred to as: Cook, *Delaware Baptists.* The Delaware Association dropped the Philadelphia Association as a corresponding body in 1834.

spiritual progress of the Baptists in all the colonies. It also had an acute interest in the physical needs of Baptists and especially of those suffering persecution in New England.[64]

This association aided needy Baptist churches in every direction and encouraged the formation of kindred associations. It was also a fruitful source of capable ministers for the Baptists in all sections of the country. These contributions of this body help to account for the many influences it was able to exert upon the Baptists of America.

Southampton Baptist meeting-house, Bucks County, Pennsylvania. This 45' x 35' building replaced the original structure.

---

[64] Backus, *A History of New England,* p. 200; Gillette, *Minutes,* pp. 459, 460.

Chapter Two

The Influence of the Philadelphia Baptist Association Upon Baptist Education in America

---

The influence of the Philadelphia Association upon Baptist education in America is of great importance. In this emphasis it has made a worthy contribution to the history of the Baptists in this country.

The first ministers of this association came to America either from England or Wales. In those countries they had an opportunity to at least the rudiments of education. The early leaders of this group were Thomas Griffith, Elisha Thomas and Enoch Morgan, all from Wales.[65] Griffith seems to have been the best trained of this group. Three other capable leaders who came from England and Wales in 1710 were Nathaniel Jenkins, John Burrows and Abel Morgan. These men were capable men and had been trained, at any rate, in "church affairs."[66] Abel Morgan (1673-1722) appears to have been the most capable of all these early men. He translated the *London Confession of Faith* into Welsh in 1716. He also prepared the first Welsh Concordance of the Bible ever published.[67]

---

[65] Benedict, *General History,* (1813 ed.), Vol. II, p. 4.

[66] Gillette, *Minutes,* p. 25.

[67] Benedict, *General History,* (1813 ed.), Vol. II, p. 6."Abel Morgan," in Sprague, *The Baptists,* p. 33.

Another work prepared by this man was a treatise on Church Discipline, however, he died before it could be published.[68]

Of all the earlier ministers who came from England and Wales more is known about Morgan Edwards than any other. He was educated at the Baptist Seminary of Bristol, England, which was at that time under the direction of Bernard Foskett. Edwards (1722-1795) was an ardent champion for the cause of an educated Baptist ministry in America throughout his life.[69]

Early Interest in Education

The early interest of this association in education was increased by word from Thomas Hollis, a business man in England and a Baptist, that he had established four scholarships at Harvard College for the education of

---

[68] Sewall S. Cutting, *Historical Vindications: A Discourse on the Province and Uses of Baptist History, with Appendixes, Containing Historical Notes and Confessions of Faith* (Boston: Gould and Lincoln, 1859), p. 200, hereafter referred to as: Cutting, *Historical Vindications.* Benjamin Griffith, in the Preface to his *Treatise on Church Discipline* adopted in 1742, in acknowledging his sources wrote, "having also found a manuscript left by my brother Abel Morgan." Morgan was his half brother.

[69] Benedict, *General History,* (1848 ed.), p. 602. Morgan Edwards lived in this country from 1761 to his death in 1795. Spencer, *Early Baptists,* pp. 96-98. Spencer cites William Roger's "Funeral Sermon of Morgan Edwards," in which he gives Edwards' views on education.

"Baptist Youth" for the ministry,[70] and asked for cooperation in the selection of worthy young men for the first vacancy. Consequently in their annual meeting of 1722 the association appointed Abel Morgan to attend to this matter and requested the churches "to make inquiry among themselves" for the purpose of discovering any "young persons hopeful for the ministry, and inclinable for learning." A report was to be made to Morgan concerning these aspiring youths as soon as possible, so that he could make the proper arrangements with "the academy" on the account of Hollis.[71] This arrangement, however, did not work out satisfactorily for the Baptists.[72]

After the failure of the plan of Hollis the Baptists did little about educational institutions. Benjamin Miller, after his conversion, "studied under a Mr. Biram."[73] John Gano was for a short period under the tutorship of a Presbyterian preacher, but this setup did not prove successful, since he and his teacher were too much inclined to debate points of doctrine than to discuss the rules of rhetoric. However, Gano affirms that this was his teacher's fault. Later Gano had an opportunity to matriculate at the College of New Jersey,[74] but he never

---

[70] Christian, *A History of the Baptists,* Vol. II, p. 157. See also Samuel Eliot Morison, *Three Centuries of Harvard 1636-1936* (Cambridge: Harvard University Press, 1936), pp. 68, 69, for a discussion of the Hollis Scholarships and the use made of them, hereafter referred to as, Morison, *Harvard.*

[71] Gillette, *Minutes,* p. 27.

[72] Morison, *Harvard,* pp. 68, 69.

[73] Edwards, *Baptists in [New] Jersey,* Vol. II, p. 71.

[74] Now Princeton University.

did.[75] James Manning and Hezekiah Smith studied in this school and graduated in the class of 1762.[76]

Isaac Eaton's Latin Grammar School

The honor of being the first Baptist to establish a school for "higher education" of young men in America goes to Isaac Eaton (1725-1772), who became the pastor of the Baptist church in Hopewell, New Jersey in the year 1748, and continued there until 1772.[77] With the "encouragement" and backing of the Philadelphia Association he established a Latin Grammar School in Hopewell "for the promotion of learning."[78] This school was established primarily to educate young men for the ministry but there was training for other professions as well. Under the leadership of Eaton this school continued to function for eleven years, from 1756-1767. It was destined to supply the Baptist denomination with some of her most competent leaders for the remainder of that period.[79]

---

[75] *Memoirs of John Gano,* pp. 37-39. Gano says, "The gentleman, under whom I studied, was a Presbyterian minister, from the State of Connecticut. He had, at that time, a number of youth studying the classics." [Gano intended to enter the senior class at the college, but was "taken sick" early in his studies. He wrote that "the doctors and my friends advised me to take a journey, and relax my mind from study" (Memoirs, p. 37), which advice he heeded.—Editor]

[76] Guild, *Life of James Manning,* p. 31-32.

[77] Backus, *A History of New England,* Vol. II, p. 346.

[78] Gillette, *Minutes,* pp. 74, 464, 465.

[79] Guild, *Life of James Manning,* pp. 41, 42. Guild lists the following as prominent leaders from this school: James Manning, Samuel Jones, Hezekiah Smith, Isaac Skillman, David Thomas,

The Hopewell school succeeded beyond the fondest expectations of her most loyal friends and promoters. A number of the churches of the Philadelphia Association were served by able ministers from this academy. This fact aided materially in the breakdown of prevalent prejudices on the part of some of the Baptists against higher learning. It convinced them of "the great usefulness of human literature to more thoroughly furnish the man of God for the most important work of the gospel ministry."[80] This served also to build up a widespread desire on the part of the leaders of this body to establish a Baptist college in order to train promising young men for a wider field of usefulness both in the ministry and in the learned professions.[81]

The Philadelphia Association was enthusiastic and loyal in supporting this school from its inception. The churches of this association raised a fund of four hundred

---

John Davis, William Williams, Robert Keith, Charles Thompson, David Jones, John Sutton, David Sutton, James Talbot, John Blackwell, Joseph Powell, William Worth, and Levi Bonnel. From Edwards it is found that some became lawyers and physicians and that one, David Howell, became a member of Congress. See Edwards, *Baptists in [New] Jersey,* pp. 49, 50.

[80] Reuben Aldridge Guild, "Charter of Brown University," *Baptist Quarterly,* IX:168, 169, April 1875. The above quotation was taken from an unsigned paper found among the papers of David Howell. In a footnote Guild says, "The author was undoubtedly Edwards." *Ibid,* p. 168. See also Henry M. King, "Education Among the Baptists of This Country During the Last Hundred Years," *Baptist Quarterly,* X:449, October, 1876.

[81] Guild, *loc. cit.*

pounds for its support.[82] In the annual meeting of 1756 the messengers of this sponsoring association appointed four of their ministers to inspect the school with Isaac Eaton.[83] This body also solicited and won the support and best interests of the Charleston Association for the Hopewell institution.[84]

Other Academies

The next academy established for the education of Baptist young men, with the favor of the Philadelphia Association, was located at Lower Dublin, Pennsylvania. It was founded by Samuel Jones, who had received his early education at the Hopewell Academy and in 1762 graduated from the College of Philadelphia with the degree of Master of Arts. Many men useful in the ministry and other "learned professions"[85] were trained in this school, which was operated for twenty-nine years or more under the competent leadership of Jones.[86]

---

[82] Gillette, *Minutes,* pp. 76, 77. See also Vedder, *Baptists in the Middle States,* pp. 207-209.

[83] Gillette, *Minutes,* p. 74. Those appointed were: Abel Morgan, Isaac Stellè, Abel Griffith, and Peter Peterson Van Horne.

[84] Guild, *Life of James Manning,* p. 41.

[85] Gillette, *Minutes* , p. 465. See also I. M. Allen, editor, *The Triennial Baptist Register* (Philadelphia: Baptist General Tract Society, 1836), p. 53.

[86] John A. Broadus, "American Baptist Ministry 100 Years Ago," *The Baptist Quarterly,* Vol. IX:7, January, 1875. Cf. also Benedict, *General History* (1848 ed.), p. 600; Gillette, *Minutes,* pp. 246, 254, 255.

One of the early students of this academy, Burgiss Allison, proceeded to Rhode Island College and after having completed his work in that institution, returned to the Philadelphia Association. He opened an academy in 1778 at Bordenton, New Jersey and operated it successfully for many years. In 1792 Morgan Edwards said of this school, "The academy is well furnished with books, globes, glasses and other pieces of apparatus for experiments."[87]

William Staughton was principal of this school in 1798, however, shortly afterward he was made principal of another academy, at Burlington, New Jersey, which he accepted, thinking it would "be more friendly to his temporal interests and ministerial usefulness." At that time there were "about eighty young gentlemen enrolled in this academy.[88]

Plans for a College

When the subject of organizing a Baptist college was first brought before the Philadelphia Association some laughed at the thought, some discouraged it, and others threatened open opposition to the move. This grew out of what Morgan Edwards called "an unhappy pre-

---

[87] Gillette, *Minutes,* pp. 142, 149, 155, 465; Edwards, *Baptists in [New] Jersey,* pp. 122, 123.

[88] Rippon, *Annual Register,* Vol. III, pp. 122, 267. In his book, *Fifty Years Among the Baptists* (New York: Sheldon & Company, 1860), p. 46, (hereafter referred to as: Benedict, *Fifty Years),* David Benedict pays a tribute to Staughton and then says of all Baptist ministers, "Their houses were then the schools of the prophets, and they cheerfully became their gratuitous teachers and models."

judice against learning."[89] In the face, however, of the growing success of the Hopewell Academy the hands of this association "were strengthened" and "their hearts encouraged" to look about for a suitable location at which to establish this college. At first this body looked favorable toward the southern colonies for this site, since there were not many colleges in that area. But some members of the association had lately visited in Rhode Island and found that it had no schools or colleges. It was pointed out by these individuals that the Baptists had grown apace there in late years and that many of the officials of the colony were Baptists.[90] These facts made it evident to the messengers that this was the proper place to found a Baptist college, "wherein education might be promoted, and superior learning obtained, free of any sectarian religious tests."[91]

As soon as the association had settled satisfactorily upon the location at which to erect the Baptist college they turned their attention to the proper man to lead the school. After some investigation "James Manning, who took his first degree in New Jersey in September of 1762, was esteemed a suitable leader in this important work."[92] Morgan Edwards said, "Manning is an excellent man,

---

[89] William R. Staples, *Annals of the Town of Providence, from Its First Settlement, to the Organization of the City Government, in June, 1832* (Providence, Rhode Island: Printed by Knowles and Vose, 1843), p. 519. Edwards is quoted at length on this subject.

[90] Reuben Aldridge Guild, "Charter of Brown University," pp. 168, 169, cites an unsigned article which he attributes to Morgan Edwards.

[91] Backus, *A History of New England,* p. 137.

[92] *Ibid.*

both as to person, parts, learning and piety."[93] The choice of Manning proved to be a happy choice. Before going to the College of New Jersey, Manning had finished preparatory work at Hopewell under the direction of Isaac Eaton. After the completion of his work at the above-mentioned college he made an extensive trip through the southern colonies for the purpose of better acquainting himself with the spiritual needs of the people and with the conditions of the Baptists in that area and "to prepare himself for more widely-extended usefulness."[94]

While on a voyage to Halifax, in July, 1763, he stopped off in Newport, Rhode Island, and laid the plans of the Philadelphia Association before Samuel Ward, John Gardner, Josias Lyndon and other "Baptist gentlemen and friends."[95] These men thought the plans for a Baptist college were well founded and readily gave their consent to enter upon the prosecution of this noble undertaking.[96]

The next important step was to formulate a charter for the proposed institution. After the matter was discussed, Josias Lyndon and Colonel Job Bennet "were appointed to draw a charter to be laid before the next General Assembly." But these men pleaded "unskill-

---

93 Morgan Edwards, *Materials Towards a History of the Baptists in Rhode Island,* in *Collections of the Rhode Island Historical Society,* Vol. VI (10 Vols.; Providence, Rhode Island: Hammond, Angell & Co., Printers, 1867), p. 343, hereafter referred to as: Edwards, *Baptists in Rhode Island.*

94 Guild, *Life of James Manning,* pp. 36, 37.

95 Backus, *A History of New England,* p. 137. See also Vedder, *Baptists in the Middle States,* pp. 210, 211.

96 Newman, *A History of Baptist Churches,* p. 261.

fulness" in such matters and suggested Doctor Ezra Stiles,[97] "a learned Congregational minister," of whom they "had a high opinion," as being well qualified "to make a draft of a charter for a college in that government."[98] At first Manning objected to asking Stiles to do the work of "other people," but when these men insisted he yielded to their desires. When approached, Stiles readily consented to render the desired service. He was given what the Baptist thought were proper instructions as to the provisions they wanted to be incorporated in the charter.[99]

When the finished draft was read and inspected by the committee it appeared to be satisfactory in its specifications, therefore, they agreed to have the charter introduced before the next General Assembly. But when it was read in the General Assembly, Daniel Jenckes discerned that the charter would eventually defeat the best interests and efforts of the Baptists, consequently he prevented it from coming to a vote until it could be studied minutely by the Baptists.[100] This intelligence

---

[97] Guild, *Life of James Manning,* pp. 46, 47. The author cites Manning's "Narrative," which is a valuable contemporary source on this subject.

[98] Backus, *A History of New England,* p. 347.

[99] Guild, *Life of James Manning,* pp. 46, 47.

[100] *Ibid.,* pp, 48-50; 52-54. James Manning, commenting upon this matter, wrote that Governor Lyndon, when finally convinced of the faults of the charter "immediately had an interview with Dr. Stiles, . . . and demanded why he had perverted the design of the charter. The answer was, 'I gave you timely warning to take care of yourselves, for that we had done so with regard to our society,' and finally observed, that 'he was not the rogue.' " *Ibid.,* pp. 48, 49. See

was transmitted immediately to the Philadelphia Association, since it was the chief mover in the affair.[101]

This body appointed Samuel Jones to go at once to Newport and to look into the matter. He was accompanied on this important mission by Robert Strettle Jones.[102] When they reached Newport, Doctor Nicholas Eyres was added to the committee to draw up a new charter. The task of drawing up the new charter seems to have been left largely to Samuel Jones, for he says in a footnote to his "Century Sermon,"

> In the fall of 1763, the writer of these sheets, on request, repaired to Newport, in Rhode Island, and new-modeled a rough draft they had of a charter of incorporation for a college which soon after obtained Legislative sanction.[103]

---

also Newman, *A History of Baptist Churches,* pp. 261, 262.

[101] Guild, *Life of James Manning,* p. 50; Backus, *A History of New England,* p. 347. Cf. Vedder, *Baptists in the Middle States,* pp. 211, 212.

[102] Guild, *Life of James Manning,* p. 50. Manning says that the Philadelphia Association "immediately sent two gentlemen hither." On this Guild says, concerning a manuscript copy of Manning's "Narrative," "On the margin of the Manuscript, in the handwriting of the Rev. Dr. Jones, . . . is the following, namely, 'Why their names are not mentioned, I cannot say. However, there was no one sent but myself, although Mr. Robert Strettle Jones was so kind as to bear me company to Rhode Island on the occasion.'—Samuel Jones." Cf. Newman, *A History of Baptist Churches,* p. 262.

[103] Gillette, *Minutes,* p. 465.

Robert Strettle Jones was a lawyer and, no doubt, gave some advice on the business at hand. At any rate the new charter was drafted in a manner calculated for the best interests of the Baptists. Morgan Edwards referred to this issue in the following words, "Thus the Baptists narrowly escaped being jockied out of their college by a set of men in whom they reposed entire confidence."[104]

Before this charter could be passed, however, there was much bickering and even name-calling by both sides. The Congregational members of the Assembly were particularly clamorous in their demands for the restoration of the first charter and strong in their accusations concerning its loss.[105] This "new-modeled" charter provoked the foxy Stiles not a little. He wrote to a friend in Boston complaining about the provisions of the charter which was finally passed by the Rhode Island General Assembly in 1764.[106] Stiles, after this "disap-

---

[104] Edwards, *Baptists in Rhode Island,* p. 351.

[105] For a good statement on this controversy in the Assembly, see Jenckes's "History of the Charter" cited by Guild, *Life of James Manning,* pp. 52-54.

[106] *Ibid.,* pp. 481, 482. Guild says, "On the back of the original draft of the Charter, . . . is written, 'For the Rev. Dr. Cha[rles] Chauncy, Boston,' in Dr. Stiles's handwriting, and also the following remarks, intended evidently for Mr. Chauncy's benefit:-

'1. This Charter was presented to the Assembly August 1763; recopied, with some alterations by the Baptists, in October; and passed the Assembly February 1764. Principal alterations were....

'2. The Baptists have shown a greater affection for all other denominations than for the Congregationalists.

pointment," would have nothing to do with the college, "though courted again and again to accept even a fellowship therein."[107]

Rhode Island College Founded

After the charter was established by law James Manning proceeded with the organization of the Rhode Island College in the city of Warren, where he had become pastor of the newly organized Baptist church. In September, 1764 he was duly chosen president of the college, and he earnestly attended to the duties connected with his new office. The first graduation exercises of this college were held in 1769, wherewith seven young men received the degree of Bachelor of Arts.[108]

'3. Instead of eight or a majority of Congregationalists in the branch of the Fellowship, according to the original agreement, they have inserted eight Baptists: thus assuming a majority of about two thirds in both branches, hereby absorbing the whole power and government of the college, and thus, by the immutability of the numbers, establishing it a party college more explicitly and effectually than any college upon the continent. This is the most material alteration.

'4. Most of what is contained between the marginal crotchets in page 6 is omitted; and the whole paragraph for securing the freedom of education with respect to religion, so mutilated as effectually to enable and empower the Baptists to practice the arts of insinuation, and proselyting upon the youth by private instruction, without the request of the parents.'

[107] Staples, *Annals,* p. 526. See also Guild, *Life of James Manning,* p. 191. Morgan Edwards could not forget the opposition put up by the Congregationalists. See Staples, *Annals,* pp. 526, 527.

[108] Backus, *A History of New England,* p. 348. Of this number two are definitely known to have been from the Philadelphia

Now that the Philadelphia Association had succeeded, with the assistance of the Rhode Island Baptists, in organizing a Baptist college there was no inclination on its part to sit idly by and see the college struggle alone for its very existence. As soon as the charter was secured in 1764 this body agreed "to inform the churches" of this fact and to encourage them to "be liberal in contributing towards carrying the same into execution."[109] Again in 1766 it agreed "to recommend warmly to our churches the interest of the College." This was brought about by informing them that "a subscription is opened all over the continent," and by requesting the churches "to forward the subscription for Rhode Island College."[110] The churches were also in-

---

[108] (Con't) Association—Charles Thompson, and William Williams. Thompson labored for a short time in the Philadelphia Association but he gave most of his life's service to the Baptist pastorate in New England. After completing his studies in Rhode Island College, Williams removed to Wrentham, Massachusetts where he operated a first rate academy, which fitted about eighty students for his Alma Mater. In 1776 he was ordained pastor of the Baptist church of that city and retained it about fifty years. See Guild, *Life of James Manning,* pp. 103-106. William Rogers, also a graduate in this class, was a New Englander by birth, but after his graduation he was the pastor of the First Baptist Church of Philadelphia for several years, after which he was professor in Philadelphia College and later in the University of Pennsylvania. *Ibid.*, pp. 91-96, and Gillette, *Minutes,* pp. 123 ff.

[109] Gillette, *Minutes,* p. 91.

[110] Gillette, *Minutes*, p. 99. The name of Rhode Island College was changed to Brown University in memory of Nicholas Brown, a liberal benefactor of the institution, in the year 1804.

formed that the college "has. . . three promising youths under the tuition of President Manning."[111]

In 1773 John Gano attended the Charleston Association as a messenger of the Philadelphia Association. He headed a committee composed of Oliver Hart and Francis Pelot, which was to address "the Baptist Association throughout America in favor of a plan of contribution, for augmenting the funds of Rhode Island College."[112] At the annual meeting of 1774 this plan[113] was taken up by the Philadelphia Association and recommended to the churches of that body. John Gano and William Rogers were appointed by this association to receive the money and forward it to the treasurer of the college.[114]

Gano must have taken the responsibility of raising money for the college seriously, before he was appointed to this committee, because in that same year one reads, "The church at New York," of which he was pastor, "raised above what was proposed by the plan adopted." Only two other churches and two individuals are listed as donors to the college fund that year.[115]

---

[111] Ibid., pp. 99, 101.

[112] Wood Furman, *A History of the Charleston Association of Baptist Churches in the State of South Carolina* (Charleston, South Carolina: J. Hoff, 1811), pp. 14, 15, hereafter referred to as: Furman, *Charleston Association.*

[113] Guild, *Life of James Manning,* p. 277.

[114] Gillette, *Minutes,* p. 140.

[115] *Ibid.,* p. 142. The churches and individuals were: Cohansie, fifteen shillings; Salem, four shillings and six pence; Hugh Glassford, seven shillings; Andrew Bray, five shillings. The following year only one church—Pennepek—is listed as a donor. Guild says, "In

In the *Minutes* for 1782 it is stated that this association:

> Voted, That the seventh article of the Warren Association minutes be adopted by us, which is as follows: "The Association, from a representation made to them by the corporation of the College in Providence, of the low state of the funds of said College, and the urgent necessity of increasing them, in order to support suitable instructors therein, and from an idea of the great importance of good education, have taken into consideration, as the most probable method to accomplish this valuable end, the recommendation of a subscription throughout all the Baptist societies on this continent, as well as to all the friends of literature of every denomination."[116]

---

[115] (Con't) the language of the record, the recommending to every member to pay sixpence sterling (12½¢), annually, for three years successively to their elder, or some suitable person: this money to be paid to the treasurer of the college." [It should be noted that the drop in donations was undoubtedly caused by concerns brought about by the onset of the Revolutionary War, which began in April of 1775. Guild states that "In the printed minutes [of the Warren Association, 1774], which are brief, we notice the following relating to the College: The meetings were on October 10, 1775. Adopted the plan proposed by the Association in Charleston, South Carolina, to raise a fund for Rhode Island College, viz., by recommending to every member to pay sixpence sterling annually for three years successively to their elder, or some suitable person: This money to be paid to the Treasurer of the College. This shows a commendable disposition. No large fund, however, was raised in this way." —Editor]

[116] *Ibid.*, p. 181.

There are no references in the *Minutes* of the association concerning any response to this action.

Of all the men in the Philadelphia Association there was not a more ardent supporter of Rhode Island College than Morgan Edwards.[117] Backus gives the information that Edwards made a trip to England and Ireland for the purpose of collecting funds for this infant institution.[118] In two years of earnest soliciting Edwards obtained 888 pounds, 10 shillings and two pence sterling. In speaking of his efforts on this trip a few years later he said that he "succeeded pretty well, considering how angry the mother country then was with the colonies for opposing the stamp act."[119] In after years Edwards always spoke with an air of deep satisfaction concerning his efforts for this college. In fact, in one of his articles "he deems" the efforts he put forth to endow it, "the greatest service he has done or hopes to do for the Baptist interest."[120]

Manning appreciated the influence of the Philadelphia Association in behalf of the Baptist college. He looked to it not only for financial aid but also for counsel when important decisions were to be made in connection with the school. Before moving the college from Warren to Providence, Rhode Island he said, "I must

---

[117] Benedict, *General History,* (1848 ed.), p. 602; Spencer, *Early Baptists in Philadelphia,* p. 96.

[118] Backus, *A History of New England,* p. 494.

[119] Edwards, *Baptists in Rhode Island,* p. 354. See also Staples, *Annals,* p. 524.

[120] Edwards, *Baptists in Pennsylvania,* p. 48.

consult my westward friends in a matter of so much consequence as moving or not moving with the college."[121]

Education Fund

The Philadelphia Association went even farther in its efforts to promote education among the Baptists by a concerted effort to establish an education fund. This is shown in the Minutes of 1789 where it is stated,

> After conferring upon the necessity and importance of raising a fund for the education of pious and promising young men for the ministry,—we, the members present, do engage to promote subscriptions in our respective churches and congregations, for said purpose and to bring in the moneys raised, with the subscription papers to the next Association, to be at their disposal.[122]

Before this a certain Mrs. Hub had left a generous legacy to the association, which had been applied by this body to the education fund.[123] In 1787 Samuel Jones

---

[121] Reuben Aldridge Guild, *Chaplain Smith and the Baptists, or Life, Journals, Letters, and Addresses of the Rev. Hezekiah Smith, D. D. of Haverhill, Massachusetts, 1737-1805* (Philadelphia: American Baptist Publication Society, 1885), p. 132, in a letter to Hezekiah Smith dated, February 12, 1770; hereafter referred to as: Guild, *Chaplain Smith.*

[122] Gillette, *Minutes,* p. 246.

[123] *Ibid.,* pp. 101, 104, 110, 114, 119, 131, 142, 149, This legacy for five years produced fourteen pounds each year. The years 1773-1775 it produced eighteen pounds each year. After this the amount of interest on this legacy is not mentioned. The name of Mrs. Hub

reported to the association that Reese Jones had demised a "real estate in New Castle County, in the State of Delaware . . . to the ministers of this association," for the education of young men. The messengers of the association at once agreed to recover the said estate even though it should involve some expense.[124] It became necessary to take the case to a court of law; so the following year the association again voted to be amenable to all expenses incurred by these proceedings.[125]

Silas Hart, a brother of Oliver Hart and a native of Pennsylvania, moved to Virginia where he became a member of the Lynville's Creek Baptist church. In his last will he left fifty pounds to the Philadelphia Association "to be kept in the hands of trustees and applied to the education of young preachers."[126] This body appointed David Jones to gain possession of this legacy, but when he approached the executors of Hart's estate they refused to surrender the money to him. A suit was commenced in chancery in Rockingham Court, which was decided in 1802 in favor of the executors, because the Philadelphia Association was not legally incorporated at the time the prosecution of the suit began. The case was appealed to

---

could not be found.

[124] *Ibid.,* p. 228.

[125] *Ibid.,* p. 239.

[126] Robert B. Semple, *A History of the Rise and Progress of the Baptists in Virginia,* Revised and Extended by G. W. Beale (Richmond, Virginia: Pitt & Dickinson, Publishers, 1894), p. 252; hereafter referred to as: Semple, *Virginia Baptists,* (1894 ed.).

higher courts but each time it was decreed to stand as decided in the Rockingham Chancery Court.[127]

After this case was first decided by the Rockingham Chancery Court the Philadelphia Association was legally incorporated[128] but this was too late to alter the decrees of the higher courts. The High Court of Appeals in 1807, however, left the case open for the Philadelphia Association to reopen the suit in the Rockingham Chancery Court and Semple says, "So that by resorting to another original action the association will ultimately receive the money."[129] The above proceedings proved costly, consequently in the annual meeting of 1804 the messengers of this association,

> Resolved, That the future collections for the education fund, be applied to discharge the debts contracted by borrowing from that fund, for the

---

[127] *Ibid.,* pp. 252, 253.

[128] Gillette, *Minutes*, p. 325. In 1791 this association appointed a "committee to effectuate the incorporation of the Association by charter." This committee was continued the following year, however, it did not "effectuate" the act of incorporation until 1797. *Ibid.*, pp. 271, 284, 316, 325.

[129] Semple, *Virginia Baptists,* p. 253. Semple observes further, "This is certainly an important case to the Baptists of Virginia. From the decision above mentioned it would seem doubtful whether any property holden by the Baptists as a religious society is safe. It remains, therefore, for them hereafter to decide whether it will be best to suffer their meeting-houses and other property to continue thus jeopardized, or to become incorporated." See also Robert B. Semple, *A History of the Rise and Progress of the Baptists in Virginia* (Richmond, Virginia: John O'Lynch, Printer, 1810), pp. 192, 193; hereafter referred to as: Semple, *Virginia Baptists,* (1810 ed.)

> prosecution of the suit against the executors of Silas Hart, late of Virginia, deceased.[130]

Beginning with the annual meeting of 1800 the messengers of the Philadelphia body recommended to the churches, "That a sermon be annually preached among them," in behalf of education and that "a collection be taken for the purpose of increasing the education fund."[131] Each year thereafter an urgent reminder of the recommendation was made in the *Minutes* of this body to all the churches composing its constituency.[132] This reminder was further emphasized by listing all churches that had given to the fund during the past year with the amount donated by each church.[133] In the *Minutes* of 1804, the following interesting entry is found:

> This Association, aware of the great benefits arising from a regular contribution of the churches to the education fund, do hereby most affectionately recommend its continuance.[134]

---

130 Gillette, *Minutes,* pp. 395, 396.

131 *Ibid.,* p. 350.

132 *Ibid.,* pp. 350, 361, 370, 380, 395.

133 *Ibid.,* pp. 361, 370, 380, 395, 412, 424. The total amount given each year was: in 1801, $59.54; in 1802, $65.11; in 1803, $57.91; in 1804, $84.37; in 1805, $53.15; in 1806, $39.50.

134 *Ibid.,* p. 395.

Ministerial Aid

The purpose of the education fund was to make it possible for the "education of such pious young men as appear promising for usefulness in the ministry of the gospel."[135] Only the interest on the principal was used for the purpose of granting aid to the ministerial students desiring such,[136] thus guaranteeing a permanent fund.

At first this aid seems to have been an outright gift to the person making application, provided he was deemed a worthy candidate. Beginning in 1769, however, the applicant was required to give "bond to return the money in case the Association should be disappointed in him."[137] The following year an additional requirement was voted by this association, namely, to require the applicant to "produce a recommendation from the church he belongs unto relative to his ministerial gifts,"[138] and to present it to the trustees at the time of his application for aid. Hereafter no additional requirements were added by this body for those needing financial assistance. But each year it was clearly stated

---

[135] *Ibid.,* p. 350.

[136] *Ibid.,* pp. 101, 104, 110, 395, 396. Due to the expense connected with the suit to recover the fifty pounds, which was willed to this body by Silas Hart, a considerable sum was borrowed from the principal of this fund. In the annual association meeting of 1804 provision was made to restore the borrowed money to the fund.

[137] *Ibid.,* p. 110.

[138] *Ibid.,* p. 114.

that the person receiving this aid must "give the usual obligations to the trustees" of the fund.[139]

Some of the leading ministers among the Baptists of the last three decades of the eighteenth century and the first quarter of the next century received aid from the education fund of the Philadelphia Association. The first person to receive the benefit from this fund was Charles Thompson, of New Jersey, who had formerly completed his preparatory work at the Latin Grammar School in Hopewell.[140] He graduated in the class of 1769 from Rhode Island College, in which class he was valedictorian.[141] He served as pastor of the Baptist church in

---

[139] *Ibid.*, pp. 119, 131, 142, 149, 155. A plan similar in many respects, to the above has been used by some of the State Conventions and associations in the present day in granting aid to ministerial students having a difficult time financially to obtain an education.

[140] *Ibid.*, pp. 101,104. See also Guild, *Life of James Manning,* p. 42.

[141] Guild, *Life of James Manning,* pp. 88-90. Guild cites in full the account of the "First Commencement" from *The Providence Gazette and Country Journal.* The seven members of this first class receiving the Bachelors of Arts were: Joseph Belton, Joseph Eaton, William Rogers, Richard Stiles, Charles Thompson, James Mitchell Barnum, and William Williams. "Then the following gentlemen (graduated in other colleges) at their own request received the honorary degree of Master in the Arts; namely, Rev. Edward Upham, Rev. Morgan Edwards, Rev. Samuel Stillman, Rev. Hezekiah Smith, Hon. Joseph Wanton Jun. Esq., Mr. Jabez Bowen, and Mr. David Howell, Professor of Philosophy in said college."

"The following gentlemen, being well recommended by the faculty for literary merit, had conferred on them the honorary degree of Master in the Arts;" namely, Abel Morgan, Oliver Hart, David Thomas, Samuel Jones, James Bryson, James Edwards, William Boulton, John Ryland, William Clark, Joshua Toulmin, and Caleb Evans, ministers; and John Davis, Robert Strettle Jones and John Stiles.

Warren, Rhode Island and later in Swansea, Massachusetts.[142] Testimony has been given that Thompson was a useful Baptist minister.[143]

The next in line to receive aid from this fund was Thomas Ustick,[144] who after the completion of his work at Rhode Island College returned to the Philadelphia Association and became pastor of the First Baptist Church of Philadelphia. In this position he was able to render valuable service to the Baptists. His counsel and services were often sought in the affairs of this association and he seems to have been ready to give his time and services freely when needed. Consequently, he filled many places of responsibility during the twenty years of his pastorate in that city.[145]

William VanHorne was the third recipient of aid from the education fund established and maintained by this association. Beginning in 1771 he was pastor in this association for more than twenty years. During these years he rendered valuable service both in his pastorate and in the association.[146] He only left this association when his church and other churches of New Jersey

---

142 Gillette, *Minutes,* pp. 103, 197.

143 Backus, *A History of New England,* p. 348. He calls three of the class "useful Baptist ministers." The three listed in the footnote are: "William Rogers, D. D. , Charles Thompson, and William Williams.

144 Gillette, *Minutes,* p. 110.

145 *Ibid.,* pp. 180 ff. Thomas Ustick's ministry was cut short by his untimely death in 1802. He was in his fiftieth year and had given thirty of these to the ministry of the Gospel. He was converted under the ministry of John Gano in New York. See *Memoirs of John Gano,* p. 91.

146 Gillette, *Minutes,* pp. 114 ff.

became members of the newly organized New York Association in 1791.[147]

Burgiss Allison was another[148] ministerial student to reap the benefit from the education fund of this association while attending Rhode Island College.[149] He returned to the association a few years after having completed his work in that institution. He served both as pastor and head of an academy until after the turn of the eighteenth century.[150]

---

[147] *Ibid.,* p. 271. VanHorne was pastor of the Scotch Plains Baptist Church, which had formerly been under the pastoral direction of Benjamin Miller.

[148] *Ibid.,* pp. 119, 131, 149, 155. There were other ministerial students, attending Rhode Island College, who received aid from this fund. But these did not play an important role in the Philadelphia Association during the time of this study. They may have filled useful fields of service elsewhere. Others who received aid from this fund were: Ebenezer David, Peter Smith, Thomas Gier, Enoch Morgan, and James Darrah.

[149] *Ibid.,* pp. 142, 149, 155.

[150] *Ibid.,* pp. 235 ff. Other works which were read for a background but not quoted are: *Biographical Sketches of the Founders and Principal Alumni of the Log College,* collected and edited by Archibald Alexander (Princeton, New Jersey: Printed by J. T. Robinson, 1845), hereafter referred to as: Alexander, *Log College; Extracts from the Itineraries and Other Miscellanies of Ezra Stiles, 1755-1794 with a Selection from His Correspondence,* edited by Franklin Bowditch Dexter (New Haven, Connecticut: Yale University Press, 1916), hereafter referred to as: Dexter, *Extracts;* Reuben Aldridge Guild, *History of Brown University with Illustrative Documents* (Providence, Rhode Island: Providence Press Company, 1867), hereafter referred to as, Guild, *Brown University;* Torbet, *A Social History;* Reuben Aldridge Guild, "The Denominational Work of President Manning," *The Baptist Review,* III

Summary

This association in its infancy looked to schools outside its jurisdiction for trained men. Some of the early leaders also came from abroad. For a short period Harvard was looked to with high hopes by this body as an institution in which its men could be trained. These hopes, however, proved to be wishful thinking.

In 1756 this training problem was tackled by Isaac Eaton, with the approval and encouragement of the Philadelphia Association, when he established his Latin Grammar School. It was the trial balloon for Baptist education in America. In this category the school served its purpose nobly. It was successful enough to excite high hopes in those who were advocates of an educated Baptist ministry. Other Baptist schools to prove successful within the boundaries of the association were those operated by Samuel Jones, Burgiss Allison and William Staughton.

When the members of this association saw the happy results of Isaac Eaton's school, they began to make plans for an institution on the college level. These plans were realized when Rhode Island College was established in the year 1765 under the direction of James Manning. Although this college had to struggle it was a successful venture from its inception.

The education fund instituted by the Philadelphia Association proved to be more than a noble experiment. The interest from this fund enabled at least a dozen men

---

[150] (Con't) (January, 1881); "Ministerial Education," editor, *The Christian Review,* II (June, 1837).

to carry on their studies at Rhode Island College and enabled several others to secure private instruction.

From the foregoing material it can be seen that the Philadelphia Association, by pioneering in Baptist education, has made a very significant contribution to the history of Baptists in America.

Isaac Eaton's Hopewell Academy, founded in 1756 under the auspices of the Philadelphia Association. Like the famous Log College of the Presbyterians, out of such experimental and modest beginnings grew wide support for an educated ministry for the Baptist churches.

An early view of Rhode Island College, later renamed Brown University, showing the college on the right and the President's house on the left. The small structure to the right of the college building is a well from which graduates recalled "cool refreshing water was drawn." The little building left or south of the house is the barn where James Manning kept his horse, "with which he was accustomed to journey during vacations." Reuben A. Guild. *Early History of Brown University, Including the Life, Times and Correspondence of James Manning, 1756-1791* (Providence: Snow & Farnham, 1896) pp. 156-157.

Chapter Three

The Influence of the Philadelphia Association Upon Baptist Doctrine in America

---

During the eighteenth century the Philadelphia Association wielded a strong influence upon Baptist doctrine in this country. This influence was more widespread and even stronger than that which it exerted upon Baptist education during the same period.

In order to obtain a proper perspective of the doctrinal influence of this association, it will be necessary to gain some knowledge of its doctrinal background. At the very outset it can be said that the members of this body had strong doctrinal convictions. Throughout the period covered by this study these people seem to have been fully assured that they had *the truth* and that they *must* propagate it in all directions. With this dominating drive the ministers and other church members of this association were urged to perform their work.

The London Confession of Faith of 1689 Adopted

When the London Confession of Faith[151] was brought to America is not known. It was translated into the Welsh language by Abel Morgan, Pastor of Pennepek,

---

[151] The full title is: *Confession of Faith Put Forth by the Elders and Brethren of Many Congregations of Christians (Baptized upon Profession of Their Faith) In London and the Country*. It was first published in London in 1689.

before February 4, 1716, because on that date it was adopted by the Welsh Tract Baptist Church and signed by one hundred twenty-two of its members.[152]

The date commonly accepted for the adoption of this Confession of Faith by the Philadelphia Association is 1742. John Leland, in his *The Virginia Chronicle,* says that the Regular Baptists "adhered to a confession of Faith first published in London, 1689, and afterwards adopted by the Baptist Association of Philadelphia, in 1742."[153] James Manning, in the "Plan of the Association," says also that it was adopted by this association in 1742.[154] This date has been accepted by various church historians down to this day, apparently without any misgivings.[155] The statement in *The Minutes of the Philadelphia Baptist Association,* however, does not warrant such a clear-cut conclusion. The statement in the *Minutes* for 1742 is:

> A motion was made in the Association for reprinting the Confession of faith, set forth by the elders of Baptized congregations, met in London, A. D. 1689, with a short treatise of Church discipline, to be annexed to the Confession of faith. Agreed,

---

[152] Benedict, *General History,* (1813 ed.), Vol., II, p. 6. McGlothlin, *Confessions,* p. 294.

[153] *Leland,* p. 105. *The Virginia Chronicle* was first published in Virginia in 1790, in book form. It is a valuable source for early American Baptist history.

[154] Guild, *Life of James Manning,* p. 80.

[155] Edwards, *Baptists in Pennsylvania,* p. 5; Cook, *Delaware Baptists,* p. 89; William Warren Sweet, *Religion in Colonial America* (New York: Charles Scribner's Sons, 1942), p. 141. See also Vedder, *Baptists in the Middle States,* p. 91.

> that the thing was needful and likely to be very useful; and in order to carry it on it is ordered to send it to the several churches belonging to this Association; to make a trial of what sums of money can be raised, and to send an account to Mr. Jenkin Jones, to the intent, that when the several collections are computed, if it be found sufficient to defray the charges of the work, that then it shall go on; if not, then to drop it for this year; and if it be carried on, that then an addition of two articles be therein inserted: that is to say, concerning singing of psalms in the worship of God, and laying of hands upon baptized believers. Ordered, also, that the said Mr. Jones and Benjamin Griffith do prepare a short treatise of discipline, to be annexed to the said Confession of faith.[156]

There are three other entries in the *Minutes* which seem to have some bearing upon this question. In answering a query addressed to this body in 1724 the messengers replied, "We refer to the Confession of faith, set forth by the elders and brethren met in London, 1689, and owned by us; chapter 22, sections 7 and 8."[157] Three years later it answered a question concerning marriage "by referring to our Confession of faith." Again in 1729

---

[156] *Minutes,* p. 46.

[157] *Ibid.,* p. 27. Cf. Also Vedder, *Baptists in the Middle States,* p. 91 In a footnote Vedder says, "This may have been only a readoption, since there is an entry under date of 1724 to the effect that the Confession was at that time accepted by the Association. The record is not known to be based on an original document, and cannot be regarded as conclusive." Newman, however, refers to this entry of 1724 as though it were authentic. Newman, *A History of Baptist Churches,* p. 213.

after answering a question they continued, "We also refer to the Confession of faith."[158]

The four entries listed above leave some doubt as to the exact time of the adoption of this Confession of Faith and lead one to agree with Cutting when he says, "The common impression that this adoption occurred in 1742, is manifestly a mistake."[159] However, there is more to be said on the subject. Benjamin Griffith, in the opening words of the preface to his treatise on Church Discipline, says:

> Our last Association, met at Philadelphia, September 25, 1742, taking into consideration the general interest of the gospel, and especially the interest of the churches they were related unto and did then represent, judging it expedient to reprint the *Confession of Faith* put forth by the Elders and Brethren of one hundred Congregations baptized upon profession of faith in England and Wales, met in London, September 3, 1689, with the additions concerning Imposition of Hands, and singing of Psalms in the worship of God.[160]

Since one reads, "A motion was made . . . for reprinting the Confession of faith" in the previous quotation, and "judging it expedient to reprint the *Confession of Faith*" here, one may well raise the question,

---

[158] Gillette, *Minutes,* pp. 29, 30. McGlothlin accepts all three of these citations as authentic. McGlothlin, *Confessions,* pp. 294, 295. Cutting also accepts them as authentic. Cutting, *Historical Vindications,* p. 93.

[159] Cutting, *Historical Vindications,* p. 93.

[160] *Ibid.,* p. 199. The "Confession of Faith" is italicized by Cutting.

how did "the common impression" arise that the Confession of Faith was adopted in 1742 by the Philadelphia Association? This impression no doubt arose because on the title page of the Confession of Faith published by Benjamin Franklin in 1743 these words occur, "*Adopted* by the Baptist Association *met at* Philadelphia, Sept. 25, 1742."[161] The same impression is given by the later Philadelphia as well as the Charleston editions of this Confession of Faith.[162]

From all that has been said it is certain that the Philadelphia Association at an early date, came to accept this Confession of Faith as a reasonably clear statement of what it considered to be the New Testament teaching for Christians. The adoption of the Confession of Faith indicated that the Philadelphia body would follow Calvinistic theology rather than Arminian, and this Confession of Faith basically "agreed in its doctrinal sentiments with the Westminster Confession."[163]

This Confession of Faith has come to be known as the Philadelphia Confession of Faith because it was first adopted by that body and published in that city. Throughout this period it was, next to the Bible, a very

---

161 McGlothlin, *Confessions,* pp. 295, 296. McGlothlin has italics as given above.

162 *A Confession of Faith put forth by the Elders and Brethren of Many Congregations of Christians (Baptized upon Profession of their faith) In London and the Country* (seventh edition; Philadelphia: Printed by John Dunlap, 1773), title page; *A Confession of Faith put forth By the Elders and Brethren of Many Congregations of Christians, (Baptized upon Profession of their faith) In London and The Country* (second Charleston edition; Charleston, South Carolina: J. Hoff, 1813), title page.

163 Benedict, *Fifty Years,* p. 137.

important doctrinal statement among the Baptists in most sections of this country.[164] This, no doubt, tended to give them a uniformity of doctrine as nothing else could when they were so loosely organized.

Distinctive Doctrine

The ministers of this body preached and emphasized all of the doctrines as listed in their Confession of Faith. On one occasion the learned Henry Muhlenberg said that William Marsh of Newtown "discoursed very powerfully and edifyingly on the article of justification."[165] However, believer's baptism was considered to be the distinctive doctrine of the Baptists. Morgan Edwards said, "If this be taken away we shall differ from the Independents in no point whatsoever."[166] Consequently questions on some aspect of this doctrine were constantly coming before the association for consideration.[167]

The article on baptism in the Confession of Faith clearly set forth that it was "a sign" of the believer's "fellowship" with Jesus Christ,

---

164 *Ibid.*, pp. 47, 137.

165 *The Journals of Henry Melchoir Muhlenberg,* Translated by Theodore G. Tappert and John W. Doberstein (Philadelphia: The Muhlenberg Press, 1942), Vol. I, p. 603. Muhlenberg was an outstanding Lutheran leader in the American colonies during the eighteenth century.

166 Edwards, *Baptists in Pennsylvania,* Preface, p. iii.

167 Gillette, *Minutes,* pp. 33, 42, 43, 49.

in his death, and resurrection; of his being engrafted into him; of remission of sins; and of his giving up unto God through Jesus Christ, to live and walk in newness of life.

This article further states that, "Those who do actually profess repentance towards *God*, faith in, and obedience, to our Lord Jesus, are the only proper subjects of this ordinance." It concludes, "Immersion, or dipping of the person in water, is necessary to the due administration of this ordinance."[168]

The early leaders of this association were emphatic in their proclamation of the doctrine of believer's baptism, very much to the displeasure of the leaders of other religious groups. One leader laments their success in challenging the baptism of the "clergy" and says, "in consequence of which numbers have suffered themselves to be baptized."[169] Muhlenberg once said, to a woman whose mother was a Baptist, that if we "insisted upon immersion and fostered it with false doctrines, like the Baptists, we would lose the substance and hang on to the shadow." He also wrote that the Baptists "despise and argue against infant Baptism."[170]

Samuel Finley, a Presbyterian minister and later president of Princeton, challenged Abel Morgan, the pastor of the Baptist church in Middletown, New Jersey, to a debate on the subject of baptism. Morgan is reported

---

[168] McGlothlin, *Confessions,* p. 270.

[169] *Historical Collections Relating to the American Colonial Church,* edited by Wm. Stevens Perry, Vol. II, *Pennsylvania* (Hartford, Connecticut: The Church Press, 1871), p. 448.

[170] *The Journals of Henry Melchoir Muhlenberg,* Vol. I, p. 210 and also Vol. II, p. 437.

to have won this debate after which Finley countered with a pamphlet, *A Charitable Plea for the Speechless*. As a result of this a pamphlet war ensued, however, after each party had fired two volleys Edwards said that the "war ended."[171] "By reading the dispute between Dr. Finley and Mr. Abel Morgan" Rachel Furman, a Presbyterian, "received favorable impressions respecting the sentiments of the Baptist, with whom she at that time had no personal acquaintance." She later became a Baptist and her son Richard became a national leader among the Baptists.[172]

Modes of Indoctrination

This body was uncompromising in its doctrinal position and it was concerned about the doctrinal views held by every member within its jurisdiction. In a word, these men believed that they had the pure doctrine of God and therefore thought it should be accepted and propagated by every person in its membership. This is evident from the pleas of the annual circular letters. In 1756 the fathers were exhorted to "be careful of the instruction of youth and those under your care," again in 1759 they were asked to "instruct" those in their households. In 1760 the plea was to "instruct them in the principles of religion." The following year the parents

---

[171] Edwards, *Baptists in [New] Jersey*, Vol. II, pp. 18, 19; see also Alexander, *Log College*, p. 316. Abel Morgan was a nephew of the pastor of Pennepek church by the same name and was a son of Enoch Morgan, pastor of the Baptist church in Welsh Tract, Delaware.

[172] Rippon, *Annual Register*, Vol. II, pp. 282, 283.

were also warned "against introducing such books among" their children "as will have a tendency to corrupt their minds."[173] Again in 1774 the messengers of the Philadelphia Association lamented the fact "that the catechising or instructing" of their "youth in the principles of the Christian religion" had been too "generally neglected." This body "thought it expedient to recommend to the churches, seriously to consider and promote the same" principles throughout their membership.[174]

From the time this association was founded it was customary to have a sermon preached at the opening of the annual associational meetings. At first it seems that the preacher was allowed to choose any Scripture or topic that appealed to him for his sermon. In 1759, however, it was decided that it would be more profitable to have a doctrinal sermon preached "upon one of the fundamental articles of the Christian faith." The sermon topic was to be assigned "the year before" and was to be preached by one of the "ministering brethren . . . who is esteemed qualified in some competent measure."[175]

The *Minutes* of this body reveal that sermons were assigned and preached from a wide selection of the

---

[173] Gillette, *Minutes*, pp. 73, 79, 80, 84.

[174] *Ibid.*, p. 141. [As David Benedict wrote, "The old Baptists in New England, although for the most part, they held with their brethren elsewhere the doctrines of Depravity, Election, Divine Sovereignty, Final Perseverance, etc., yet they were not in the habit of enforcing them so strongly as were those in New York, Philadelphia, and further south."—*Fifty Years Among the Baptists,* p. 137.—Editor]

[175] *Ibid.*, p. 79.

doctrines listed in the Confession of Faith.[176] These sermons seem to have had the desired effect upon those present at the meetings.[177] This custom was soon adopted by the other associations and is practiced in a modified manner by most associations throughout the country today.

The Philadelphia Association adopted the plan for the circular letters presented at its annual meeting in 1774 by Abel Morgan. This plan proposed in part,

> I. That the contents of the general letter shall consist of observations and improvements of some particular article of faith, contained in our Confession, beginning with the first, and so on in order, unless occasion require the contrary; . . . .
>
> II. Let diligent care be used to caution the churches against innovation in doctrine and practice, and to watch against errors and avoid them wherever they rise, and by whomsoever they may be propagated.[178]

This decision proved to be the most acceptable way of disseminating the doctrines of this body among its members. In a day when there were no denominational periodicals, these circular letters seem to have served their purpose in the indoctrination of the Baptists of the Philadelphia Association. The letters were assigned one year in advance of their presentation and publication, thus giving the author ample time to make a careful

---

[176] *Ibid.*, pp. 79 ff.

[177] For a list of the sermons preached see Appendix A.

[178] Gillette, *Minutes,* p. 136.

treatment of the subject assigned.[179] They cover the doctrines of the Confession of Faith and have been pronounced "a fund of rich theology."[180]

Another way in which the leaders of the Philadelphia Association sought to indoctrinate its members was through the answering of various questions sent in by the churches on some doctrinal problem that was confronting them.[181] These questions and answers often went to the very heart of the Confession of Faith. The questions taken up and answered by this body must often have had more appeal to the members than some of the circular letters and doctrinal sermons had, because they arose out of vital problems that concerned the members of the churches.[182]

The practice of the Philadelphia Association of sending out circular letters was taken up by most if not all the early associations of America as a means of teaching Bible doctrine to their membership. The same bodies also adopted the custom of answering doctrinal

---

[179] For a list of the doctrines treated in these circular letters see Appendix A.

[180] Gillette, *Minutes,* p. ii. This is found in the Notice given by the committee appointed to gather and publish this material. The committee was composed of Horatio G. Jones, Howard Malcom, A. D. Gillette, Wilson Jewell, Joseph Taylor and William Shadrach. For an illustration of the statement made concerning these circular letters see *Minutes,* pp. 136 ff.

[181] Gillette, *Minutes,* pp. 43, 58, 68, 70 ff. These questions deal with baptism, the foreknowledge of God, unconditional election, original sin, the final perseverance of the saints, the assurance of faith and other doctrines.

[182] *Ibid.,* pp. 42, 43, 49, 70, 95, 238. All of these questions deal with baptism. See also pp. 200, 256.

queries sent to the annual meetings by perplexed churches.[183] Most of the Baptist associations continued this practice well into the nineteenth century.

The Confession of Faith was printed and distributed for the purpose of instructing the people in Baptist doctrine.[184] The catechism was also published for the same reason.[185] As late as 1794 the Philadelphia body recommended to the churches that they "institute the catechising of children in their respective congregations, at stated seasons."[186] The Charleston Association also adopted this practice.[187]

Attitude Toward False Doctrine

The association of Philadelphia was zealous to spread what it considered to be true doctrine, while at the same time it had no time or place in its program for any doctrine contrary to its Confession of Faith. After all precautions had been taken against the inroads of doctrines considered by it to be false to the Scriptures and to the Confession, there still were men who not only strayed but endeavored to lead others astray with them.

In the annual session of the association for 1743 much of the time was taken up in dealing with two

---

[183] See the Minutes of the Charleston, Warren, Shaftsbury, New York and other associations for a confirmation of this statement.

[184] Gillette, *Minutes*, p. 46.

[185] *Ibid.*, pp. 39, 83, 163.

[186] *Ibid.*, p. 297.

[187] See *A Confession of Faith,* second Charleston edition. This work also contains the Catechism.

ministers who had taught doctrines concerning Jesus Christ contrary to the Philadelphia Confession of Faith. After this issue had been debated "in love and meekness" at some length, Joseph Eaton, one of the ministers involved, "stood up, and freely, . . . recanted, renounced, and condemned all expression," which had led many to believe that he had "departed from the literal sense and meaning of that fundamental article" in the Confession of Faith. Subsequently the messengers voiced the desire that all its constituency would "have a tender regard for him in his weak and aged years."[188] The other minister involved was Simon Butler, who gave his acknowledgment in writing, in which he expressed his sorrow for everything said and for "every other misconduct."[189]

In 1748 there were some who denied the foreknowledge of God, "concerning all future evil as well as good." This form of teaching was looked upon by the messengers of the association as being "directly repugnant to Scripture" and for that reason it was pronounced by them to be "exceeding erroneous and pernicious." They concluded that the promulgation of this type of doctrine would "oppose and tend to overthrow the whole Christian religion."[190]

---

[188] Gillette, *Minutes,* p. 47.

[189] *Ibid.,* p. 48. [The issue was over the Eternal Sonship of Christ, which Eaton and Butler had denied. For a fuller discussion of this incident, the reader is referred to the biographical work on Benjamin Griffith in Terry Wolever, ed., *A Noble Company: Biographical Sketches of Notable Particular-Regular Baptists in America,* Vol. I. (Springfield, Missouri: Particular Baptist Press, 2001).]

[190] *Ibid.,* p. 58.

The messengers of the Philadelphia Association in 1781 saw fit to notify their constituency that the Reverend Robert Morris had been excommunicated by the church of Stamford because of "gross immoralities, and departure from the faith as held by us." They warned the churches to "beware of him." In the same year they also authorized an advertisement concerning one David Branson, who, posing as a Baptist preacher, "is an excommunicated person, and ought not, by any means, to be countenanced."[191]

Universal Restoration Opposed

The espousal of doctrine contrary to the Confession of Faith that caused the most consternation in this association was the doctrine of "universal restoration." In 1781 its messengers received "proposals and queries" from the churches in Pennepek, Hopewell, and Philadelphia respecting this doctrine. Samuel Jones, Oliver Hart, Abel Morgan, and James Manning, president of Rhode Island College, were appointed a committee to investigate these "proposals and queries" and to "report thereon in the afternoon."[192]

---

[191] *Ibid.,* p. 173.

[192] *Loc. cit.* [The controversy began when Elhanan Winchester (1751-1797) removed from the church at Welsh Neck, South Carolina to become pastor at First Baptist in Philadelphia in October of 1780. Less than six months later, in a sermon delivered on March 5, 1781, Winchester was accused of holding the doctrine of the "final restoration of bad men and angels from hell." That same evening, 97 members of the church signed a protest which was entered into the Minute Book, stating that, "We whose names are underwritten do in the most solemn manner from real conviction of

When the session was convened in the afternoon the committee gave the following report,

> First. That the proceedings of the protesters in that business were regular and fair.
>
> Secondly. That the declaration of the ministers who were called to their assistance, respecting the protesters, was weighty, full and decisive.
>
> Thirdly. That although the nonsigners are virtually excluded, yet, in order to their more formal excommunication, the Philadelphia church be advised to appoint at their meeting of business, two of their regular male members to go with the protest to the non protestors, one by one, in order to their signing it, and warn them, that in case they refuse to sign, should openly and formally, by name, be excommunicated.[193]
>
> Committee { Samuel Jones, Oliver Hart
> Abel Morgan, James Manning

This report of the committee was approved unanimously by the messengers.[194] The instructions of the committee were followed by the "protesters," that is, the opposers of this doctrine in the Philadelphia church, however, there were no excommunications until 1784 when forty-six

---

duty seriously protest against the same, as a most dangerous heresy."—Editor]

[193] Gillette, *Minutes*, pp. 173, 174. Protesters was the name given to ninety-seven members of the First Baptist Church of Philadelphia who signed a protest against the proclamation of the doctrine of universal restoration in that church.

[194] *Ibid.*, p. 174.

were publicly expelled from the church.[195] Elhanan Winchester, the pastor and leader of this movement, said of the action taken by this group,

> They took uncommon pains in carrying about a *protest* against me, to every member of the church, both in the city and in the country, and threatening all with excommunication who would not sign it; by which some were intimidated, and by these and other means they strengthened their party. . . .But I believe near an hundred of the members suffered themselves to be excommunicated rather than to sign the *protest* against me, and the doctrine that I preached.[196]

The Philadelphia Association at its meeting in 1781 advised all the churches to "beware of Elhanan Winchester, and not admit him or any who advocate 'universal salvation,' " to teach or preach in any of their services. It further recommended that any individuals "who avow the same" to be put out of the communion of the church.[197] These admonitions were followed so closely that three years later (1784), when John Leland came from Virginia to Philadelphia in the company of Winchester, he was not allowed to preach in any of the Baptist churches. Leland says, that they "were so fearful that I was a Universalist, that I was not invited by them to preach in their meeting-house." When Leland returned to the city, however, in 1790, at a time when the

---

[195] Spencer, *Early Baptists in Philadelphia,* p. 131.

[196] Winchester, *Universal Restoration,* Preface, pp. xx, xxi. The first edition of this work came from the press in 1788. The italics are Winchester's.

[197] Gillette, *Minutes,* p. 174.

controversy was still alive over this doctrine, he was invited to preach in the Philadelphia church, much to his satisfaction.[198]

A council of Baptist ministers advised the protesting or orthodox group to secure the services of another pastor, since Winchester had departed from the faith. When Winchester was "requested to desist from supplying the pulpit" his friends broke into the church and took possession of it. Control of the church was regained by the protesters and as a result Winchester and his party entered suit to gain possession of the building, however, they lost the suit in 1784.[199] Winchester said that they were kept out of the house by force until it was at "last confirmed" to the protesters "by law, though I think unjustly, as we were the majority at first."[200]

Winchester seems to have been well pleased with himself because on one occasion when giving the arguments in favor of the doctrine of universal restoration, he said that he did so in "such a manner as astonished all present, and I was amazed at myself, I spoke with so much ease."[201] The committee of the protesters said, "Popular applause, the idol which too many worship, was soon discovered to be an object

---

198 Leland, p. 24.

199 Spencer, *Early Baptists in Philadelphia,* pp. 131 ff. Spencer says, "About fifty pages of the church records are taken up with the proceedings relative to this case."

200 Winchester, *Universal Restoration,* Preface, p. xx. [Winchester and his deluded followers held their meetings at the University of Pennsylvania.—Editor]

201 *Ibid.*, Preface, p. xi.

zealously sought for and courted by Mr. Winchester."[202] Benedict reported that many believe Winchester would have abandoned this doctrine if it had not "been for the difficulty of saying, *I was* mistaken."[203] Manning wrote to John Rippon, "Self-exaltation was the rock on which he split. . . . but I think he is now at the end of his tether."[204]

The Philadelphia Association in 1789 also cautioned its "churches to beware" of the Reverend William Worth and Artist Seagraves of Pittsgrove. The following year this association lamented that "they have occasion again to call the attention . . . to another awful instance of departure from the faith" in the person of the Reverend Nicholas Cox who had served in places of responsibility.[205] He had been a messenger in 1788 from this body to the Shaftsbury Association.[206] The situation became so irritating to this association that it appointed

---

[202] Guild, *Life of James Manning,* p. 333. Guild cites excerpts from the sixteen page pamphlet, *An Address from the Baptist Church in Philadelphia, to Their Sister Churches of the Same Denomination, Throughout the Confederate States of North America, Drawn up by a Committee of the Church Appointed for the Said Purpose* (Philadelphia: Printed by Robert Aitkin, 1781).

[203] Benedict, *General History,* (1813 ed.), Vol. I, pp. 275, 276. Italics are Benedict's.

[204] Guild, *Life of James Manning,* p. 327. Winchester went to London in 1787, where he died in 1797 at the age of forty-six. Spencer, *Early Baptists,* p. 133.

[205] Gillette, *Minutes,* pp. 247, 256.

[206] Stephen Wright, *History of the Shaftsbury Baptist Association from 1781 to 1853* (Troy, New York: A. G. Johnson, Steam Press Printer, 1853), p. 20, hereafter referred to as: Wright, *Shaftsbury Association.*

Samuel Jones, of Lower Dublin, to draw up a circular letter on this doctrine for the 1790 session of the association.[207] In 1793 Joseph Stephens, the pastor of the Upper Freehold church was excommunicated for holding the "erroneous doctrine of universal salvation."[208] This is the last case of this kind spoken of in the *Minutes of the Philadelphia Baptist Association.*

Influence on Southern Churches

The influence exerted by this body upon Baptist churches in other areas makes far more interesting reading than the doctrinal battles which raged constantly for a decade within its borders. There is no record that this association influenced the early doctrinal background of the Charleston and Ashley Creek Baptist churches in South Carolina. The former adopted the Confession of Faith of 1689 at the "beginning of the eighteenth century" and the latter "adopted it March 18, 1737."[209] However, Oliver Hart, a native son of the northern body, was pastor of the First Baptist Church of Charleston for thirty years, from 1749-1779. The church at Welsh Neck, South Carolina was made up largely of members who had come south from the church at Welsh Tract, Delaware.[210] It cannot be concluded, therefore,

---

[207] Gillette, *Minutes,* pp. 257-260.

[208] *Ibid.,* p. 293.

[209] Furman, *Charleston Association,* p. 12.

[210] Benedict, *General History,* (1848 ed.) pp. 704, 705. See also Furman, *Charleston Association,* p. 70.

that the influence of this association upon the doctrine of these churches was negligible because at the time of the formation of the Charleston Association every minster, with the exception of one, was a native of the Philadelphia Association.[211]

In North Carolina the story is different. The first Baptist churches here were first established upon "Arminian or Free-will doctrines." These churches admitted members to baptism "without requiring an experience of grace." They practiced baptism by immersion only, but they were very loosely organized and were also lax in their discipline.[212]

The church at Fishing Creek reported to the Charleston Association, at the time it was admitted to that body in 1758, that it had had a large membership "but without discipline or a proper acquaintance with Christian doctrines, and the majority destitute of real

---

[211] Furman, *Charleston Association,* pp. 5-9, 70, 71, 75-78. Philip James and John Brown were co-pastors of Welsh Neck; John Stephens was pastor of Ashley Creek; and Oliver Hart was pastor of Charleston; Joshua Edwards was ordained to the ministry in 1751. All of these men were from the Philadelphia Association. Only Francis Pelot, pastor of Euhaw, was not from the northern body. [Pelot was a Swiss immigrant—Editor.]

[212] Lemuel Burkitt and Jesse Read, *A Concise History of the Kehukee Baptist Association, From Its Original Rise to the Present Time* (Halifax, North Carolina: A. Hodge, 1803), p. 28, hereafter referred to as: Burkitt & Read, *Kehukee Association.* Cf. Also George W. Purefoy, *A History of the Sandy Creek Baptist Association From Its Organization in A. D. 1758 to A. D. 1858* (New York: Sheldon & Co., Publisher 1859), p. 42, hereafter referred to as: Purefoy, *Sandy Creek Association.*

religion." From this report it was also evident that the same condition was prevalent in the churches at Three Creeks and Kehukee.[213]

These conditions continued in the churches in this manner until they "were partially reclaimed by Robert Williams of Welsh Neck, South Carolina" in 1751.[214] John Gano came and preached to them in 1754 under the auspices of the Philadelphia Association and later "at their request represented their case" to the body sponsoring his missionary tour.[215] Consequently, this body appointed Benjamin Miller from New Jersey, and Peter Peterson VanHorne from Pennsylvania, to journey to North Carolina in order to indoctrinate the lax churches in that area.[216] These men were accompanied on this important mission by John Gano. Together they were able to reorganize the churches along the lines of Regular

---

213 Furman, *Charleston Association,* pp. 13, 62.

214 Purefoy, *Sandy Creek Association,* pp. 42, 43.

215 Furman, *Charleston Association,* p. 62. See also *Memoirs of John Gano,* pp. 69 ff.

216 Gillette, *Minutes,* p. 72. [See Morgan Edwards, *Materials Towards a History of the Baptists in the Province of North Carolina,* reprinted in materials *Towards a History of the Baptists,* edited by Eve B. Weeks and Mary B. Warren (Danielsville, Georgia: Heritage papers, 1984), Vol. I, pp. 85, 89]

Baptist doctrine and discipline.[217] The newly organized churches adopted the Philadelphia Confession of Faith.[218]

This was a notable accomplishment for the ministers from the North as well as for their association. One author, however, has nothing but condemnation for this group, because they "proselytized to the Particular Baptist faith" the Arminian Baptists of eastern North Carolina. When the ministers of this area were "schooled in the rigid Calvinism of the Philadelphia Confession" he laments that the "wonderful progress of the Baptists of eastern North Carolina was at an end."[219] The plain statements in the various accounts, however, seem to conflict with these inferences of Paschal.[220]

---

[217] Benedict, *General History,* (1848 ed.), p. 682. Cf. also Burkitt and Read, *Kehukee Association,* pp. 28, 29; Purefoy, *Sandy Creek Association;* B. F. Riley, *A History of the Baptists in the Southern States East of the Mississippi* (Philadelphia: American Baptist Publication Society, 1898), p. 25, hereafter referred to as: Riley, *Baptists in the Southern States.*

[218] Burkitt and Read, *Kehukee Association,* pp. 29, 30.

[219] Paschal, *Shubal Stearns,* pp. 43, 44.

[220] For a different view see Burkitt and Read, *Kehukee Association,* pp. 28, 29; Furman, *Charleston Association,* p. 62; Benedict, *General History* (1848 ed.), pp. 682, 683; Purefoy, *Sandy Creek Association,* pp. 42-44. Cf. also Riley, *Southern States,* pp. 19, 25. Purefoy says, "After 1827 this body *changed its position,* and condemned these revival measures." *op. cit.,* p. 51. This was seventy years after its acceptance of the Philadelphia Confession of Faith. It would seem, therefore, that Paschal's remarks are groundless. [Editor's note: For a more extended refutation of Paschal's views on these events, see Terry Wolever, *The Life and Ministry of John Gano,* Vol. I, Particular Baptist Press, Springfield, Missouri, 1998, pp. 234-267 and Appendix A, "The Particular Baptists in North Carolina: An Appraisal Appraised," pp. 315-346].

A group of General or Arminian Baptists settled in Virginia in 1743 and organized a Baptist church at Opekon. For a period of several years this church seemed to prosper but their pastor—Henry Loveall—became careless and "licentious in his life" consequently he was excluded by the church in 1751. In their distress the members of this church petitioned the Philadelphia Association for assistance.[221] Subsequently Benjamin Miller and John Thomas were appointed for this urgent mission. They were accompanied by John Gano who had only recently considered favorable the "call" to the Baptist ministry.[222]

When they arrived in Virginia and investigated the condition of the church they found that it had been "remiss in government" and that it was Arminian in doctrine. After several conferences the church was "new-modeled" along the lines of the Philadelphia Confession of Faith and discipline. This church joined the Philadelphia Association in 1754.[223]

The Opekon church remained true to the doctrines which it had received from these ministers. After coming into contact with the Separates[224] its members became

---

[221] Semple, *Virginia Baptists* (1894 ed.), p. 375. See also *Memoirs of John Gano,* p. 40.

[222] Benedict, *General History* (1848 ed.), p. 643. See also *Memoirs of John Gano,* pp. 39. 40.

[223] Semple, *Virginia Baptists* (1894 ed.), pp. 375-376. Cf. Also *Minutes,* p. 71; *Memoirs of John Gano,* pp. 48-50.

[224] Separates was a name applied first to the converts of George Whitefield in New England who refused to remain in fellowship with the Standing Order in that locality. Even after some of this group became Baptists they retained the title of *Separate.*

very zealous and animated in both their preaching and religious exercises. So much so that a complaint was lodged with the Philadelphia Association by some of the "less engaged members" of the church. Consequently Benjamin Miller was sent to investigate the complaints and to assist them in solving the problem. When he arrived and saw what the situation was, he joined wholeheartedly into the services with the "engaged members." Before returning north he informed those who had registered the complaints that if he had such members he would not "take gold for them."[225]

Other churches in Virginia which were strongly influenced by the Philadelphia Association were Ketocton, Mill Creek, and Smith's Creek. These churches, when constituted, joined the association to the north, since they were of the "same religious sentiments."[226]

After making several missionary journeys into Virginia, David Thomas, of Pennsylvania, settled at Broad Run as the pastor of the Baptist church there. He journeyed over all of this area proclaiming the doctrines contained in the Scriptures and the Philadelphia Confession. In this way he strongly influenced both churches and young preachers to accept these doctrines.[227] He was the instrument used to raise up the Fristoe brothers, Daniel and William, besides other

---

[225] Semple, *Virginia Baptists,* (1894 ed.), p. 376; Benedict, *General History,* (1848 ed.), p. 644.

[226] Fristoe, *Ketocton Association,* p. 6. Cf. also Gillette, *Minutes* , pp. 71, 72.

[227] Fristoe, *Ketocton Association,* p. 7; Benedict, *General History,* (1848 ed.), p.644; Semple, *Virginia Baptists,* (1894 ed.), pp. 378, 379.

useful preachers. When Thomas later seemed to accept Arminian doctrine his younger disciples chose William Fristoe to talk with him about this problem. Fristoe evidently won his point because Thomas came back into line in his doctrinal stand.[228]

The doctrinal influence of this association upon the churches in the South was widespread because Miller and Gano as well as other ministers made numerous preaching tours through the area. Of course they did not find and reorganize Baptist churches on each of these tours, however, they did exercise a positive influence on the Regular Baptist churches in their preaching and teaching.[229]

The Kentucky Baptist churches felt the doctrinal influence of the Philadelphia Association as early as 1788 when John Gano took over the pastorate of the Town Fork church near Frankfort.[230] The Bullittsburg Baptist Church was organized in 1794 and it too adopted the doctrines "set forth in the Philadelphia Confession of Faith."[231]

---

[228] Edward W. and Spencer W. Cone, *Some Account of the Life of Spencer Houghton Cone, a Baptist Preacher in America* (New York: Livermore & Rudd, 1856), pp. 179, 180, hereafter referred to as, *Life of Spencer Cone.*. A paper drawn up by Doctor John L. Dagg on this period is cited at length. Dagg and Cone were strongly influenced in their early ministry by William Fristoe.

[229] *Memoirs of John Gano,* pp. 39 ff.

[230] *Ibid.,* pp. 118 ff.

[231] J. A. Kirtley, *History of Bullittsburg Church with Biographies of Elders Absalom Graves, Chichester Matthews, James Dicken and Robert Kirtley* (Covington, Kentucky: Printed by Davis, 1872), p. 3.

Influence on Associations

In tracing the doctrinal influence of the Philadelphia Association on churches and associations one runs into many difficulties. In the first place, many of the available records give little data concerning this influence. In the second place, there were many churches dismissed from this body down through the years to join other associations. Again, many prominent ministers journeyed through and preached in many associations. There were other preachers from this body and many members who took up residence in other associations. This association also made a practice of sending letters and its *Minutes* to many of the associations.

Of the first four associations formed in the south it is fairly easy to trace the influence of this association in three. The Charleston Association was organized in 1751 largely through the efforts of Oliver Hart, a product of the Philadelphia Association and pastor of the Baptist church in Charleston.[232] Many members of the Welsh Neck church were from the Welsh Tract Baptist Church in Delaware.[233] John Gano and Hezekiah Smith of the Philadelphia Association preached extensively in this association.[234] It did not, however, adopt a confession of faith until 1767 when it adopted the Confession of Faith of London of 1689."[235]

---

[232] Furman, *Charleston Association,* pp. 7-9; Benedict, *General History,* (1848 ed.), pp. 703, 707, 708. [Hart was a Pennsylvanian—Editor]

[233] Benedict, *General History* (1848 ed.), pp. 704-706.

[234] Furman, *Charleston Association,* pp. 10-12, 62, 71, 74.

[235] *Ibid.,* p. 12.

Through the efforts of Benjamin Miller, Peter Peterson VanHorne, and John Gano the Kehukee Association was firmly established along the lines of the Philadelphia Confession. Its churches, however, had adopted this Confession at the time they were reorganized.[236] This body, it is true, went on to a very rigid form of Calvinism by 1832. But Paschal seems to be wrong when he speaks of the "blight of Hyper-Calvinism which the ministers of the Philadelphia Association imposed" upon these churches.[237] One author gives a good idea of the later position of this body in relating the instance of a Baptist preacher coming into this association in the year 1791 and preaching free will doctrines. A committee called upon him and asked him to desist from preaching such doctrines but to no avail. Finally in the words of this author,

> when Frost went to preach again, and took his text, which was, *He shall thoroughly purge his floor, and gather his wheat into his garner;* and coming to the words "purge his floor," his tongue failed, he cried, "let us pray," but sunk in his knees, and spoke not another word. He was dead in less than three hours. Thus did God avenge his suffering church in these towns, for this fox was spoiling the tender grapes.[238]

---

[236] Burkitt and Read, *Kehukee Association,* pp. 29, 30.

[237] Paschal, *Shubal Stearns,* p. 56. Cf. also Purefoy, *Sandy Creek Association,* pp. 51, 53.

[238] Burkitt and Read, *A Concise History of the Kehukee Association, From Its Original Rise to the Present Time,* edited and enlarged by Joseph Biggs (Tarborough, North Carolina: George Howard, 1834), pp. 151, 152, hereafter referred to as: Burkitt & Read, *Kehukee Association, enlarged edition.*

The Sandy Creek Association had been organized before the above association, but it was a Separate Baptist and not a Regular Baptist association. When John Gano visited this association in 1759, he was at first treated rather coldly by all except Shubal Stearns. Finally, at the insistence of Stearns, he was allowed to preach, but nothing came of these efforts other than perhaps a better understanding.[239]

In 1765 three churches, Ketocton, Mill Creek, and Smith's Creek of Virginia, were dismissed by the Philadelphia Association to form a new association, "provided they go on the same plan."[240] "After a good deal of deliberating" on the matter, the Ketocton Baptist Association agreed to adopt the "Regular Baptist Confession of Faith." But this Confession was not "to hold tyrannical sway over the conscience of any member."[241]

The second Regular Baptist association organized in the North was the Warren, composed of churches in Rhode Island and Massachusetts. This association was organized as a result of the efforts of James Manning and with the assistance of Hezekiah Smith of Haverhill, Massachusetts—both were from the Philadelphia Association. This association adopted the same Confession of Faith held by the Philadelphia body.[242]

---

[239] Benedict, *General History,* (1848 ed.), p. 686.

[240] Gillette, *Minutes,* p. 95.

[241] Fristoe, *Ketocton Association,* p. 22.

[242] *A Compendium of the Minutes of the Warren Baptist Association, from its Formation in 1767 to the Year 1825,* Inclusive, p. 3. Cf. also Guild, *Life of James Manning,* p. 80.

The Elkhorn Association was formed in Kentucky in 1785,[243] and in the same meeting the question was asked,

> Whether the Philadelphia confession of faith adopted by the Baptists shall be strictly adhered to as the rule of our communion or whether a suspension thereof for the sake of Society be best?

When put to a vote the body decided that this "confession of faith should be strictly adhered to."[244]

John Gano, of the city of New York and the Philadelphia Association, came into this association when he accepted the pastorate of the Town Fork Baptist Church in 1788 and continued there until his death in 1804. He no doubt exerted a strong influence upon this body as preacher, moderator, and member of many important committees.[245] One informant says of Gano in 1790, "he is a blessing to our new country."[246] Another wrote in 1794, he is "an instructing and animating preacher" and he "has been singularly useful to the churches in Kentucky."[247] After his death this association agreed to

---

243 Asplund, *Annual Register,* p. 51.

244 William Warren Sweet, *Religion on the Frontier: The Baptists* (Chicago: The University of Chicago Press, 1931), p. 417.

245 *Ibid.,* pp. 428 ff.

246 Rippon, *Annual Register,* Vol. I, p. 117. A letter from Kentucky is cited without the name of the author, dated 1790.

247 Rippon, *Annual Register,* Vol. II, p. 202. Again a letter from Kentucky is cited without the name of the author, dated 1794.

insert in the Minutes a tribute to him—"he lived and died an ornament to religion."[248]

The Holston Association was for a while united with the Sandy Creek Association, but in 1786 it became an independent body. The same year it adopted the Philadelphia Confession of Faith, and in 1847 it still adhered to the "doctrinal sentiments contained in that instrument."[249]

The Warwick Association, (New York), organized in 1791, stated that it agreed with all of the Confessions, "but that they prefer, to all other human compositions" the one "adopted by the Philadelphia Association and others in America."[250] The New York Association, organized the same year, decided that "they approve" the Confession of Faith, "adopted and held" by the Philadelphia Association, "as happily expressing the sentiments contained in the holy Scriptures . . . which are the only certain rule of faith and practice."[251] "The faith and order" of the Danbury Association of Con-

---

[248] Sweet, *op. cit.,* p. 504.

[249] Benedict, *General History,* (1848 ed.), pp. 791, 792. See also Asplund, *Annual Register,* p. 52; Semple, *Virginia Baptists,* (1810 ed.), pp. 192, 193. See Wesley M. Gewehr, *The Great Awakening in Virginia, 1740-1790* (Durham, North Carolina: Duke University Press, 1930), pp. 9, 107. Gewehr says, "The great revivals . . . increased dissent . . . and brought on many schisms . . . the Baptists split into Regulars and Separates." p. 9. The two were never united in the first place and did not unite until 1787. Gillette, *Minutes,* p. 227.

[250] Rippon, *Annual Register,* Vol., I, p. 211. See also *Gillette, Minutes,* pp. 281, 296, 297, 305, 333, 341.

[251] Rippon, *Annual Register,* Vol. I, p. 299.

necticut "is essentially contained" in the same Confession of Faith.[252]

The Delaware Association was formed in 1795 largely of churches which had been dismissed from the Philadelphia Association for that purpose.[253] The churches which formed this body adopted a Constitution that year, the final article of which was,

> we approve of the confession of Faith adopted by the Philadelphia Association, September 25, 1742, as generally expressing our opinion of the Holy Scriptures, which we hold above all as the only certain rule of faith and practice.[254]

Other associations which were influenced directly by the Philadelphia Association in their doctrinal position were the Shaftsbury,[255] Baltimore[256] and Redstone.[257] The first two of these associations received both ministers and churches from it, while the latter received several capable ministers.[258]

---

[252] *Ibid.,* Vol. I., p. 111.

[253] Benedict, *General History,* (1848 ed.), pp. 630, 631. See also Gillette, *Minutes* pp. 341 ff.

[254] Cook, *Delaware Baptists,* pp. 89, 90.

[255] Gillette, *Minutes,* pp. 236, 254, 270. Cf. also Asplund, *Annual Register,* p. 49; Wright, *Shaftsbury Association,* p. 28.

[256] Gillette, *Minutes,* p. 305.

[257] *Ibid.,* pp. 409, 437. Cf. also Asplund, *Annual Register,* pp. 49, 50.

[258] Other associations which adopted the Philadelphia Confession of Faith were: Bowdoinham (Maine), New Hampshire, Meredith (New Hampshire), Woodstock (New Hampshire and Vermont),

Summary

When the Philadelphia Association adopted the London Confession of Faith of 1689 it took a step that was to shape the doctrinal sentiments of the Baptists throughout America.

The efforts of this body to thoroughly inculcate these doctrines into its own membership were wisely planned. One method of approach was through the home—with the parents giving the instruction. Another way was through doctrinal sermons, which were preached by capable ministers at the annual meetings. A third method was the doctrinal circular letters that were sent out once each year. Another approach was through the doctrinal questions which were taken up and answered by this body in its yearly meetings. A fifth method of indoctrination was through the printing and distribution of the Confession of Faith and a catechism based upon the Confession.

The Philadelphia Association had no sympathy whatsoever with that which it considered to be false doctrine. Those who had strayed from the doctrines which had been delivered "once for all to the saints" were first approached on the subject and given opportunity to reconsider and then if they saw fit to repudiate the erroneous doctrine they were forgiven. But, if they decided to maintain the new doctrine they were immediately excluded from the membership of their church by its members.

---

[258] (Con't) Stonington (Connecticut and Rhode Island), Vermont, Chappawamsic District (Virginia), Salem (Kentucky), and Georgia.

This body did not, however, spend all of its efforts upon itself. As early as 1751 it sent some of its preachers to Virginia to assist two churches that had requested aid in solving their doctrinal and disciplinary difficulties. After this, its ministers and missionaries ranged throughout the colonies aiding needy churches in whatever way they could.

The doctrinal influence of this body was strongly felt by many of the early associations. This was especially true in their early and formative years. In the South the Charleston, Ketocton, Kehukee, Holston and Elkhorn were associations influenced in this manner. The Warren, New York, Warwick and others in the North were likewise influenced by the Philadelphia Association.

Samuel Jones (1735-1814), who was characterized according to a contributing writer to Cathcart's *Baptist Encyclopedia (*1881, p. 619), as "the most influential Baptist minister in the Middle Colonies, and probably in the whole country."

Baptist Meeting-house at Hopewell, New Jersey. John Hart, later a signer of the Declaration of Independence, had donated a three-quarter acre of land to the congregation to build on. The 40' x 30' structure was completed in 1747. It was here that member John Gano, later a noted pastor/evangelist of the Philadelphia Association, was ordained on May 29, 1754.

Chapter Four

The Influence of the Philadelphia Association Upon Baptist Organization in America

The influence of the Philadelphia Association upon Baptist organization in the English speaking colonies of North America and later the United States has been generally neglected if not entirely overlooked by writers in the field of American Baptist history. This fact is difficult to understand since this body exerted considerable influence in this field as well as in the realm of Baptist education and doctrine. A possible explanation of this is the fact that usually writers in Baptist history have written surveys instead of treating special fields of the subject.

The Background for This Influence

By the middle of the eighteenth century this association began to lay the foundation for bringing its influence to bear upon Baptists in the English colonies of North America. In 1750 it appointed two of its ministers[259] to write to some people in Fairfax County, Virginia for the association. Shortly after this, two of its

---

[259] Gillette, *Minutes,* p. 65.

ministers, John Thomas of Montgomery, Pennsylvania and Benjamin Miller of Scotch Plains, New Jersey went into Virginia on a preaching tour. Thomas succeeded in organizing a church at Ketocton. This church and the Arminian Baptist church at Opekon, sent a request to the Philadelphia Association for help. It readily agreed to send Thomas and Miller, who were accompanied by John Gano and Isaac Sutton. These ministers in due time examined the members at Opekon and found that it was "not a regular church" as most of them had been baptized before they had experienced salvation. Three were found to have "experienced grace" and so were constituted a church, to which six converts were added by baptism upon their profession of faith and request to unite with this church.[260] These churches along with other Virginia churches were later received into the Philadelphia Association.[261]

In 1755 the Philadelphia Association appointed Benjamin Miller of New Jersey and Peter Peterson Van Horne of Pennsylvania to go into North Carolina for the purpose of assisting churches in need. John Gano, a missionary under the auspices of both the Philadelphia and Charleston Associations, had made the request to the former body for its help in behalf of these destitute churches. Together these men and one Williams preached and taught at several General Baptist churches, which had not required an "experience of grace previous to their baptism" and as a result of these efforts they

---

[260] *Memoirs of John Gano,* pp. 39, 40, 49; Benedict, *General History,* (1848 ed.) p. 643.

[261] Gillette, *Minutes,* pp. 71, 72, 86; Semple, *Virginia Baptists,* (1894 ed.), pp. 251, 252; Fristoe, *Ketocton Association,* p. 6.

reorganized a number of these churches along the Regular Baptist lines.[262]

In 1757 the churches were informed by this body that it had received "many pressing calls from vacant places for ministerial helps." This fact was stated with the hope that it would be an "inducement to all our churches to spare their ministers as much as possible to supply them."[263] When Gano took the pastorate of the First Baptist Church in the city of New York he did so with the understanding that he could spend three months out of the first year preaching in North Carolina.[264]

Organization of Associations

The influence of the Philadelphia Association upon the organization of associations was as widespread as its influence in the organization of churches. This influence was manifested in various ways in the different associations.

The Charleston Association, organized in 1751, was the second Baptist association to be organized in this

---

[262] Gillette, *Minutes,* pp. 72, 73; Burkitt and Read, *Kehukee Association,* pp. 28, 29; Furman, *Charleston Association,* p. 62; Benedict, *General History,* (1848 ed.) pp. 682, 683; Purefoy, *Sandy Creek Association*, pp. 42, 43; Riley, *Southern States,* pp. 19, 25. For a view diametrically opposed to all the above writers on this subject see, Paschal, *Shubal Stearns.*

[263] Gillette, *Minutes,* p. 75.

[264] *Memoirs of John Gano,* p. 87. [Gano had organized a church in North Carolina at the Jersey Settlement, so named for the number of families from New Jersey who came there. Gano himself was a native of New Jersey. He and his family had been driven from this field by the French and Indian War.—Editor]

country. The influence of the Philadelphia Association in this organization was paramount. Oliver Hart, a native of Pennsylvania, became pastor of the church at Charleston in the latter part of 1749. Furman gives Hart the honor of being the chief mover in the organization of this association. He says, "Mr. Hart had seen, in the Philadelphia Association, the happy consequences of union and stated intercourse among churches maintaining the same faith and order." With this desire in mind he worked and planned until it became a reality.[265]

Hart, however, did not accomplish this union singlehandedly, nor was he the only contribution from the northern association. In 1737 several Welsh Baptists from the Welsh Tract Baptist Church in Delaware settled in South Carolina. The following year they organized the Welsh Neck Baptist Church. This church was one of the three churches—the messengers from the Euhaw church were prevented from attending the first meeting and so they came in the following—that organized the Charleston Association. Three of the four pastors who came into this association were products of the older body to the north, Francis Pelot being the only exception. Two other ordained ministers who signed the instrument were also from the Philadelphia Association.[266] It is possible that each of these sons also had observed the "happy

---

[265] Furman, *Charleston Association,* p. 8.

[266] *Ibid.,* pp. 5-9, 70, 71, 75-78. Philip James and John Brown were co-pastors of Welsh Neck; John Stephens was pastor of Ashley Creek; and Oliver Hart was pastor of Charleston. Joshua Edwards was ordained into the ministry in 1751. Each of these men was from the Philadelphia Association. See also Newman, *A History of Baptist Churches,* pp. 309-311.

consequences of union" in the parent body and were ready, therefore, to cooperate in this undertaking.

It is doubtful whether the Philadelphia Association had any influence in the organization of the next association—the Sandy Creek, since it was of the Separate Baptist connection.[267] It is true that Daniel Marshall and his wife were converted to Baptist doctrine by coming into contact with the work being done in Virginia by the northern body and that Shubal Stearns was in contact with the Opekon church which was a member of that body.[268] But in the absence of any direct statements of influence received from the above body it must not be assumed because they were influenced very slightly in other ways by these contacts.

The influence of the Philadelphia Association upon the Kehukee Association, which was formed in 1765 was certainly not predominant. The Charleston Association seems to have exerted the stronger influence; however,

---

[267] The leaders of the Separate Baptists came from the Separates of New England. The Separates were converts of George Whitefield, who felt they could not find a cordial church home in the Congregational Churches, consequently they became Independents and for that reason were called Separates. When they were converted to the Baptist position they became known as Separate Baptists. They were zealous and highly emotional in their services. They were Calvinistic in doctrine. Fristoe, *Ketocton Association,* pp. 22, 23. See also, *The Life of the Rev. James Ireland, Who was, for Many Years Pastor of the Baptist Church at Buck Marsh, Waterlick and Happy Creek, in Frederick and Shenandoah Counties, Virginia* (Winchester, Virginia: J. Foster, 1819), pp. 136 ff.

[268] Newman, *A History of Baptist Churches,* pp. 292, 293.

Gano, VanHorne and Miller did have a strong formative influence upon some of its member churches.[269]

In the organization of the Ketocton Association the influence of the Philadelphia Association was more direct than it had been in any of the other associations mentioned thus far. In the *Minutes* of the latter association for the year 1765 the following entry is found: "Agreed, that the churches in Virginia have our leave to form themselves into an association, provided they go on the same plan, and hold union with us."[270] As stated above these churches had been members of the Philadelphia Association since the time of their organization. They found the distance and inconvenience of attending the Philadelphia annual meeting to be too great, therefore, they requested leave of that body for permission to form their own association. Consequently they met in August of the following year and formed an association "in order to transact business that might be conducive to the interest of religion and glory of God." They also determined that the union with the parent body would be by "messenger and letter."[271]

The Warren was the first Regular Baptist association organized in New England. The hand of the Philadelphia Association looms large in its organization.

---

[269] Burkitt and Read, *Kehukee Association,* pp. 28, 29; Furman, *Charleston Association,* p. 62; Benedict, *General History,* (1848 ed.) pp. 682, 683; Purefoy, *Sandy Creek Association,* pp. 42, 43; Riley, *Southern States,* p. 25; Newman, *A History of Baptist Churches,* pp. 290, 293.

[270] Gillette, *Minutes,* p. 95.

[271] Fristoe, *Ketocton Association,* pp. 6, 7; Newman, *A History of Baptist Churches,* pp. 287-289.

The chief mover in this movement was James Manning, the pastor of the recently constituted Baptist church of Warren, Rhode Island and president of the newly-founded Rhode Island College. He was a son of the Philadelphia Association and an alumnus of Isaac Eaton's Latin Grammar School which had been a pet project of this body. His biographer says, "It was Manning's wish to unite all the churches of his faith and order in New England in an Association similar to the one formed in Philadelphia."[272]

He first secured the backing of his church in this matter and then set about the task of winning other Baptist ministers of Rhode Island and Massachusetts to the idea. He did this through letters and personal contacts. As a result of these efforts a preliminary meeting was held in August of 1766 but adjourned to reassemble in September of 1767. For this latter meeting Manning sent out invitations to the churches and eleven responded by sending messengers to Warren.[273]

When the meeting convened in 1767 Manning was ably assisted in the effort to organize by Hezekiah Smith, pastor of the newly organized Baptist church of Haverhill, Massachusetts. Smith, like Manning, was a native son of the Philadelphia Association. Before the Warren meeting his church in its business session drew up a letter of encouragement to the other churches. This letter stated its desire that all messengers and churches would be "directed to form a regular and useful association which shall conduce to the benefit of Christ's cause and the Baptists' interest in general." His church

---

[272] Guild, *Life of James Manning,* p. 74.

[273] *Ibid.,* pp. 74, 75.

was one of the four that entered union and thus formed the Warren Association.[274]

In the annual meeting of the Philadelphia Association in 1766 the messengers, when informed of the meeting in Warren for the year following, took steps to assist Manning in his efforts. Samuel Jones, the pastor of the Lower Dublin church, was appointed to write a letter[275] to this group encouraging them to organize a new association. They also appointed three of their most capable men—John Gano, Samuel Jones and Morgan Edwards—as messengers to represent them at this important meeting in Warren,[276] but for some reason the latter two did not attend. Abel Griffith and Noah Hammond went in their place. Gano, Manning's brother-in-law, preached the opening sermon which was based upon Acts 15:9. After that he was promptly chosen moderator by the delegates of this meeting.[277]

The letter written by Jones was presented to the gathering in Warren. In this letter Jones goes directly to the point:

> When we understood that you had concluded to meet . . . with a view to lay the foundation-stone of an associational building, it gave us peculiar joy, in

---

[274] Guild, *Chaplain Smith,* p. 120; Backus, *A History of New England,* Vol. II, p. 409.

[275] This letter is given in full in Appendix A.

[276] Gillette, *Minutes,* p. 97.

[277] Guild, *Life of James Manning,* p. 75; Backus, *A History of New England,* pp. 408, 409.

> that it opened to our view a prospect of much good being done.[278]

Lest the purpose of the letter should be misconstrued he continues,

> we are still in hopes you will not forget that our embracing the first opportunity of commencing Christian fellowship and acquaintance with you, afford the strongest evidence of our approbation of your present meeting, and how fond we should be of a mutual correspondence between us in this way.[279]

He observes further, "A long course of experience and observation has taught us to have the highest sense of the advantages which accrue from association." In this letter he also took note of the possibility of difficulties that "may call for the exercise of the greatest tenderness and moderation" in order that all minor differences may subside and a "more general union commence."[280]

From these facts it can be seen that the Philadelphia Association was fully committed to the organization of the Warren Association. This seems to be the most aggressive step taken by this body to obtain the formation of a new association.

The Philadelphia body met in October, 1767 and was happy to report in the circular letter to the churches, "We received comfortable letters from the Associations in Virginia and Rhode Island." It also appointed Benjamin

---

[278] Samuel Jones, "Letter to Warren," cited by Guild, *Life of James Manning,* p. 76.

[279] *Ibid.,* p. 76.

[280] *Ibid.,* pp. 76, 77.

Miller and Isaac Stellè, ministers from New Jersey and close friends of Manning and Smith, messengers to the Warren Association at its meeting in 1768.[281] The latter body in 1768 adopted Manning's "Plan of the Association" which set forth the purpose, time and meeting, powers of an association and other related items. Section 6 is interesting and has a bearing upon this chapter. It reads, "A connection to be formed and maintained between this Association and that at Philadelphia, by annual letter and messengers from us to them and from them to us."[282] The influence exerted upon this body by the senior association remained evident for many years.

As late as 1789 the Philadelphia Association covered a large area. In addition to Pennsylvania it had churches in Connecticut, New York, New Jersey, Delaware and Maryland. The leaders of the association realized, however, that this was too wide an area to cover efficiently and for the best interests of all concerned. After stating these conclusions in the annual session of 1789, the messengers recommended that the churches in New York and vicinity "give their opinion at the next association on the expediency of the eastern churches forming a new Association at New York."[283]

As a result of this recommendation, the following year, permission was granted to six churches, at their request, to withdraw in order to "join other Associations, if it should be found more convenient."[284] These churches

---

[281] Gillette, *Minutes,* p. 102.

[282] This is cited in full by Guild, *Life of James Manning,* pp. 78-80.

[283] Gillette, *Minutes,* p. 248.

[284] *Ibid.,* p. 256.

along with others formed two associations in 1791, namely, the Warwick and the New York.[285] The latter was organized upon "the plan and principles of the association of Philadelphia."[286] This is not stated of the Warwick, but it is evident from the close relations between the two associations.[287]

Later this same process was repeated in New Jersey, Delaware and Maryland as well as in Pennsylvania, thus the influence of this body was going on to other associations, which would be difficult to treat adequately in so brief a scope. Another way the parent body influenced associational activities was through ministers and members of its churches moving into other districts. This has already been indicated in the case of the associations to the south and east. With all facts before us it is easy to see why an eminent Baptist historian could say, "Philadelphia, a half a century since, and for a long time before that date . . . both by the North and South, was regarded as the emporium of Baptist influence."[288]

Early Efforts at National Organization

The time came, however, when the leaders in the Philadelphia Association began to see the need for going beyond that of forming churches and associations to that of a national organization of the Baptists. The first hint

---

[285] Rippon, *Annual Register,* Vol. I, pp. 211, 294, 299.

[286] *Ibid.,* Vol. I, p. 299.

[287] Gillette, *Minutes,* pp. 281 ff.

[288] Benedict, *Fifty Years,* pp. 46, 47.

of this is seen in the *Minutes* of 1765 when this body granted permission to the four churches in Virginia to form the Ketocton Association on the conditions that "they go on the same plan, and hold union with us."[289] The new association took the latter condition into consideration and decided that the "union" would be by "letter and messengers" between the two bodies and that it was not to be construed to involve any external power over the new body.[290] The Philadelphia Association in 1766 voted, "That a yearly intercourse between the Associations to the east and west of us be, by letters and messengers, now begun, and hereafter maintained."[291]

In his letter to the messengers gathered at Warren, Rhode Island in 1767, for the purpose of forming the Warren Association, Samuel Jones gave a wider application to this conception of a national organization than had yet been presented. In this letter he indicated both the value and desirability of associations. With this background he proceeded to the question of a national organization and made his position clear on the subject by saying, "a union of associations will still increase the body in weight and strength."[292]

As far as could be determined, five years elapsed before anything else was written on this important subject. Morgan Edwards, pastor of the Baptist church in Philadelphia, was the next to raise the subject. In the

---

289 Gillette, *Minutes,* p. 95.

290 Fristoe, *Ketocton Association,* pp. 7, 8.

291 Gillette, *Minutes,* p. 97.

292 Jones, "Letter to Warren" cited by Guild, *Life of James Manning,* p. 77.

preface to his invaluable book, *Materials Towards a History of the Baptists in Pennsylvania Both British and German,* published in 1772, he gave the fullest treatment of this matter that had appeared to that time. He advocated each congregation of baptized believers being organized into churches and groups of churches into associations. He concluded that the associations should be "multiplied so as to have one in every province." He was not content, however, to stop here for he longed for a union of all these associations on the order of that of the Ketocton and Warren to the Philadelphia.[293]

In Edwards' day Philadelphia was considered the center of things in the colonies. This is not difficult to understand because few settlers had pressed beyond the mountains into what is now Ohio, West Virginia, Kentucky and Tennessee. So it can be seen why Edwards would hold that the Philadelphia Association, from its very location, was central and for that reason should be the headquarters of the national Baptist organization. To him this organization was to be advisory and a collector and dispenser of letters and messengers sent from the churches to the associations and from the associations to the center. This information was there to be digested before being sent back to the associations and thence to the churches and on to the individuals.[294]

---

[293] Edwards, *Baptists in Pennsylvania,* pp. i, ii. [A facsimile reprint of this important work is available from Regular Baptist Publishing—Editor]

[294] *Ibid.,* pp.ii, iii. [Edwards' view would be realized years later when what became known as the Triennial Convention was organized at Philadelphia—Editor]

Edwards maintained that this system would be of value not only in the gathering of important knowledge of the Baptist growth in the colonies and in the contributions arising from the "mutual advice" of these various bodies but would be of inestimable value in bringing the far-flung groups of Baptists into a closely knit unit.[295]

He does not claim to be the originator of a new or revolutionary plan, but readily admits that he is only calling to the attention of his readers a plan that already had been put to the test in the case of the Ketocton and Warren Associations. This plan had been set in motion in 1765 and 1767, respectively—the time of the organization of the two associations. He declares that both of these bodies had adopted the "Philadelphia plan." To him the practicability of the plan had been amply proven by its working over a period of five to seven years.[296]

Edwards insisted that this plan needed only to be perfected to be put into practice on a widespread scale. For the perfection of the plan he presented, in substance,[297] the following five-fold program:

> 1. That the association of Philadelphia be embodied by charter; and that one person from every provincial association be made a member of that body.
> 2. That an able preacher be appointed to visit all the churches in the character and office of an evangelist.

---

[295] *Ibid.*, pp. ii-iv.

[296] *Ibid.*, pp. 1, 11.

[297] This plan is given in full in Appendix A.

> 3. That the nature of associations among the Baptists be made public.
> 4. That all the Baptist churches from Nova Scotia to Georgia be made sufficiently known one to another.
> 5. That the terms of the proposed union should be so general as not to preclude any Baptist church of fair character, though differing from others in "unessential points of faith or order."[298]

As can readily be seen, this plan left much to be desired in the way of a national organization of Baptists. In a day, however, when Baptists were thinking and writing little on the subject, this plan seems to be worthy of full consideration. It was, like the earlier efforts, an attempt to organize on the federation or federal union basis and in this respect it was similar to the political efforts to organize the thirteen colonies of that day.

The idea set forth in this plan of chartering the Philadelphia Association and making it the corporate body probably did not set too well with many of the Baptist associations of that day, however, the idea of messengers in a modified form is used today by all of the Baptist bodies—the messengers are appointed by the churches instead of the associations. Most of these associations had evangelists. The point of disseminating knowledge of what was being done by the Baptists was good. Today it may be confined to various reports, minutes, tracts and to the many denominational papers. Edwards realized that this point was strategic to the success of any form of Baptist organization. Point

[298] Edwards, *Baptists in Pennsylvania,* pp. ii, iii.

number five, undoubtedly, provided the most difficult hurdle for Baptists of that day, for many of the Baptists, just as they are today, were not willing to concede anything on "unessential points."[299]

Edwards was willing to admit, and rightly so, that he was "anxious to render the said combination of Baptist churches universal upon this continent." He considered the undertaking so important and worthy of his best efforts that he said, "should God give me success herein, as in the affair of the Baptist college, I shall deem myself the happiest man on earth."[300]

There doesn't seem to have been any immediate response to these proposals. Edwards died in 1795 without having seen his desire in this matter fulfilled. William Rogers preached his funeral sermon, in which he referred to this plan of Edwards and continues, "but, finding this impracticable, at that time, he visited the churches from New Hampshire to Georgia, gathering materials towards the history of the whole." He adds rather succinctly, "this plan of union, as yet, has not succeeded."[301]

Later Efforts of The Association

It was not until four years after Edwards death and twenty-nine years after he had submitted his plan of national organization to the Baptists that another serious

---

[299] *Ibid.,* p. iii.

[300] *Ibid.,* p. 128.

[301] Sprague, *The Baptists,* p. 84; Davis, *Welsh Baptists,* p. 80.

effort was put forth by the Philadelphia Association to effect an organization of the Baptists on a nationwide scale. In the associational meeting of 1799 this subject was introduced and seriously considered. The decision that it made is so important that it is given in full,

> Apprehensive that many advantages may result from a general conference, composed of one or more members from each Association, to be held every one, two or three years, as may seem most subservient to the general interests of our Lord's kingdom; this Association respectfully invites the different Associations in the United States to favor them with their views on the subject.[302]

In order to put this important decision before the Baptists the association appointed Thomas Ustick, the pastor of the First Baptist Church of Philadelphia, to send a copy of the minutes, with this request, to every association in the United States. [303] The following year it appointed a committee composed of William Rogers, Thomas Ustick, Burgiss Allison, William Staughton and Peter Wilson "to receive and answer all communications from the different associations" concerning this important business "in order that we may bring the whole to a conclusion."[304]

Response of the Associations

In the Minutes of 1800 the Philadelphia Association reported that "three of their sister" associations had

---

[302] Gillette, *Minutes,* p. 343.

[303] Loc. cit.

[304] Gillette, *Minutes,* pp. 349, 350.

sent "approving resolutions" in reply to its request of the year before concerning a general conference. There is no definite indication given in the minutes as to the identity of the associations which sent these "approving resolutions" and the author has been unable to discover which they were.[305] A strong appeal is given again to the other associations to consider this "important subject." They are also solicited in their replies to give "their views as to the time when, and the place where," the first general conference should convene.[306]

The Philadelphia Association was so anxious to get this organization under way that it recommended to the different associations that they authorize their messengers to confer with a committee, to be appointed by it the following year, on this subject and to assist it in "digesting a plan relative to the general conference." This effort was made to clear up anything that had been a hindrance and to "do whatever may have a tendency to

---

[305] In the *Minutes* of 1800 it is stated that letters and minutes were received from the Warwick, Delaware, New York and Charleston Associations. The Charleston Association did not meet and make its decision until November after the Philadelphia meeting in October, so it could not be one of the three. This is not conclusive proof, however, that the others were the three spoken of, though possibly they might have been. Minutes were also received from the following associations: Shaftsbury, Middle District, Neuse, Dover, Flat River, Goshen, Roanoke District, Kehukee and Culpepper. Gillette, *Minutes,* p. 348. [The New York Association, at its meeting on May 23, 1800, agreed as a body that "a general conference of members from the different Baptist associations in the United States is desirable." *Minutes of the New York Baptist Association,* 1800, p. 3.—Editor]

[306] Gillette, *Minutes,* p. 349.

accelerate this beneficial design."[307] But for some unknown reason there is no reference to this item of business in the minutes of the following year. It is probable that the other associations did not make the provisions requested by the association at Philadelphia.*

This proposition was taken up for consideration in the annual meeting of the Charleston Association in 1800. After due consideration this body decided, that, "If a well digested plan should be devised" in which the objects for such an organization be clearly defined or stated and if proper steps be taken to prevent any usurpation of authority or other abuses by the said organization it might consider it further. As if this were not enough, it further stipulated that if the plan became universally accepted or approved by the churches and associations in the United States it would be "disposed to give it their support."[308] It certainly did not take a Philadelphia lawyer of that day to see that the messengers of the churches of the Charleston Association wanted to have ample guarantee of its freedom before entering into a national organization of Baptists in America.

---

[307] *Ibid.*, p. 349.

* [The messengers appointed by the New York Association, to the Philadelphia (Reune Runyan, William VanHorne, Peter Bryant and Francis Davis), "were instructed to concert measures with the committee appointed by that [the Philadelphia] Association; together with delegates who may be appointed by other Associations, respecting the establishment of a *general conference* of members from the different Baptist Associations in the United States of America." *Minutes of the New York Baptist Association,* 1801, p. 3.—Editor.]

[308] Furman, *Charleston Association,* p. 29.

The same year this proposition was introduced in the Shaftsbury Association for consideration at its annual meeting. After the matter had been discussed for some time this body decided to turn it over to the churches within its boundaries to obtain their opinions on the issue. The churches, after discussing the proposition, were instructed to forward their decisions to the next session in 1801. After considering the decisions of the churches this association reported it would give its answer to the enquiring association.[309]

After due consideration of the decisions of the churches the following year this body decided, "That at present we have not sufficient light on the subject, to see the utility of such a combination." In consequence of the above decision the messengers of this body "voted not to engage therein till we have further light thereon."[310]

This proposition was not brought before the Georgia Association until its annual session in 1801 or at any rate it did not decide to close the issue until that year. The contemporary historian of this association states that it was taken up at this session, however, he adds, "the Body from prudential considerations, forbade to express an opinion upon the subject at that time."[311] What the "prudential considerations" were which "forbade" this association to make a decision Mercer does not say.

If the conclusions of the Charleston, Georgia and Shaftsbury Associations, as listed above, are indicative of

---

[309] Wright, *Shaftsbury Association,* pp. 71, 72.

[310] *Ibid.,* p. 79.

[311] Jesse Mercer, *History of the Georgia Baptist Association* (Washington, Georgia: No Printer, 1838), p. 40.

the majority of associations and if no more than the "three sister associations" approved the proposition of the Philadelphia Association it is not at all surprising that the Philadelphia body in 1802 came to the conclusion that a General Conference of Baptists was not "likely to be accomplished."[312] On the other hand it is possible that this body gave up too easily on this issue.

It seems that this noble dream failed to be realized for several basic reasons. The chief reason for this failure appears to have been a lack of clarification, as to the purpose and power of the proposed organization as well as the time of meeting. Another hindrance to the realization of the plan was too exclusive reliance upon correspondence and interchange of associational minutes to accomplish the gigantic task instead of also sending men who were thoroughly sold on the issue to explain and plead for it as well as to secure the suggestions of others on the subject in the associational meetings. A third reason for the failure seems to have been a lack of men with the drive of Gano, Miller, and Edwards to push the issue to a successful realization.[313] A final reason for not realizing the organization was the lack of a rallying point or popular slogan. At any rate, these were prominent features in the formation of the Triennial Convention years later.

---

[312] Gillette, *Minutes,* pp. 349, 370.

[313] In 1800 Gano was the only one living of this list. He was in Kentucky in his seventy-third year. Samuel Jones, although a leader of note in the Philadelphia Association, seems never to have been the traveler and organizer that the above were.

A New Plan—The Committee of Correspondence

The Philadelphia Association did not give up all hope for a national organization of Baptists. In the 1802 meeting a new, long range plan was introduced which was "designed to answer" all the purposes of the proposed general conference. A committee was appointed to examine this new plan, make recommendations and report these to that session of the association. This committee, composed of four ministers[314] of the association, reported on the plan. Its recommendations, after being amended, were adopted. The provisions, in substance, were:

> 1. For a General Committee of Correspondence composed of not more than fifteen members.
> 2. Members to be selected from ministers and laymen of Philadelphia and vicinity.
> 3. That it open a correspondence with all associations for the purpose of securing reliable statistics.
> 4. The Committee to meet at least once a year but more if the business warranted.
> 5. That it publish the vital facts.
> 6. That all money saved be used for deceased ministers' families or other "laudable purposes."
>
> This examining committee appointed a fourteen man committee to "carry the same into execution."[315]

---

[314] The Examining Committee was composed of Samuel Jones, Reune Runyan, William Rogers and Thomas Montanye. Gillette, *Minutes,* p. 370.

[315] Gillette, *Minutes,* pp. 370, 371. The Committee of Correspondence was composed of: Samuel Jones, Burgiss Allison, William Rogers, Thomas Ustick, William Staughton, William White, Thomas Montanye, John Peckworth, Silas Hough, M. D., George Ingles, Thomas Holmes, John McLeod, John Holmes, and William M'Gee.

In 1803 the Correspondence Committee reported that it had received short histories of three associations, namely, Otsego, of New York, Roanoke District and Middle District, both of Virginia and a letter and minutes from the Rensselaerville Association in New York and a short account of the churches in Wayne and Luzerne Counties in Pennsylvania.[316]

This committee did not make a report to the Philadelphia Association in 1804, but in 1805 it made up for this by giving full reports of all meetings held since its report in 1803. It reported that five associations had adopted its latest idea, namely, Charleston, Warren, Danbury, New York, and Warwick. The first three of these associations along with the Savannah sent minutes. A further indication of the success of this latest move was the numerous letters received from leading Baptist ministers and laymen in all sections of the United States reporting on the activities of Baptists in their particular locality.[317]

In the report of the Committee for 1805 there was news of pleasing revivals in New England, New York, South Carolina and Virginia. There was also a letter from Henry Holcombe, of Savannah, in behalf of the General Committee of Georgia Baptists. But the big news came from Maine where most of the members of a Congregational church and its pastor were converted to the Baptist position.[318]

---

[316] *Ibid.,* pp. 381, 382.

[317] *Ibid.,* pp. 411, 412.

[318] *Ibid.,* p. 412. The church was located in Sedgwick, Maine. [It is mistakenly stated in the Minutes as being in New Hampshire. The pastor's name was Daniel Merrill. His son, Moses Merrill, would

In 1806 this Committee reported letters concerning the work of four associations, the Danbury in Connecticut, the Redstone, in Pennsylvania and Ohio, the Bethel in South Carolina, and the Sarepta in Georgia. The Bethel reported that it had dismissed fourteen churches in 1800 to form the Broad River Association and in 1802 nine more to assist in the formation of the Saluda Association—all of these associations were located in South Carolina. There was also a letter from Newport, Rhode Island, with news of a revival in that city.[319]

Response to The Latest Plan

This latest effort of the Philadelphia Association to bring about a fuller understanding and a closer relationship among the Baptists throughout the United States was met with various reactions by the different associations. The response of individuals throughout the country was more spontaneous than to the first plan.

In 1803 the Charleston Association, after considering this proposal, appointed a similar committee to correspond with the various associations in the United States for the purpose of giving as well as receiving valuable information, "and in particular to correspond with the Committee of the Philadelphia Association, to aid their design of publishing general religious information."[320]

---

[318] (Con't) later pioneer Baptist work in the Nebraska Territory. —Editor]

[319] *Ibid.*, p. 425.

[320] Furman, *Charleston Association,* p. 31.

This proposal was taken up the same year by the Warren Association at its regular meeting. The plan was approved and later recommended by this association to all the churches composing its constituency. The associations which corresponded with the Warren body were also urged "to send their minutes, and such other information as they may judge proper, to the Committee" in Philadelphia.[321]

In 1804 the Georgia Association took the circular from the "Philadelphia General Committee requesting intelligence relative to the state of religious and other matters" and after discussing the request it decided to refer the question to the "General Committee of this State, as the most suitable medium through which the desired information might be obtained."[322]

From the reports of the General Committee of Correspondence of the Philadelphia Association to its annual meetings and from action taken by other bodies it can be seen that this effort made a greater impression on the Baptists of the United States than any of its previous efforts had made.[323]

One must not come to the conclusion that the efforts put forth by the Philadelphia Association to effect a national organization of the Baptists in this country were in vain. They were not. In speaking of the system instituted by the Philadelphia Association of exchanging minutes and letters with other associations, the editor of

---

[321] *Minutes of the Warren Association* 1803, p. 7.

[322] Mercer, *op. cit.,* p. 43.

[323] For response of other associations see the "Reports" of the Correspondence Committee, Gillette, *Minutes,* pp. 381, 382, 411, 412, 425. *Cf. Ante,* pp. 120, 121.

The Baptist Magazine of London wrote that:

> The Minutes and Letters of which correspondence are reported to each Association at their several annual assemblies. We should be happy to see a plan of this kind adopted in England; by extending the mutual knowledge of each other's circumstances, it would draw closer the cords of fraternal affection among the brethren of our denomination.[324]

These were the last serious efforts in this direction until 1813 when Luther Rice returned from India, newly converted to Baptist principles, to win the backing of Baptists for Adoniram and Ann Judson, also recently converted to the Baptist faith. It is not too much to say that these efforts by the Philadelphia body had prepared the ground for the monumental work of Rice in effecting the old Triennial Convention.

Summary

The influence of the Philadelphia Association upon organization began to be felt in Virginia soon after 1750 when some of its ministers were authorized to go there to assist churches with doctrinal difficulties. These ministers reorganized many of these churches, especially those which were considered by them to be too loosely organized.

---

[324] "American Baptists," *The Baptist Magazine* (London: 1809), p. 469.

First Baptist meeting-house, Philadelphia as it appeared after the enlargement of 1808. While the work was being done, the members met for worship in the State House, now called Independence Hall. The sister Pennepek meeting-house was located about 11 miles northwest of Independence Hall. It was in the above building that what became known as the Triennial Convention was organized on May 14, 1814. In America as well as previously in Great Britain it was the Calvinists who initiated foreign missionary endeavors among the Baptists.

Present at this organizational meeting of the American Baptists was William Staughton (1770-1829), right, a native of England who was pastor of the Samson St. Baptist church in Philadelphia, and former pastor at First Baptist. Staughton had also been present at the organizational meeting of "The Particular Baptist Society for Propagating the Gospel Among the Heathen" in Kettering, England in 1792 which commissioned William Carey to India. Staughton had removed to America the following year of 1793.

When other associations began to be organized the influence of this body was again felt. This was partially true when the Charleston and Ketocton Associations were organized in the South. It was also brought to bear upon the organization of the Warren, Warwick and New York Associations when they were formed in the North.

The first hints from this association regarding a national organization came when the Ketocton and Warren Associations were formed respectively in 1765 and 1767. Morgan Edwards further developed this idea in 1772 by giving five points, which he considered to be a necessary yardstick for this purpose.

The Philadelphia Association put forth its first serious effort to effect a national organization in 1799. These efforts were continued through 1801. In 1802 it came to the conclusion that a "general conference not being likely to be accomplished" a plan was laid before it, which was a Committee of Correspondence. The purpose of the new plan was to gather and disseminate information concerning Baptists in all parts of the United States and thus draw the Baptists closer together. The response to this idea was more spontaneous than that given to the initial efforts to form a national organization.

In the efforts put forth in various phases of Baptist organization the Philadelphia Association rendered invaluable service to the cause of the Baptists in this country.

Chapter Five

The Influence Of The Philadelphia Association Upon Baptist Associational Discipline

The influence which the Philadelphia Association exercised upon the discipline of Baptist associations in this country played an important role in the history of Baptists. The word "discipline" is used in this chapter to indicate the powers and limitations as well as the duties of an association. This influence, like that upon organization, has been too generally overlooked by many of our Baptist historians.

It must be understood at the outset that the Philadelphia Association did not adopt a fully developed system of discipline at the time of its formation. Some of the decisions and rules of its first meetings came to be seriously questioned and altered as a result of years of experience.

Early Decisions Affecting Discipline

At the time of the organization of this body, in 1707, the messengers decided that the five churches composing the association should choose capable brethren "to meet at the yearly meeting to consult about such things as were wanting in the churches, and to set them in order." Apparently no qualifications or limitations were made at that time upon this decision. The messengers at this first meeting also decided that a person, grieved by his church, could "appeal to the brethren of the several congregations" who in turn would "nominate" a committee to decide upon their differences, stating that " the church and the person so grieved do fully acquiesce in their determination."[325]

As far as the records reveal these decisions were first put to the test in 1712, when "one Thomas Selby made a disturbance and rupture in the church at Philadelphia and Pennepek." Consequently an application was made by the church to the Philadelphia Association for its assistance in finding a solution to the problem. The latter body appointed a committee in response to the application, subsequently both parties agreed to abide by the decision of the committee. This committee made a full report and recommendations to the association after it had investigated the case. The first decision was that the conduct of both parties was "unbecoming Christians in many respects." With regard to Selby the committee decided that he should "be paid the money subscribed to him" and that he was a person deemed "not likely for the promotion of the Gospel in those parts of the country." Selby's conduct after this seems to have borne out the latter decision concerning himself.[326]

The Philadelphia body first used the word "advise" in answering a query in 1726. After 1733 it was used with more regularity to show the relation of the association to the churches,[327] that is, as an *advisory* body.

---

[325] Gillette, *Minutes,* p. 25.

[326] *Ibid.,* p. 26.

[327] *Ibid.,* pp. 28, 34 ff.

Some of its other decisions seem to have been given in more direct terms, however, as in 1730, when the Piscataqua church in New Jersey asked this body for ministerial assistance, it answered,

> we judge it necessary that our ministering brethren do supply such general meetings; nevertheless, we not knowing who, nor how to bind any of them, we think it necessary that the church, where such are held, send to them, that, if possible, they may be certain of some help.[328]

The following year the "distracted condition" of this church was reported to the Philadelphia Association, consequently it appointed Jenkin Jones and Joseph Eaton "to give them a visit before the winter." The visit was made and "proved a means to reduce that church to peace and order."[329]

The Great Valley Baptist Church in 1741 reported to the association the case of two of its members who had been at variance and had submitted their case to the church for solution, however, when the solution was given one refused to abide by the decision. Its question was: "What may be done with the brother so contending?" The association "maturely considered the matter," and concluded,

> we judge the contending person worthy of reproof, because he, having submitted and preferred the matter to the church for final determination, yet contrary to what might be expected from him as a

---

[328] *Ibid.,* p. 31.

[329] *Ibid.,* p. 32.

> man, much more as a Christian, refused to comply with the church's determination.[330]

This church further reported that a member had been excluded, but had afterward given "satisfaction to the majority of the church, by confession of his fault;" but some were not "satisfied" although they had no "substantial reason to render for the same." The question again was, "What may the church do in such a case?" The association advised "the church and the persons dissatisfied to use moderation for some time," and privately to endeavor to win the dissatisfied party but if this should fail, this body further recommended, "at your monthly meeting, urge such persons to produce sufficient reasons for their dissatisfaction." If these members failed to have "such reasons, or upon their refusing to produce such reasons," then the "church may deal with such as disorderly persons."[331]

The Montgomery Baptist Church sent a proposal to the association in 1739, "concerning the keeping of the present Association, whether it be as usual, or altered?" The messengers decided that the association "be continued as usual the present year" and concluded, "if the churches desire the method of the Association altered, let them consult unanimously, and insert the same in next year's letters."[332] This decision gives some idea of the early conception of the powers of an association held by the Baptists in the middle colonies.

---

[330] *Ibid.,* p. 44.

[331] *Ibid.,* p. 45.

[332] *Ibid.,* p. 40

Later Decisions Affecting Discipline

In 1766 an application or appeal was made by an excommunicated person to the Philadelphia Association for it to consider his case. The association voted to postpone the question until the following year. Subsequently the question was taken up in 1767 when it decided that such a person could "appeal" to that body for the consideration of his case. At the meeting in 1768, however, the question was reopened because of "some jealousy arising on account of" the use of "appeal." It was decided that "the word appeal" was unfortunate, since the association "claims no jurisdiction, nor a power to repeal any thing settled by any church." It also concluded that if any parties agreed "to refer matters to the Association" before a settlement of the case was made that the association could "give their advice."[333]

The church of Newtown requested the Philadelphia Association in 1771 to "set the time and ministers" to ordain Nicholas Cox; the messengers of this body replied, that the "appointment of both properly belongs to the church."[334] A similar request was presented to the association in 1775 by the Coram church in New York when it "desired this body to ordain Ebenezer Ward as an itinerant." The reply of the association was that it claimed "no such right."[335]

In 1794 two questions came before the Philadelphia body affecting the independency of local

---

[333] *Ibid.,* pp. 99, 101, 102, 105.

[334] *Ibid.,* p. 119.

[335] *Ibid.,* pp. 148, 149.

churches. The first question was: "Shall the evidence of a non-member be taken as valid against a member?" The messengers "determined, that it be left to every church to judge for themselves in every instance of this nature."[336] The other question concerned the right of churches to withdraw to unite with another association. The answer was,

> It is considered and decided that the churches have an undoubted right to depart from this Association, and join any other they may see fit; but this Association, having been happy in their connection, wish them to continue in union with them as long as . . . they can; but if they choose to withdraw and join any other, we consent.[337]

The messengers decided in 1800, "that the regular business of the Association" is to consider "those matters which are introduced by the churches;" yet, they felt at liberty "to take up any matter of consequence introduced by any individual member."[338] However, in 1805, when a question arose regarding an individual, the messengers decided, "That this Association cannot take up a question that relates to an individual member of any church without interfering with the independence of such church."[339]

---

[336] *Ibid.,* p. 297.

[337] *Ibid.,* p. 297. The churches which requested to be dismissed to unite with the Delaware Association were: Cow Marsh, Welsh Tract, Duck Creek, and Wilmington–all in Delaware.

[338] *Ibid.,* p. 350.

[339] *Ibid.,* p. 410.

As can readily be seen all of these decisions vitally affected both the power and authority of the association and the independency of the churches. This body, as a whole, seems to have been more willing to sacrifice the former than the latter. Since the decisions have been taken from this entire period, one can see that this body has been fairly consistent in not assuming unto itself power over the churches. On this point Benedict says, "It has now been in operation 106 years, and I do not find that it was ever complained of for infringing on the independency of any church."[340]

A Treatise of Church Discipline Adopted

The association took a decisive step in 1742 when a motion was made and carried "to reprint the Confession of faith, set forth by the elders of baptized congregations, met in London, A. D. 1689, with a short treatise of church discipline, to be annexed to the Confession of faith." Jenkin Jones and Benjamin Griffith were appointed by the association to "prepare a short treatise of discipline."[341] "By reason of his other avocations" Jenkin Jones was unable to aid in this task, so it became the responsibility of Griffith to prepare the treatise. For this task he had a tract on the subject by Elias Keach, as well as a manuscript copy from his half brother Abel Morgan, which had been prepared for publication but not printed due to his premature death in 1722. In addition to these treatises he had access to the works of John Owen and

---

[340] Benedict, *General History* (1813 ed.), Vol. 1, p. 596.

[341] Gillette, *Minutes,* p. 46.

Thomas Goodwin.[342] His treatise was presented to the association at its annual meeting in 1743 and "approved by the whole house."[343]

In the treatise on discipline Griffith treated the subject of the powers and limitations of an association under the heading, "Of Communion of churches." He maintained that the church had "sufficient power from Christ to call and ordain its own officers," and he continued "no man or set of men, have authority to choose officers for them . . . without their previous knowledge and voluntary consent." He came to the crucial point when he stated that the local church is,

> independent of any other church power superior to itself, or higher judicatory lodged in any man or any set of men, by any institution of Christ: and therefore, the elders of a church, meeting in the absence of the members, or convened with the elders of other churches, are not intrusted with a power to act for a church in admission of members, ordination, or censures.[344]

He also emphasized the desirability of groups of churches meeting together by messengers or delegates by "mutual agreement" for the purpose of considering the things "as may be for the common benefit of all such churches" that is, for their peace, prosperity and edification, and "what may be for the furtherance of the gospel, and the interest of Christ in the world." He concluded,

---

[342] Cutting, *Historical Vindications,* pp. 199, 200.

[343] Gillette, *Minutes,* p. 48.

[344] Cutting, *Historical Vindications,* pp. 221, 222.

> Yet such delegates thus assembled, are not intrusted or armed with any coercive power, or any superior jurisdiction over the churches concerned, so as to impose their determinations on them or their officers, under the penalty of excommunication, or the like.[345]

Griffith's Essay

The language of Griffith's essay was clear enough, and the messengers in 1749 "unanimously approved and agreed to an essay of Benjamin Griffith," respecting "The Power and Duty of An Association." After "mature deliberation" they ordered the "contents of the same" to be transcribed in the "Association book, to the end and purpose that it may appear what power. . . and duty is incumbent on an Association." It was also to be recorded "to prevent the contempt" some have for such an "assembly" as well as to "prevent any future generation from claiming more power than they ought—lording over the churches."[346]

Griffith, in his essay, said that an "Association is not a superior judicature, having such superior power over the churches" but each church had "a complete power" to "administer all gospel ordinances" since it was "independent of any other church." The association, he maintained was "subservient to the churches," yet he concluded, "that an Association of the delegates of associate churches have a very considerable power in their hands" to maintain "sound doctrine and regular practice." Of course this was not construed to mean that

---

[345] *Ibid.,* pp. 223, 224.

[346] Gillette, *Minutes,* p. 60.

an association could coerce a church into conformity of doctrine or practice but merely to withdraw fellowship from such a "disorderly" church. This, according to Griffith, was not "exceeding the bounds of their power and duty."[347]

This essay began to exert a strong influence upon other associations in this country soon after its adoption by the Philadelphia Association. The Charleston Association when organized in 1751 at Charleston, South Carolina, at that time also "concluded" that Griffith's essay should "be inserted in their Book, as judging it most expressive of the Power and Duty of an Association; and worthy to be adhered to by all our future Associations."[348] The language of the delegates who met in 1751 at Charleston is clear on the value of this document. Basil Manly, Sr., in 1830, thought the essay was important enough for him to copy it, with the above decision, on the flyleaves of his *Confession of Faith.*[349]

---

[347] *Ibid.,* pp. 60-63. See also Daniel Sheppard, *Baptist Confession of Faith: and a Summary of Church Discipline* (Charleston, South Carolina: Printed by W. Riley, 1831), pp. 231-237. Griffith's Essay is cited in Appendix VI, hereafter referred to as: Sheppard, *Confession of Faith.*

[348] Sheppard, *Confession of Faith,* p. 231.

[349] *A Confession of Faith, Put Forth by the Elders and Brethren of Many Congregations of Christians. (Baptized upon Profession of Their Faith.) In London and the Country* (second Charleston edition; Charleston, South Carolina: J. Hoff, 1813). He copied the essay on the flyleaves in the back of this book from the original *Minute Book* of the Charleston Association, which was in his possession October 13, 1830. This *Confession of Faith,* owned by Manly, is now property of the New Orleans Baptist Theological Seminary, New Orleans, Louisiana.

During the same year Daniel Sheppard thought the essay would make a worthwhile contribution to the edition of the *Confession of Faith* which he was editing, therefore, he included it with the above decision of the Charleston Association.[350]

Another Discipline Adopted

Sometime previous to 1774 Morgan Edwards drew up a treatise on church discipline with the imposing title, *The Customs of Primitive Churches, or A Set of Propositions Relative to the Name, Materials, Constitution, Powers, Officers, Ordinances, etc., of a Church,* which he intended for the use of the Philadelphia Association. He published it "in hopes they would have improved on the plan, so that their joint productions might have introduced a full and unexceptionable treatise of Church Discipline."[351] For some unknown reason this body never did accept Edwards' treatise on church discipline, however, the opinion seems to have been widespread that it had been adopted by the Philadelphia body. Consequently, this body in 1774 appointed a committee of four[352] "to form a minute in answer" to this opinion, which was,

---

[350] Sheppard, *Confession of Faith,* pp. 231-237.

[351] Davis, *Welsh Baptists,* p. 79.

[352] The committee was: Abel Morgan, Isaac Backus, Isaac Stellè and Samuel Jones.

> Whereas, a book was published, entitled, *The Customs of the Primitive Churches,*[353] which the author proposed should be altered, amended, and corrected, by his ministering brethren, and then reprinted for the use of the churches, which was never done; and whereas, we have reason to think, that it is understood by many abroad to have been adopted by us in its present form, as our custom and mode of church discipline and practice; it is therefore thought meet, that we should thus publicly testify to the contrary, as it is not, nor ever has been adopted by us, or by any of the churches belonging to the Association.[354]

Gradually Griffith's discipline began to lose its hold on the association and many saw the need for a new treatise on the subject as indicated by the work of Edwards. Consequently, in 1792, the church at Marcus Hook posed this question to the Philadelphia Association, "Would it not be expedient for this Association to republish Dr. Gill's *Nature, Order and Discipline of a Gospel Church*[355] or some other equally good, and recommend the same to the churches?" The association answered that, "most of the churches are unacquainted" with this treatise but it recommended "that they make themselves acquainted therewith against next annual association," in order that they may "be prepared to determine upon the expediency" of adopting Gill's

---

[353] The italics are not in the original record.

[354] Gillette, *Minutes,* p. 141.

[355] The italics are not found in the original records.

work.[356] No further record is given in the *Minutes* concerning this subject.

These efforts, however, were not in vain for in 1795 the association "committed" its "system of discipline to Dr. Samuel Jones for revision and amendment."[357] Jones was instructed to bring his revised treatise before the association at its next meeting, but he was unable to complete the work. After he had "given satisfactory reasons why he had not" he was "appointed to go on in the business."[358] The revised treatise was brought forward and read at the annual meeting in 1797, after which a committee consisting of one member from each church was appointed to consider and alter any point in the treatise that seemed proper before it was published. The first edition of this treatise was published in 1798 with the approval of the committee appointed by the association for that purpose.[359]

The new discipline maintained that the "delegates" of an association "are not armed with coercive power, to compel the churches to submit to their decisions" nor "have they any control over the acts or doings of the churches" since each "church still remains independent." However, they could exclude a church "that may act an unworthy part" or "become unsound in their principles or act irregularly and disorderly," and further, they could "call any delinquent church to account." It concluded

---

[356] Gillette, *Minutes,* p. 282. "against", i.e. *before* the next associational meeting.

[357] *Ibid.,* p. 306.

[358] *Ibid.,* pp. 306, 317.

[359] Gillette, *Minutes,* pp. 325, 334.

that an excluded church would "still remain an independent church though an heterodox and irregular one."[360]

The language of Griffith's treatise was simplified and interpreted here, consequently the First Baptist Church of Philadelphia in 1806 contended that some "rules in the new system of discipline" were discordant with the old. The association, however, exercised its Baptistic prerogative by voting to postpone the consideration of the question until the next year. The following year it voted, "That it is not expedient" to appoint a committee to harmonize the conflicting points.[361]

Influence on Other Associations

As already indicated[362] the Charleston Association at its formation voted to insert Benjamin Griffith's essay on "The Power and Duty of an Association" in its *Minute Book,* since it judged, "it most expressive of the power and duty of an Association, and worthy to be adhered to by all our future Associations."[363]

When this body printed its own discipline it took cognizance of the fact that many of its constituency would question the wisdom of such an edition, since "there is such a valuable treatise on church-discipline, published some years ago by the Philadelphia Association." It

---

[360] Samuel Jones, *A Treatise of Church Discipline and a Directory* (Lexington, Printed by T. Anderson, 1805), pp. 32, 33.

[361] Gillette, *Minutes,* pp. 422, 438.

[362] *Cf. ante,* pp. 136, 137.

[363] Sheppard, *Confession of Faith,* p. 231.

explained that it did not "mean to depreciate the value of that piece," because "it has merited much from the Baptist churches." The reasons given for issuing the Charleston edition were, the Philadelphia edition was "out of print," it was "not so explicit as this" and finally "some things therein appear to us exceptionable." The editors admitted "we have borrowed many hints" from the Philadelphia discipline.[364]

A close check on the chapter "Of the Association of Churches" reveals that the committee, on this point at least, used language closely resembling that of Griffith's essay and discipline. It concluded that an association was "by no means to be deemed a superior judicature vested with coercive power, or authority over the churches" and it cannot threaten or impose its sentiments upon its constituents with excommunication, nor can it "anathematize those who do not implicitly submit to its determinations." It further concluded,

> The Baptist Association, therefore, arrogates no higher title than that of an Advisory Council, consistent with which epithet it ought ever to act, when it acts at all; without intruding on the rights of independent congregational churches; or usurping authority over them.[365]

Sheppard in his 1831 edition of the Confession of Faith not only included the discipline first adopted by the

---

[364] *A Confession of Faith,* second Charleston edition. Preface (only one page) to "A Summary of Church Discipline."

[365] *Ibid.,* p. 28.

Charleston Association, but one by Andrew Fuller as well as that by Samuel Jones.[366]

The Ketocton Association was organized in Virginia in 1766 by four Baptist churches, three of which had been dismissed from the Philadelphia Association for that purpose the previous year, "provided they go on the same plan."[367] What regulations or discipline this body adopted in its early days is not known, however, in its first meeting a resolution was drawn up to send "to the Philadelphia Association for instructions with regard to this Association," the historian continued, "by which they probably meant such rules and regulations as had been, or should be, advised by the mother Association."[368] It must not be forgotten that these churches had been members of the Philadelphia Association for a decade or more when they were dismissed by that body.[369] Each had also adopted the Philadelphia Confession of Faith which carried with it the "Treatise on Church Discipline" by Benjamin Griffith.[370] In addition to this, David Thomas, pastor of the Broad Run church in Virginia was

---

[366] Sheppard, *Confession of Faith,* pp. 228-230. [Fuller's work was titled, *The Discipline of Primitive Churches.*—Editor]

[367] Gillette, *Minutes,* p. 95.

[368] Semple, *Virginia Baptists,* (1894 ed.), p. 388.

[369] Gillette, *Minutes,* pp. 71, 72. The Ketocton and Opekon churches joined it in 1754; and the Mill Creek church joined in 1755.

[370] *Ibid.,* p. 84. In a "Letter Sent to the Board of Ministers in London," May 16, 1762, one reads, "Our numbers in these parts multiply; for when we had the pleasure of writing to you, in 1734, there were but nine churches in our Association, yet now there are twenty-eight, all owning the Confession of faith put forth in London, in 1689."

a veteran of the parent body and knew much of its discipline and practice.[371] Therefore, the action spoken of by Semple did not indicate ignorance on the part of all the members of the newly formed association.

The Warren Association, which was organized in 1767, had as its leaders James Manning and Hezekiah Smith; both had been brought up in the Philadelphia Association and seemingly were well schooled in its discipline. In his "Sentiments Touching an Association,"[372] Manning said that an association was a "combination of churches" which "is consistent with the independency and power of particular churches," and this is true "because it pretends to be no other than an *advisory council,* utterly disclaiming superiority, jurisdiction, coercive right, and infallibility."[373] This is a good summary of both the discipline and essay put forth by Griffith.

The Warren Association went on to accept the "faith and order"[374] of the Philadelphia Association as set forth in its Confession of Faith. Isaac Backus and his church in Middleborough, Massachusetts did not join the Warren body until they were "satisfied that this association did not assume any jurisdiction over the

---

371 *Ibid.,* p. 86.

372 This is given in full in Appendix A.

373 Guild, *Life of James Manning,* p. 78.

374 *Ibid.,* p. 80. See also *A Compendium of the Minutes of the Warren Baptist Association, from Its Formation in 1767 to the Year 1825, Inclusive,* p. 3.

churches."[375] This body informed its constituency in 1809,

> we are happy to discover, notwithstanding the apprehensions of some, that our oldest Associations are as far from usurping any authority over the churches as when they were first established; and pretend to no prerogative on account of their combination but that of modest and friendly advice.[376]

In response to a letter sent out by the First Baptist Church in the city of New York, representatives of eight Baptist churches met April 12, 1790, for the purpose of "forming a new Association" of churches "adjacent to said city upon the plan and principles of the association of Philadelphia."[377] Most of the churches, which formed this new association, had been dismissed from the Philadelphia Association,[378] consequently they were well acquainted with its discipline.

The Minutes of the Danbury Association in 1790, the year of its formation, declared, "The faith and order of this association is essentially contained in a confes-

---

[375] Backus, *A History of New England,* Vol. II, p. 409.

[376] *Minutes of the Warren Association 1809,* p. 14.

[377] Rippon, *Annual Register,* Vol. I, p. 299; [Rippon mistakenly gives the date as 1791 and states only seven churches met. See *Minutes of the Baptist Convention Met at New York For the Purpose of Constituting An Association.* (New York: W. Durrell, 1790) —Editor]

[378] Gillette, *Minutes,* pp. 256, 271.

sion. . . adopted by the Association of Philadelphia."[379] The same year it sent a letter to the latter association requesting "union and correspondence" with it; "after the usual inquiries respecting their doctrine and practice," the Philadelphia Association agreed wholeheartedly to the request.[380]

The Warwick and Delaware Associations were also strongly influenced by the Philadelphia Association. The former body preferred the Philadelphia Confession of Faith "to all other human compositions."[381] The Delaware Association adopted a Constitution and Rules in 1795 and at the same time approved "the confession of Faith adopted by the Philadelphia Association."[382] Many of the churches which formed these two bodies had long been members of the Philadelphia Association[383] and for that reason were well trained in its discipline.

Discipline Through the Confession of Faith

On the powers and duties of an association the Philadelphia Confession of Faith stated that,

---

[379] Rippon, *Annual Register,* Vol. I, p. 111. The Danbury Association was located in Connecticut.

[380] *Gillette, Minutes,* p. 254.

[381] Rippon, *Annual Register,* Vol. I, p. 211. The Warwick Association was formed in 1791 by churches in New York and Connecticut.

[382] Cook, *Delaware Baptists,* pp. 89, 90.

[383] Gillette, *Minutes,* pp. 256, 271, 297.

> ...the churches, when planted by the providence of God, as they enjoy opportunity and advantage for it, ought to hold communion among themselves for their peace, increase of love and mutual edification.[384]. . .it is according to the mind of Christ that many churches holding communion together, do by their messengers meet to consider and give their advice on or about the matter in difference, to be reported to all the churches concerned; howbeit these messengers assembled, are not intrusted with any church-power properly so called; or with any jurisdiction over the churches themselves, to exercise any censures either over any churches, or persons; or to impose their determination on the churches or officers.[385]

From the language used it can be seen that Griffith, Jones and the committee of Charleston all borrowed much from the Confession of Faith when they drew up their respective disciplines, especially that section dealing with the powers and duties of an association.

By 1814 many Baptist associations in the United States had adopted the Philadelphia Confession of Faith as briefly setting forth their view of the Scriptures, which all Baptists seem to have agreed was "the only certain

---

[384] McGlothlin, *Confessions,* p. 268; Cutting, *Historical Vindications,* p. 169; *A Confession of Faith,* second Charleston edition, pp. 57, 58; Sheppard, *Confession of Faith,* pp. 110, 111. This is taken from the *Philadelphia Confession of Faith,* Chapter XXVII "Of the Churches."

[385] McGlothlin, *Confessions,* p. 268; Cutting, *Historical Vindications,* p. 170; *A Confession of Faith,* second Charleston edition, p. 58; Sheppard, *Confession of Faith,* p. 111.

rule of faith and practice." The sources at hand, however, do not state what their decisions were toward the discipline held by the Philadelphia Association.[386]

Summary

The Philadelphia Association began to set the pattern concerning the powers and duties of an association in its early decisions, which limited its powers to infringe upon the independency of the churches. This pattern set by the early decisions was further clarified and reinforced by other decisions throughout the first century of its existence. Even when the opportunity presented itself this body continually refused to usurp authority over any of the churches.

The determination of this association not to assume any jurisdiction over the churches was strengthened in 1743 when it adopted a treatise on discipline drawn up by Benjamin Griffith. The independency of the local Baptist church was made more certain by the acceptance of his essay on "The Power and Duty of an Association" which was unanimously adopted in 1749. The position of this body on this issue was reasserted in 1798 in a treatise on church discipline drawn up by Samuel Jones.

---

386 Since this information is not given there is no point in speculating upon what these associations may have done. The other associations which adopted the Philadelphia Confession of Faith were: Baltimore, Bowdoinham, Chappawamsic District, Elkhorn, Georgia, Holston, Kehukee, Meredith, New Hampshire, Redstone, Salem, Shaftsbury, Stonington, Vermont, and Woodstock.

This influence was strongly felt in the Charleston Association, which was organized in 1751. One of its first transactions after organizing was to adopt Griffith's essay on "The Power and Duty of an Association." When a committee of this association drew up a treatise on discipline it drew heavily from Griffith's essay and from his treatise on discipline.

The Ketocton and Warren Associations were the next to be directly influenced by this association in their discipline. These bodies drew capable leaders from the older association who were thoroughly schooled in its position relative to the independency of the local churches.

Other associations which were directly influenced by this association were the Danbury, New York, Warwick, and Delaware. With the exception of the Danbury, each of these associations received churches and leaders from the Philadelphia Association, and all were close enough to observe its practice in this matter.

The Philadelphia Association, by exerting a strong influence upon the powers and limitations of an association, and exalting the independency of the local church, has exercised a definitive role in the history of the Baptists throughout the United States.

Chapter 6

Conclusion: The Legacy of the Philadelphia Association

The Philadelphia Association was organized in 1707 with five churches located in Pennsylvania, New Jersey and Delaware. It was the first Baptist association formed in the new world. It grew out of "General Meetings" which were held quarterly in the church at Lower Dublin, Pennsylvania or its branches from 1688, or 1689 to the formation of the association.

The strongest concentration of Baptists in the colonies was found in this area at the time of the formation of the Philadelphia Association. This, however, ceased to be the case about the middle of the eighteenth century.

The Philadelphia Association from its inception had in its midst some of the most capable leaders to be found among the Baptists of this country. The wise leadership of these men made this body a model for other associations which were formed during the remainder of the eighteenth century. The geographical expansion of the association also enabled it to exert a strong influence upon Baptists in all directions. Another feature that enhanced its influence in the early days was its central location in the colonies. The cordial relations this association eagerly maintained with other associations was a fourth factor in its influence upon the Baptists of the United States.

The groundwork for the influence of the association upon Baptist education was laid in 1756 when Isaac Eaton established his Latin Grammar School at Hopewell, New Jersey. The formation of this school had the approval and support of the Philadelphia Association. In this small effort the association was trying its wings. The success of the school encouraged them to attempt greater things in the field of education. Consequently Rhode Island College was established in 1765 through the promotion of this body.

The Philadelphia Association further influenced Baptist education by establishing an education fund. The interest from this fund was used wisely to aid needy and worthy ministerial students in their struggle to obtain an education. Most of these men later showed that the confidence the association had in them had not been misplaced.

The doctrinal influence of this body upon Baptists was even greater than its influence upon education. The first step in this direction took place when the association, early in its history, adopted the confession of Faith of 1689, which was Calvinistic in its emphasis. This influence was also made possible because this body had thoroughly indoctrinated its members through the teaching in the home, doctrinal sermons in its annual meetings, circular letters that were short treatises of doctrines found in their Confession, through a liberal use of the catechism on its Confession, and through doctrinal queries submitted to the annual meetings by perplexed churches. Every effort was put forth to maintain a pure interpretation of these doctrines.

The ministers of the Philadelphia Association were not content to remain in their own territory and hold fast their doctrines, but looked for and gladly accepted every opportunity to propagate these doctrines. From 1751 to 1756 its missionaries traveled through the Carolinas and Virginia remodeling General (Arminian) Baptist churches into Regular (Calvinistic) Baptist churches. During the years following this period these men wielded a predominate influence upon the doctrinal position of associations in all sections of the United States.

A third major influence of the Philadelphia Association upon the Baptists of America was exerted in the field of organization. Soon after 1750 some of its ministers, with the approval of this association, went into Virginia and reorganized some Baptist churches, which were reportedly loosely organized. Later this process was repeated in North Carolina.

This body played a dominant role in the organization of many of the early associations in this country. Its hand is seen clearly in the organization of the Charleston and Ketocton Associations in South Carolina and Virginia. In the formation of the Warren Association in New England in 1767 it took a very active part. It dismissed churches for the purpose of organizing the New York, Warwick and Delaware Associations, thus demonstrating a keen interest in the welfare of the Baptist churches on the outer fringes of its territory.

The first indications from this body concerning its interest in a national organization came at the time of the organization of the Ketocton and Warren Associations in 1765 and 1767 respectively. Morgan Edwards hailed these gestures on the part of the Philadelphia Association as strategic forward steps in the Baptist cause in America. He further developed the idea in 1772 and gave five points, which he considered to be a necessary yardstick for the purpose.

The Philadelphia Association put forth its first serious effort in 1799 to effect a national organization of the Baptists. The response to this effort was not as gratifying as the leaders of the association had hoped, consequently the movement died in 1802. At that time a new plan was launched, namely, a Committee of Correspondence, for the purpose of gathering and disseminating vital information concerning the Baptists in all parts of the United States, which was calculated to draw the Baptists closer together. The response to the new effort judged by the reports of the Committee was most gratifying.

The last influence of the Philadelphia Association which is treated in this study was that which it brought to bear upon Baptist associational discipline, that is, the powers and limitations as well as the duties of an association relative to independent Baptist churches and their members.

This association seems to have arrived at its position on this subject through three methods. In the first place its messengers made a series of decisions ranging throughout the period covered, which vitally affected the powers and limitations of an association in relation to the individual churches. The next determining factor was the adoption in 1743 of a treatise on discipline drawn up by Benjamin Griffith. The most far-reaching step, however, was taken by this body when it adopted Griffith's essay on "The Power and Duty of an Association" in 1749. Although some of the churches after this were seemingly willing to surrender their rights the association would never assume any jurisdiction or infringe upon the rights of the churches.

After the Charleston Association was formed one of its first transactions was to adopt Griffith's essay, which it ordered to be transcribed in the minute book. Later when a committee of the association set about the task of drawing up a treatise of church discipline it drew heavily from this essay as well as from Griffith's treatise on the subject. The influence of these documents upon the Charleston Association remained very much in evidence throughout this period.

The Ketocton and Warren Associations were the next to be significantly influenced in their discipline by this body. The Ketocton drew three churches and at least one pastor from the Philadelphia Association. The Warren Association had two prominent leaders from the latter association. It concluded that an association was an advisory council which was not infallible in its decisions. This association was happy to report in 1809 that Baptist churches were still independent.

The Philadelphia Association also exerted a direct influence over the Danbury, New York, Warwick and Delaware Associations. Many other associations felt the influence of this association upon its discipline directly through churches, ministers or the printed page.

The Philadelphia Association exercised influences upon the Baptists in this country other than the four listed in this study, but these seem to have been the most important. No effort has been made to claim influence in the above realms upon any association unless it has been admitted or claimed by some source at hand. Neither has there been any conscious effort to minimize the influence of any other association in any of the fields treated in this work, nor has there been any denial of influence exerted upon the Philadelphia Association by other associations.

In championing the cause of an educated ministry, even in the face of adverse criticism, the Philadelphia Association rendered a notable service to the cause of the Baptists and by so doing redirected their entire history. Through fostering a uniform pattern of doctrine among the Baptists throughout the country it was actually laying the foundation stone for a national Baptist organization. By advocating the movement for a national organization of the Baptists in the United States, this body tended to mitigate any tendency on the part of the Baptists toward provincialism and to direct their attention to nationwide and worldwide issues; and consequently prepared the way for the monumental work of Luther Rice. Finally, by upholding the independency of the local church against any inclination toward centralizing authority vested in the association, this body tended either to retard Baptist organization or to direct it along democratic lines.

"...TO SET THEM IN ORDER :"

I. THE PHILADELPHIA CONFESSION OF FAITH, 1742

The Historical Background of Why the Association Added the Two Additional Articles to the London Confession of 1689[1]

by William L. Lumpkin

Elias Keach returned to England from America in 1692, and assumed the pastorate of the Tallow Chandler's Hall Church in London. There, in 1697, he concurred with his father to publish a set of articles of faith in the name of his church. These articles were almost exactly the Assembly Confession of 1689 with the addition of articles on hymn-singing and the laying on of hands upon baptized believers. Concerning both of the additions, Benjamin Keach had been an innovator among Particular Baptists. He began to use vernacular hymns in his Horsleydown Church by 1691, and he urged the laying on of hands as a "sacred Ordinance" in a book written in the 1670's and reissued in 1697.[2]

This so-called Keach's Confession is the first generally used Baptist confession of which we hear in America.[3] When the church at Middletown, New Jersey, experienced doctrinal difficulty in 1712, a council of neighboring Baptists called in to help settle the dispute recommended that the members "should subscribe to Elias Keach's Confession of Faith, at least the Covenant annexed to it." The subscribing majority became the reconstituted church. Records of

---

[1] Excerpted from William L. Lumpkin. *Baptist Confessions of Faith.* (Philadelphia: The Judson Press, 1959), pp. 348-349.

[2] *Laying on of Hands upon Baptized Believers* was written in answer to a book by Danvers. Keach taught toleration of differences in churches on the subject, though he urged the practice.

[3] A local confession was prepared for the Lower Dublin (Pa.) Church in 1700. It was used for instructional purposes. Even earlier, in 1697, a community of Keithian Baptists (former Quakers) in the same area had published a confession based upon the Apostles' Creed.

the Welsh Tract Church, in New Jersey, show that the Assembly Confession in 1716 was translated into Welsh by Abel Morgan, a Philadelphia minister. To the Confession he added "An article relative to Laying on of hands; Singing Psalms; and Church Covenants." This Confession then was signed by members at the quarterly meeting (May 4, 1716), though it may never have been published. The Welsh had earlier refused to enter into friendly relationship with the pioneer Pennepack Church because Pennepack did not acknowledge the Laying on of Hands.

* * * * * * *

The new edition [paid for by the churches and printed by Benjamin Franklin in 1743] had two additional articles, indications of the influence of Keach's Confession and of the Welsh Baptists. They are in fact reprints of Articles 27 and 28 of Keach's Confession. One numbered XXIII, concerned the singing of Psalms, hymns, and spiritual songs as of "divine institution," and the other, numbered XXXI, considered the imposition of hands upon baptized believers as "an ordinance of Christ."[4] This brought the number of articles in the Philadelphia Confession to 34, and caused the renumbering of the articles from XXIII to XXXIV.

On the following pages is a facsimile reprint of the earliest extant copy of the Philadelphia Baptist Confession, the Sixth Edition of 1743, containing Benjamin Griffith's "A Short Treatise of Church Discipline." It is reproduced here in full from a copy in the collections of the Library of Congress.

---

[4] William J. McGlothlin in his *Baptist Confessions of Faith* (Philadelphia: American Baptist Publication Society, 1911), p. 295, noted that "There had been tremendous controversy among English Baptists over singing in public worship and the imposition of hands upon the newly baptized, and articles in favor of both practices had found place in Keach's Confession. Imposition of hands was not general among Calvinistic Baptists in England, or in America in the earliest times; but the influence of Keach's Confession and of the Welsh Baptists (Minutes of Welsh Tract Church) had been decisive, and the Philadelphia Baptists now incorporate the practice in their doctrinal statement."

A CONFESSION OF FAITH,

Put forth by the *Elders* and *Brethren* Of many CONGREGATIONS OF *CHRISTIANS* (Baptized upon Profeſſion of their Faith) In *London* and the *Country*.

Adopted by the Baptiſt ASSOCIATION *met at* Philadelphia, Sept. 25. 1742.

The SIXTH EDITION.

To which are added,
Two Articles *viz.* Of Impoſition of Hands, and Singing of Pſalms in Publick Worſhip.
ALSO
A Short Treatiſe of Church Diſcipline.

With the Heart Man believeth unto Righteouſneſs, and with the Mouth Confeſſion is made unto Salvation, Rom. 10. 10.
Search the Scriptures, John 5. 39.

PHILADELPHIA: Printed by B. FRANKLIN.
M,DCC,XLIII.

WE the Ministers and Messengers of, and concerned for, upwards of one hundred Baptized Congregations in *England* and *Wales* (denying *Arminianism*) being met together in *London* from the Third of the Seventh Month, to the Eleventh of the same 1689. to consider of some things that might be for the Glory of God, and the good of these Congregations; have thought meet (for the Satisfaction of all other Christians that differ from us in the Point of Baptism) to recommend to their perusal the Confession of our Faith; Printed for, and Sold by *John Marshall*, at the *Bible* in *Grace-Church Street*. Which Confession we own, as containing the Doctrine of our Faith and Practice; and do desire that the Members of our Churches respectively do furnish themselves therewith.

Hanserd Knollys.
William Kiffin.
John Harris,
William Collins.
Hercules Collins.
Robert Steed.
Leonard Harrison.
George Barret.
Isaac Lamb.
Richard Adams.
Benj Keach.
Andrew Gifford
Tho. Vaux.
Tho Winnel.
James Hitt.
Richard Tidmarsh.
William Facey.
Samuel Buttall.
Christopher Price.
Daniel Finch.
John Ball
Edmond White.
William Prichard.
Paul Fruin.
Richard Ring.
John Tomkins.
Toby Wilkes
John Carter.
James Web,
Richard Sutton.
Robert Knight.
Edward Price.
William Phips.
William Hankins.
Samuel Ewer.
Edward Man.
Charles Archer.

In the Name and Behalf of the whole Assembly.

To the Judicious and Impartial

READER.

Courteous Reader,

IT is now many Years ſince divers of us (with other ſober Chriſtians then living, and walking in the way of the Lord, that we profeſs) did conceive our ſelves to be under a neceſſity of Publiſhing a *Confeſſion* of our *Faith*, for the information and ſatisfaction of thoſe, that did not throughly underſtand what our Principles were, or had entertained Prejudices againſt our Profeſſion, by reaſon of the ſtrange repreſentation of them, by ſome Men of Note, who had taken very wrong Meaſures, and accordingly led others into Miſapprehenſions, of us, and them: And this was firſt put forth about the Year 1643. in the Name of Seven Congregations then gathered in *London*; ſince which time, divers Impreſſions thereof have been diſperſed abroad, and our end propoſed, in good meaſure anſwered, in aſmuch as many (and ſome of thoſe Men eminent both for Piety and Learning) were thereby ſatisfied, that we were no way guilty of thoſe Hetero-

A 2 doxies

doxies and fundamental Errors, which had too frequently been charged upon us without ground, or occasion given on our Part. And forasmuch, as that Confession is not now commonly to be had, and also that many others have since embraced the same Truth which is owned therein, it was indeed necessary by us to joyn together in giving a Testimony to the World, of our firm adhering to those wholsom Principles, by the Publication of this which is now in your Hand.

And forasmuch as our method and manner of expressing our Sentiments, in this, doth vary from the former (although the substance of this Matter is the same) we shall freely impart to you the Reason and Occasion thereof. One thing that greatly prevailed with us to undertake this Work was (not only to give a full account of our selves to those Christians that differ from us about the Subject of Baptism, but also) the Profit that might from thence arise, unto those that have any account of our Labours, in their Instruction and Establishment in the great Truths of the Gospel; in the clear understanding, and steady belief of which our comfortable walking with God, and fruitfulness before him, in all our ways, is most nearly concerned; and therefore we did conclude it necessary to express our selves the more fully, and distinctly; and also to fix on such a Method as might be most comprehensive of those things we designed to explain our sense and belief of; and finding no defect, in this regard, in that fixed on by the Assembly, and after them, by those of the

Con-

Congregational way, we did readily conclude it beſt to retain the ſame *Order* in our preſent Confeſſion ; and alſo when we obſerved, that thoſe laſt mentioned, did in their Confeſſions (for Reaſons which ſeemed of weight both to themſelves and others) chuſe not only to expreſs their Mind in Words concurrent with the former in Senſe, concerning all thoſe Articles wherein they were agreed, but alſo for the moſt part, without any variation of the Terms, we did in like manner conclude it beſt to follow their Example, in making uſe of the very ſame Words with them both, in theſe Articles (which are very many) wherein our Faith and Doctrine is the ſame with theirs, and this we did, the more abundantly, to manifeſt our conſent with both, in all the fundamental Articles of the Chriſtian Religion, as alſo with many others, whoſe Orthodox Confeſſions have been Publiſhed to the World, on the behalf of the *Proteſtants* in divers Nations and Cities: And alſo to convince all, that we have no itch to Clog *Religion* with new Words, but do readily acquieſce in that form of ſound Words, which hath been in conſent with the *Holy Scriptures*, uſed by others before us ; hereby declaring before *God*, *Angels*, and *Men*, our hearty agreement with them, in that wholeſome *Proteſtant Doctrine*, which with ſo clear evidence of Scriptures they have aſſerted : Some things indeed, are in ſome places added, ſome Terms omitted, and ſome few changed ; but theſe Alterations are of that Nature, as that we need not doubt, any charge or ſuſpicion of unſoundneſs in the Faith, from any of our Bretheren upon the account of them.

A 3 In

In thofe things wherein we differ from others, we have expreft our felves with all candor and plainnefs, that none might entertain jealoufie of ought fecretly lodged in our Breafts, that we would not the World fhould be acquainted with; yet we hope we have alfo obferved thofe Rules of modefty and humility, as will render our freedom in this refpect inoffenfive, even to thofe whofe Sentiments are different from ours.

We have alfo taken care to affix Texts of Scripture at the Bottom, for the confirmation of each Article in our *Confeffion*; in which *Work* we have ftudioufly endeavoured to felect fuch as are moft clear and pertinent, for the proof of what is affert-ed by us: And our earneft defire is, that all into whofe Hands this may come, would follow that (never enough commanded) Example of the Noble *Bereans*, who fearched the *Scriptures* daily that they might find out whether the things preached to them were fo or not.

There is one thing more which we fincerely profefs, and earneftly defire credence in, *viz.* That Contention is moft remote from our Defign in all that we have done in this matter: And we hope, the Liberty of an ingenuous unfolding our Princi-ciples, and opening our Hearts unto our Brethren, with the Scripture-grounds on which our Faith and Practice will by none of them be either denied to us, or taken ill from us. Our whole defign is accomplifhed if we may obtain that Juftice, as to be meafured in our Principles, and Practice, and the judgment of both by others, according to what

we

we have *now* Publiſhed; which the *Lord* (*whoſe Eyes are as a flame of Fire*) *knoweth* to be the *Doctrine*, which with our Hearts we moſt firmly believe, and ſincerely endeavour to conform our Lives to. And oh that other Contentions being laid aſleep, the only *Care* and *Contention* of all, upon *whom* the Name of our *Bleſſed Redeemer* is called, might for the future be, to walk humbly with their God, in the Exerciſe of all *Love* and *Meekneſs* towards each other, to perfect Holineſs in the fear of the *Lord*, each one endeavouring to have his Converſation ſuch as becometh the *Goſpel*; and alſo ſuitable to his place and capacity, vigorouſly to promote in others the Practice of true Religion, and undefiled in the ſight of *God* our *Father*. And that in this back-ſliding Day, we might not ſpend our Breath in fruitleſs complaints of the Evils of others, but may every one begin at home, to reform in the firſt place our own Hearts and Ways, and then to quicken all, that we may have Influence upon, to the ſame *Work*; that if the Will of God were ſo, none might deceive themſelves, by reſting in, and truſting to a form of Godlineſs, without the *Power* of it, and inward experience of the efficacy of thoſe Truths that are profeſſed by them.

And verily there is one ſpring and cauſe of the decay of Religion in our Day, which we cannot but touch upon, and earneſtly urge a redreſs of, and that is the neglect of the Worſhip of God in Families, by thoſe to whom the charge and conduct of them is committed. May not the groſs Ignorance

A 4 and

and Inſtability of many, with the Profaneneſs of others, be juſtly charged upon their Parents and Maſters who have not trained them up in the *Way* wherein they ought to Walk when they were young? But have neglected thoſe frequent and ſolemn Commands which the Lord hath laid upon them ſo to Catechize and Inſtruct them, that their tender Years might be ſeaſoned with the *Knowledge* of the Truth of God, as revealed in the Scriptures; and alſo by their own omiſſion of Prayer, and other Duties of Religion of their Families, together with the ill example of their looſe Converſation, have inured them firſt to a neglect, and then contempt of all Piety and Religion; we know this will not excuſe the *Blindneſs* and *Wickedneſs* of any; but certainly it *will* fall heavy upon thoſe that have been thus the occaſion thereof; they indeed die in their Sins, but will not their Blood be required of thoſe under whoſe Care they were, who yet permitted them to go on without *Warning*, yea, led them into the Paths of Deſtruction? and will not the Diligence of Chriſtians, *with* reſpect to the diſcharge of theſe Duties, in Ages paſt, riſe up in judgment againſt, and condemn many of thoſe who would be eſteemed ſuch now.

We ſhall conclude with our earneſt Prayer, That the God *of all Grace, will pour out theſe meaſures of his holy Spirit upon us, that the* Profeſſion *of truth may be accompanied with the ſound belief, and diligent practice of it by us, that his name may in all things be glorified, through Jeſus Chriſt our Lord.* Amen.

The

A CONFESSION OF FAITH.

CHAP. I.

Of the HOLY SCRIPTURES.

HE Holy Scripture is the only sufficient, certain, and infallible (*a*) Rule of all Saving Knowledge, Faith, and Obedience; altho the (*b*) light of Nature, and the works of Creation

(*a*) 2 Tim. 3. 15, 16, 17. Isa. 8. 20. Luke. 16. 29, 31. Eph. 2. 20. (*b*) Rom. 1. 19, 20, 21, &c. ch. 2. 14, 15. Psalm 19. 1, 2, 3.

and

and Providence do ſo far manifeſt the Goodneſs, Wiſdom and Power of God, as to leave Men unexcuſable; yet are they not ſufficient to give that Knowledge of God and his Will, which is neceſſary unto Salvation. (*c*) Therefore it pleaſed the Lord at ſundry times, and in divers manners, to reveal himſelf, and to declare That his Will unto his Church; and afterward for the better preſerving, and propagating of the Truth, and for the more ſure Eſtabliſhment, and Comfort of the Church againſt the corruption of the Fleſh, and the malice of Satan, and of the World, to commit the ſame wholly unto (*d*) Writing; which maketh the Holy Scriptures to be moſt neceſſary, thoſe former ways of God's revealing his Will unto his People being now ceaſed.

2. Under the Name of Holy Scripture, or the Word of God written, are

---

(*c*) Heb. 1. 1. (*d*) Prov. 22. 19, 20, 21. Rom. 15. 4. 2 Pet 1. 19, 20.

now

now contained all the Books of the Old and New Teſtament, which are theſe:

Of the OLD TESTAMENT.

Geneſis, Exodus, Leviticus, Numbers, Deuteronomy, Joſhua, Judges, Ruth, 1 *Samuel,* 2 *Samuel,* 1 *Kings,* 2 *Kings,* 1 *Chronicles,* 2 *Chronicles, Ezra, Nehemiah, Eſther, Job, Pſalms, Proverbs, Eccleſiaſtes, The Song of Songs, Iſaiah, Jeremiah, Lamentations, Ezekiel, Daniel, Hoſea, Joel, Amos, Obadiah, Jonah, Micah, Nahum, Habakkuk, Zephaniah, Haggai, Zachariah, Malachi.*

Of the NEW TESTAMENT.

Matthew, Mark, Luke, John, The Acts of the Apoſtles, Paul's Epiſtle to the Romans, Corinthians, 2 *Corinthians, Galatians, Epheſians, Philippians, Coloſſians,* 1 *Theſſalonians,* 2 *Theſſalonians,* 1 *Timothy,* 2 *Timothy, to Titus, to Philemon, the Epiſtle to the Hebrews, the Epiſtle of James, the*

firſt

first and second Epistles of Peter, the first, second and third Epistles of John, the Epistle of Jude, the Revelation. All which are given by the (*e*) Inspiration of God, to be the Rule of Faith and Life.

3. The Books commonly called *Apocrypha*, not being of (*f*) Divine Inspiration, are no part of the Canon (or Rule) of the Scripture, and therefore are of no Authority to the Church of God, nor to be any otherwise approved, or made use of than other Humane Writings.

4. The Authority of the Holy Scripture, for which it ought to be believed, dependeth not upon the testimony of any Man, or Church, but wholy upon (*g*) God, (who is Truth it self) the Author thereof; therefore it is to be received, because it is the Word of God.

5. We may be moved and induced by the testimony of the Church of God, to an high and reverent Esteem of the

(*e*) 2 Tim. 3. 16. (*f*) Luke 24. 27, 44. Rom. 3. 2. (*g*) 2 Pet. 1. 19, 20, 21. 2 Tim. 3. 16, 22. Thess. 2. 13. 1 John 5. 9.

Holy

Holy Scriptures; and the heavenliness of the Matter, the efficacy of the Doctrine, and the majesty of the Stile, the consent of all the Parts, the scope of the Whole, (which is to give all Glory to God) the full discovery it makes of the only Way of Man's Salvation, and many other incomparable Excellencies, and intire Perfections thereof, are Arguments whereby it doth abundantly evidence it self to be the Word of God; yet notwithstanding, our (*h*) full persuasion, and assurance of the infallible Truth, and Divine Authority thereof, is from the inward work of the Holy Spirit, bearing witness by and with the Word in our Hearts.

6. The whole Counsel of God concerning all things (*i*) necessary for his own Glory, Man's Salvation, Faith and Life, is either expresly set down, or necessarily contained in the Holy Scripture; unto which nothing at any time is to be

(*h*) John 16. 13, 14. 1 Cor. 2. 10, 11, 12. 1 John 1. 2, 20, 27. (*i*) 2 Tim. 3. 15, 16, 17. 9Gal. 1. 8, 9.

added,

added, whether by new Revelation of the Spirit, or Traditions of Men.

Neverthelefs we acknowledge the (*k*) inward Illumination of the Spirit of God, to be neceffary for the faving underftanding of fuch things as are revealed in the Word, and that there are fome Circumftances concerning the Worfhip of God, and Government of the Church, common to Humane Actions and Societies; which are to be (*l*) ordered by the Light of Nature, and Chriftian Prudence, according to the General Rules of the Word, which are always to be obferved.

7. All things in Scripture are not alike (*m*) plain in themfelves, nor alike clear unto all; yet thofe things which are neceffary to be known, believed, and obferved for Salvation, are fo (*n*) clearly propounded, and opened in fome place of Scripture or other, that not only the learned, but the unlearned, in a due ufe

(*k*) John 6. 45. 1 Cor. 2. 9, 10, 11, 12. (*l*) 1 Cor. 11. 13, 14. & Ch. 14. 26, & 40. (*m*) 2 Pet. 3. 16. (*n*) Pfalm 19. 7. & 119. 130.

of

of ordinary Means, may attain to a sufficient understanding of them.

8. The Old Testament in(*o*)*Hebrew*, (which was the Native Language of the People of God of old) and the New Testament in *Greek*, which (at the time of writing of it) was most generally known to the Nations, being immediately inspired by God, and by his singular Care and Providence kept pure in all Ages, are therefore (*p*) authentical; so as in all Controversies of Religion, the Church is finally to appeal unto them(*q*). But because these original Tongues are not known to all the People of God, who have a right unto, and interest in the Scriptures, and are commanded in the fear of God to read (*r*) and search them, therefore they are to be translated into the vulgar Language of every Nation, unto which they (*s*) come, that the Word of God dwelling (*t*) plentifully in

(*o*) Rom. 3. 2. (*p*) Isa.8. 20. (*q*) Acts 15. 15. (*r*)John 5. 39. (*s*) 1 Cor. 14. 6, 9, 11, 12, 24, 28. (*t*) Col. 3. 16.

all,

all, they may worſhip him in an acceptable manner, and through patience and comfort of the Scriptures may hope.

9. The infallible Rule of Interpre - tation of Scripture is the (*u*) Scripture it ſelf: And therefore when there is a queſtion about the true and full ſenſe of any Scripture, (which is not manifold but one) it muſt be ſearched by other Places, that ſpeak more clearly.

10. The ſupream Judge by which all Controverſies of Religion are to be determined, and all Decrees of Councils, Opinions of antient Writers, Doctrines of Men, and private Spirits, are to be examined, and in whoſe Sentence we are to reſt, can be no other but the Holy Scripture delivered by the Spirit, into which (*x*) Scripture ſo delivered, our Faith is finally reſolved.

(*u*) 2 Pet. 1. 20. 21. Acts 15. 15. 16. (*x*) Mat. 22. 29, 32. Eph. 2. 20. Acts 28. 23.

CHAP.

CHAP. II.

Of GOD and of the Holy Trinity.

1. THE Lord our God is but (*a*) one only living, and true God; whose (*b*) subsistence is in and of himself, (*c*) infinite in Being, and Perfection, whose Essence cannot be comprehended by any but himself; (*d*) a most pure Spirit, (*e*) invisible, without Body, Parts, or Passions, who only hath Immortality, dwelling in the Light, which no Man can approach unto, who is (*f*) immutable, (*g*) immense, (*h*) eternal, incomprehensible, (*i*) almighty, every way infinite, (*k*) most holy, most, wise, most free, most absolute, (*l*) working all Things according to the Counsel of his own immutable and most righteous

(*a*) 1 Cor. 8. 46. Deut. 6. 4. (*b*) Jer. 10. 10. Isa. 48. 12. (*c*) Exod. 3. 14. (*d*) John 4. 24.. (*e*) 1 Tim. 1. 17. Deut. 4. 15, 16. (*f*) Mal. 3. 6. (*g*) 1 Kings 8. 27. Jer. 23. 23. (*h*) Psalm 90. 2. (*i*) Gen. 17. 1. (*k*) Isa. 6. 3. (*l*) Psalm 115. 3. Isa. 46. 10.

B Will,

Will (*m*) for his own Glory, moſt loving, gracious, merciful, long ſuffering, abundant in goodneſs and truth, forgiving Iniquity, Tranſgreſſion and Sin, (*n*) the rewarder of them that diligently ſeek him, and withal moſt juſt, (*o*) and terrible in his Judgments, (*p*) hating all ſin, and will by no means clear the (*q*) guilty.

2. God, having all (*r*) Life, (*s*) glory (*t*) goodneſs, bleſſedneſs, in and of himſelf, is alone in, and unto himſelf allſufficient, not (*u*) ſtanding in need of any Creature which he hath made, nor deriving any Glory from them, but only manifeſting his own Glory in, by, unto, and upon them, he is the alone Fountain of all Being, (*x*) of whom, through whom and to whom are all things, and he hath moſt ſoveraign (*y*) Dominion over all Creatures, to do by them, for

(*m*) Prov. 16. 4. Rom. 11. 36. (*n*) Exod. 34. 6, 7 Heb. 11. 6. (*o*) Neh. 9. 32, 33. (*p*) Pſalm 5. 5, 6. (*q*) Exod. 34. 7. Nahum. 1. 2, 3. (*r*) John 5. 26. (*s*) Pſal. 148. 13. (*t*) Pſal 119. 68. (*u*) Job. 22. 2, 3. (*x*) Rom. 11. 34, 35, 36. (*y*) Dan. 4. 25. &c v. 34, 35.

them,

them, or upon them, whatſoever himſelf pleaſeth ; in his ſight (*z*) all things are open and manifeſt, his knowledge is (*a*) infinite, infallible, and independant upon the Creature, ſo as nothing is to him contingent or uncertain ; he is moſt holy in all his Counſels, in (*b*) all his Works, and in all his Commands ; to him is due (*c*) from Angels and Men, whatſoever Worſhip, Service, or Obedience, as Creatures they owe unto the Creator, and whatever he is further pleaſed to require of them.

3. In this Divine and Infinite Being there are three ſubſiſtences, (*d*) the Father, the Word,(or Son)and Holy Spirit, of one Subſtance, Power and Eternity, each having the whole Divine Eſſence, (*e*)yet the Eſſence undivided, the Father is of none neither begotten, nor proceeding, the Son is (*f*) eternally begotten

---

(*z*) Heb. 4. 13. (*a*) Ezek. 11. 5. Acts 15. 18 (*b*) Pſalm 145. 17. (*c*)Rev 5. 12, 13, 14 (*d*) 1 John 5. 7. Matt. 28. 19. 2 Cor. 13. 14. (*e*) Exod. 3. 14. John 14. 11. 1 Cor. 8. 6. (*f*) John 1. 14, 18.

B 2 of

of the Father, the Holy Spirit (*g*) proceeding from the Father and the Son, all infinite, without beginning, therefore but one God, who is not to be divided in Nature and Being, but distinguished by several peculiar, relative Properties, and personal Relations; which Doctrine of the Trinity is the Foundation of all our Communion with God, and comfortable dependance on him.

CHAP. III.

Of God's Decree.

1. GOD hath (*a*) *decreed* in himself, from all Eternity, by the most wise and holy Counsel of his own Will, freely and unchangeably, all things whatsoever comes to pass; yet so as thereby is God neither the Author of Sin, (*b*) nor hath fellowship with any therein,

(*g*) John 15. 26. Gal. 4. 6. (*a*) Isa. 46. 10. Eph. 1. 11. Heb. 6. 17. Rom. 9. 15, 18. (*b*) Jam. 1. 15, 17. 1. John 1. 5.

nor

nor is violence offered to the Will of the Creature, nor yet is the liberty, or contingency of ſecond Cauſes taken away, but rather (*c*) eſtabliſhed, in which appears his Wiſdom in diſpoſing all things, and Power, and Faithfulneſs (*d*) in accompliſhing his *Decree.*

2. Although God knoweth whatſoever may, or can come to paſs upon all (*e*) ſuppoſed Conditions; yet hath he not *decreed* any thing, (*f*) becauſe he foreſaw it as future, or as that which would come to paſs upon ſuch conditions.

3. By the *Decree* of God, for the manifeſtation of his Glory, (*g*) ſome Men and Angels are pre-deſtinated, or fore-ordinated to Eternal Life, through Jeſus Chriſt, to the (*h*) praiſe of his glorious Grace; others being left to act in their

(*c*) Acts 4. 27, 28. John 19. 11. (*d*) Numb. 23. 19. Eph. 1. 3, 4, 5. (*e*) Acts 15. 18. (*f*) Rom. 9. 11, 13, 16, 18. (*g*) 1 Tim. 5. 21. Mat. 25. 41. (*h*) Eph. 1. 5, 6.

ſin to their (*i*) juſt condemnation, to the praiſe of his glorious Juſtice.

4. Theſe Angels and Men thus pre-deſtinated, and fore-ordained, are particularly, and unchangeably deſigned; and their (*k*) number ſo certain, and definite, that it cannot be either increaſed, or diminiſhed.

5. Thoſe of Mankind (*l*) that are pre-deſtinated to Life, God, before the Foundation of the Word was laid, according to his eternal and immutable Purpoſe, and the ſecret Counſel and good Pleaſure of his Will, hath choſen in Chriſt unto everlaſting Glory, out of his meer free Grace and Love; (*m*) without any other thing in the Creature as a condition or cauſe moving him thereunto.

6. As God hath appointed the Elect unto Glory, ſo he hath by the eternal and moſt free Purpoſe of his Will, fore-

(*i*) Rom. 9. 22, 23. Jude 4. (*k*) 2 Tim. 2 19. John 13. 18. (*l*) Eph. 1. 4, 9, 11. Rom. 8. 30 2 Tim. 1. 9. 1 Theſſ 5. 9. (*m*) Rom. 9. 13. 16. Eph. 2. 6. 12.

ordained

ordained (*o*) all the Means thereunto, wherefore they who are elected, being fall'n in *Adam*, (*p*) are redeemed by Christ, are effectually (*q*) called unto Faith in Christ, by his Spirit working in due season, are justified, adopted, sanctified, and kept by his Power through Faith (*r*) unto Salvation; neither are any other redeemed by Christ, or effectually called, justified, adopted, sanctified, and saved, but the Elect (*s*) only.

7. The Doctrine of this high Mystery of Pre-destination, is to be handled with special Prudence and Care; that Men attending the Will of God revealed in his Word, and yielding Obedience thereunto, may, from the certainty of their effectual Vocation, be assured of their (*t*) eternal Election; so shall this Doctrine afford matter (*u*) of Praise, Reverence, and Admiration of God, and

---

(*o*) 1 Pet. 1. 2. 2 Thess. 2. 13. (*p*) 1 Thess. 5. 9, 10. (*q*) Rom. 8. 30. 2 Thess. 2. 13. (*r*) 2 Pet. 1. 5 (*s*) John 10. 26. John 17. 9. John 6. 24 (*t*) 1 Thess. 1. 4, 5. 2 Pet. 1. 10. (*u*) Eph. 1. 6. Rom. 11 33.

(*x*) of humility, diligence, and abundant (*y*) Conſolation, to all that ſincerely obey the Goſpel.

CHAP. IV.

Of Creation.

1. IN the beginning it pleaſed God the Father, (*a*) Son, and Holy Spirit, for the manifeſtation of the Glory of (*b*) his Eternal Power, Wiſdom, and Goodneſs, to *create* or *make* the World, and all things therein, (*c*) whether viſible or inviſible, in the ſpace of ſix Days, and all very good.

2. After God had made all other Creatures, he *created* (*d*) Man, Male and Female, with (*e*) reaſonable and immortal Souls, rendring them fit unto that Life to God, for which they were

(*x*) Rom. 11. 5, 6. (*y*) Luke 10. 20. (*a*) John 1. 1, 5. Heb. 1. 2. Job 26. 13 (*b*) Rom. 1 20. (*c*) Col. 1. 16. Gen. 2. 1, 2. (*d*) Gen. 1. 27. (*e*) Gen. 2 7.

created,

created, being (*f*) made after the Image of God, in Knowledge, Righteousness, and true Holiness; having the Law of God (*g*) written in their Hearts, and Power to fulfil it; and yet under a possibility of transgressing, being left to the liberty of their own Will, which was (*h*) subject to change.

3. Besides the Law written in their Hearts, they received (*i*) a Command not to eat of the Tree of Knowledge of Good and Evil; which whil'st they kept, they were happy in their Communion with God, and had Dominion (*k*) over the Creatures.

(*f*) Eccles 7. 29. Gen. 1. 26. (*g*) Rom. 2. 14, 15. (*h*) Gen 3. 6. (*i*) Gen. 6. 17. & Ch. 3. 8, 9, 10. (*k*) Gen. 2. 26, 28.

CHAP.

CHAP. V.

Of Divine Providence.

1. GOD the good *Creator* of all things, in *his* infinite Power and Wiſdom, doth (*a*) uphold, direct, diſpoſe, and govern all Creatures, and Things, from the greateſt even to the (*b*) leaſt, by *his* moſt wiſe and holy Providence, to the end for which they were *created*, according unto *his* infallible Foreknowledge, and the free and immutable Counſel of *his* (*c*) own Will; to the praiſe of the glory of *his* Wiſdom, Power, Juſtice, infinite Goodneſs and Mercy.

2. Athough in relation to the foreknowledge and *Decree* of *God*, the firſt Cauſe, all things come to paſs (*d*) immutably and infallibly; ſo that there is

(*a*) Heb. 1. 3. John 38. 11. Iſa. 46. 10, 11. Pſalm 13. 5. 6. (*b*) Matth. 10. 26, 30, 31. (*c*) Eph. 1. 11. (*d*) Acts 2. 23.

not

not any thing, befalls any (*e*) by chance or without *his Providence*; yet by the ſame *Providence* he ordereth them to fall out according to the nature of ſecond Cauſes, either (*f*) neceſſarily, freely, or contingently.

3. God in *his* ordinary *Providence* (*g*) maketh uſe of Means; yet is free (*h*) to work without, (*i*) above, and (*k*) againſt them at *his* Pleaſure.

4. The Almighty Power, unſearchable Wiſdom, and infinite Goodneſs of *God*, ſo far manifeſt themſelves in *his Providence*, that *his* determinate Counſel (*l*) extendeth itſelf even to the firſt Fall, and all other ſinful Actions both of Angels and Men; (and that not by a bare permiſſion) which alſo he moſt wiſely and powerfully (*m*) boundeth, and otherwiſe ordereth, and governeth, in a manifold diſpenſation to his moſt

(*e*) Prov. 16. 33. (*f*) Gen. 8. 22. (*g*) Acts. 27. 31, 44. Iſa. 55. 10, 11. (*h*) Hoſ. 1. 7. (*i*) Rom. 4. 19, 20, 21. (*k*) Dan. 3. 27. (*l*) Rom. 11. 32, 33, 34. 2 Sam. 24. 1. 1 Chron. 21. 1. (*m*) 2 Kings 19. 28. Pſalm 76. 10.

holy

holy (*n*) Ends: Yet ſo, as the ſinfulneſs of their Acts proceedeth only from the Creatures, and not from *God*; who being moſt holy and righteous, neither is nor can be, the Author or (*o*) Approver of Sin.

5. The moſt wiſe, righteous, and gracious *God*, doth oftentimes, leave for a ſeaſon his own Children to manifold Temptations, and the Corruptions of their own Heart, to chaſtiſe them for their former Sins, or to diſcover unto them the hidden ſtrength of Corruption, and deceitfulneſs of their Hearts, (*p*) that they may be humbled; and to raiſe them to a more cloſe and conſtant dependance for their ſupport upon himſelf; and to make them more watchful againſt all future occaſions of Sin, and for other juſt and holy Ends.

(*n*) Gen. 50. 20. Iſa. 10. 6, 7, 12. (*o*) Pſalm 50. 21. 1 John 2. 16. (*p*) 2. Chron. 32. 25, 26, 31. 2 Sam. 24. 1. 2 Cor. 12. 7, 8, 9.

So

So that whatſoever befalls any of his Elect is by his appointment, for his Glory, (*q*) and their good.

6. As for thoſe wicked and ungodly Men, whom God as a righteous Judge, for former Sin doth (*r*) blind and harden; from them he not only withholdeth his (*s*) Grace, whereby they might have been enlightned in their underſtanding, and wrought upon in their Hearts; but ſometimes alſo withdraweth (*t*) the Gifts which they had, and expoſeth them to ſuch (*u*) Objects as their *Corruptions* makes occaſion of Sin; and withal, (*x*) gives them over to their own Luſts, and temptations of the World, and the power of Satan, whereby it comes to paſs, that they (*y*) harden themſelves, even under thoſe means which God uſeth for the ſoftning of others.

(*q*) Rom. 8. 28. (*r*) Rom. 1. 24, 25, 28. Ch. 11. 7, 8. (*s*) Deut. 29. 4. (*t*) Matt. 13. 12. (*u*) Deut. 2. 30. 2 Kings 8. 12, 13. (*x*) Pſalm 81. 11, 12. 2 Theſſ. 2. 10, 11, 12. (*y*) Exod. 8. 15. 32. Iſai. 6. 9, 10. 1 Pet. 2. 7, 8.

7. As

7. As the *Providence* of *God* doth in general reach to all *Creatures*, ſo after a more ſpecial manner it taketh Care of his (z) *Church*, and diſpoſeth of all things to the good thereof.

CHAP. VI.

Of the Fall of Man, of Sin, and of the Puniſhment thereof.

1. ALthough *God created Man* upright, and perfect, and gave him a righteous Law, which had been unto Life had he kept it, (*a*) and threatned Death upon the breach thereof; yet he did not long abide in this Honour; (*b*) Satan uſing the ſubtilty of the Serpent to ſeduce *Eve*, then by her ſeducing *Adam*, who without any compulſion, did wilfully tranſgreſs the Law of their *Creation*, and the Command given unto them

(z) 1 Tim. 4. 10. Amos 9. 8, 9. Iſa. 43. 3, 4, 5. (*a*) Gen. 2. 16, 17. (*b*) Gen. 3. 12, 13. 2 Cor. 11. 3.

them, in eating the forbidden Fruit; which *God* was pleaſed according to *his* wiſe and holy *Counſel* to permit, having purpoſed to order it, to *his* own Glory.

2. Our firſt *Parents* by this *Sin*, fell from their (*c*) original righteouſneſs and communion with *God*, and we in them, whereby Death came upon all; (*d*) all becoming dead in *Sin*, and wholly defiled, (*e*) in all the faculties, and parts of Soul and Body.

3. They being the (*f*) Root, and, by *God*'s appointment, ſtanding in the room, and ſtead of all Mankind; the guilt of the *Sin* was imputed, and *corrupted* Nature conveyed to all their Poſterity, deſcending from them by ordinary generation, being now (*g*) conceived in *Sin*, and by nature Children (*h*) of Wrath, the Servants of *Sin*, the ſubjects (*i*) of *Death*, and all other Mi-

(*c*) Rom. 3. 23. (*d*) Rom. 5. 12. &c. (*e*) Tit. 1 15. Gen. 6. 5. Jer. 17. 9. Rom. 3. 10.---19. (*f*) Rom. 5. 12----19. 1 Cor. 15. 21, 22, 45, 49. (*g*) Pſalm 51. 5. Job. 14. 4. (*h*) Eph. 2. 3. (*i*) Rom. 6. 20. & Ch. 5. 12.

ſeries,

ſeries, Spiritual, Temporal and Eternal, unleſs the *Lord Jeſus* (*k*) ſet them free.

4. From this original *Corruption*, whereby we are (*l*) utterly indiſpoſed, diſabled, and made oppoſite to all good, and wholy inclined to all Evil, do (*m*) proceed all actual Trangreſſions.

5. This *Corruption* of Nature, during this Life, doth (*n*) remain in thoſe that are regenerated: And although it be through *Chriſt* pardoned, and mortified, yet both itſelf, and the firſt Motions thereof, are truly and properly (*o*) *Sin.*

CHAP. VII.

Of God's Covenant.

1. THE diſtance between *God* and the *Creature* is ſo great that although reaſonable *Creatures* do owe Obe-

(*k*) Heb. 2. 14 1 Theſſ. 1. 10 (*l*) Rom. 8. 7. Col. 1. 21. (*m*) Jam. 1. 14, 15. Matt. 15. 19. (*n*) Rom. 7. 18. 23. Eccleſ. 7. 20. 1 John 1. 8. (*o*) Rom. 7. 24, 25 Gal. 5. 17.

dience

dience unto him as their *Creator*, yet they could never have attained the Reward of Life, but by ſome (*a*) voluntary condeſcenſion on *God's part*, which he hath been pleaſed to expreſs, by way of *Covenant*.

2. Moreover, *Man* having brought himſelf (*b*) under the *curſe* of the Law by his fall, it pleaſed the *Lord* to make a *Covenant* of *Grace*, wherein he freely offereth unto *Sinners* (*c*) Life and Salvation by *Jeſus Chriſt*, requiring of them Faith in him, that they may be ſaved; and (*d*) promiſing to give unto all thoſe that are ordained unto eternal *Life*, his holy *Spirit*, to make them willing, and able to believe.

3. This *Covenant* is revealed in the Goſpel firſt of all to *Adam* in the promiſe of Salvation by the (*e*) Seed of the Woman, and afterwards by farther ſteps, untill the full (*f*) diſcovery thereof was

(*a*) Luke 17. 10. Job. 35. 7, 8. (*b*) Gen. 2. 17. Gal. 3. 10. Rom. 3. 20, 21. (*c*) Rom. 8 3. Mark 16. 15, 16. John 3. 16. (*d*) Ezek. 36. 26, 27. John 9. 44, 45. Pſalm 110. 3. (*e*) Gen 3. 15. (*f*) Heb. 1. 1.

C Com-

compleated in the New Teſtament; and it is founded in that (*) Eternal *Covenant* tranſaction, that was between the *Father* and the *Son* about the Redemption of the *Elect* ; and it is alone by the Grace of this *Covenant*, that all of the Poſterity of fallen *Adam*, that ever were (*g*) ſaved, did obtain Life and bleſſed Immortality ; *Man* being now utterly uncapable of acceptance with *God* upon thoſe terms on which *Adam* ſtood in his ſtate of Innocency.

CHAP. VIII.

Of Christ the Mediator.

1. IT pleaſed *God*, in his eternal purpoſe, to chuſe and ordain the *Lord Jeſus*, his only begotten *Son*, according to the *Covenant* made between them both, (*a*) to be the *Mediator* be-

(*) 2 Tim. 1. 9. Tit. 1 2. (*g*) Heb 11. 6, 13. Rom. 4 1, 2 &c. Acts 4. 12. John 8. 56. (*a*) Iſai. 42. 1. 1 Pet. 1. 9. 10.

tween

tween *God* and *Man*; the (*b*) Prophet, (*c*) Prieſt and (*d*) King; Head and Saviour of his Church, the Heir of all things, and Judge of the World; Unto whom he did from all eternity (*e*) give a People to be his Seed, and to be by him in time redeemed, called, juſtified, ſanctified, and glorified.

2. The *Son of God*, the ſecond Perſon in the *Holy Trinity*, being very and eternal *God*, the brightneſs of the Father's Glory, of one Subſtance, and equal with *him*: Who made the World, who upholdeth and governeth all things he hath made: Did, when the fulneſs of time was come, take upon him (*f*) Man's nature, with all the eſſential Properties, and common Infirmities thereof (*g*) yet without Sin; being conceived by the *Holy Spirit* in the *Womb* of the *Virgin Mary*, the *Holy Spirit* com-

(*c*) Heb. 5. 5, 6. (*d*) Pſal. 2. 6. Luke 1. 33. Eph. 1. 23. Heb. 1. 2. Acts 17. 31. (*e*) Iſai 53. 10. John 17. 6. Rom. 8. 30 (*f*) 1 John 1. 14. Gal. 4. 4. (*g*) Rom. 8. 3. Heb. 2. 14. 16, 17. Ch. 4. 15.

C 2 ing

ing down upon her, and the Power of the *most high* overshadowing her (*h*) and so was made of a *Woman*, of the Tribe of *Judah*, of the Seed of *Abraham* and *David*, according to the *Scriptures*: So that two whole, perfect, and distinct Natures, were inseparably joined together in one Person, without *Conversion*, *Composition*, or *confusion*; which Person is very *God*, and very *Man*, yet one (*i*) *Christ*, the only *Mediator* between *God* and *Man*.

3. The *Lord Jesus* in his Humane Nature thus united to the Divine, in the Person of the *Son*, was sanctified, and anointed *(k)* with the *Holy Spirit*, above measure; having in him *(l)* all the treasures of Wisdom and Knowledge; in whom it pleased the *Father*, that *(m)* all fullness should dwell; to the end, that being *(n)* holy, harmless, undefiled, and full *(o)* of *Grace*, and

---

(*h*) Luke 1. 27, 31, 35. (*i*) Rom. 9. 5. 1 Tim. 2. 5. (*k*) Psalm 45. 7. Acts 10. 38. John 3. 34. (*l*) Col. 23. (*m*) Col. 1. 19. (*n*) Heb. 7. 26. (*o*) John 1. 14.

Truth,

Truth, he might be throughly furnished to execute the Office of a *Mediator*, and *(p) Surety*; which Office he took not upon himself, but was thereunto *(q)* called by his *Father*; who also put *(r)* all Power and Judgment in his Hand, and gave him Commandment to execute the same.

4. This Office the *Lord Jesus* did most *(s)* willingly undertake, which that he might discharge he was made under the Law, *(t)* and did perfectly fulfil it, and underwent the *(u)* Punishment due to us, which we should have born and suffered, being made *(x) Sin* and a *Curse* for us; enduring most grievous Sorrows *(y)* in his Soul; and most painful sufferings in his Body; was crucified, and died, and remained in the state of the dead; yet saw no *(z) Cor-*

(*p*) Heb. 7. 22. (*q*) Heb. 5. 5. (*r*) John 5. 22, 27. Matt. 28. 18. Acts 2. 36. (*s*) Psalm 40. 78. Heb. 10. 5---11. John 10. 18. (*t*) Gal. 4. 4. Matt. 3. 15. (*u*) Gal. 3. 13. Isa. 53. 6. 1 Pet. 3. 18. (*x*) 2 Cor. 5. 21 (*y*) Matt. 26. 37. 31. Luke 22. 44. Matt. 27. 46. (*z*) Acts 13. 37.

C 3 *ruption*.

ruption: On the (*a*) third Day he arose from the Dead, with the same (*b*) Body in which he suffered; with which he also (*c*) ascended into Heaven; and there sitteth on the right Hand of *his Father* (*d*) making intercession; and shall (*e*) return to judge *Men* and *Angels*, at the end of the World.

5. The *Lord Jesus*, by his perfect Obedience and Sacrifice of himself, which he through the Eternal *Spirit* once offered up unto *God*, (*f*) hath fully satisfied the Justice of *God*, procured reconciliation, and purchased an Everlasting Inheritance in the Kingdom of Heaven; (*g*) for all those whom the *Father* hath given unto him.

6. Although the Price of Redemption was not actually paid by *Christ*, till after his *Incarnation*, (*) yet the vertue, efficacy, and benefit thereof was com-

(*a*) 1Cor. 15.3, 4. (*b*) John 20. 25, 27. (*c*) Mark 16. 16. Acts 1. 9, 10, 11. (*d*) Rom. 8. 34. Heb. 9 24. (*e*) Acts 10. 42. Rom. 14. 9, 10. Acts 1. 10 (*f*) Heb. 9. 14. Ch. 10. 14. Rom 3. 25, 26. (*g*) John 17. 2. Heb. 9. 15. (*) 1Cor. 4. 10. Heb. 4. 2. 1Pet. 1 10, 11

municated

municated to the Elect in all Ages successively, from the beginning of the World, in and by those Promises, Types, and Sacrifices, wherein he was revealed, and signified to be the Seed of the *Woman*, which should bruise the Serpent's Head; (*h*) and the Lamb slain from the Foundation of the World: (*i*) Being *the same yesterday, and to day, and for ever.*

7. Christ in the work of *Mediation* acteth according to both Natures, by each Nature doing that which is proper to itself; yet by reason of the Unity of the Person, that which is proper to one Nature, is sometimes in *Scripture* attributed to the Person (*k*) denominated by the other Nature.

8. To all those for whom Christ hath obtained Eternal Redemption, he doth certainly and effectually (*l*) apply, and communicate the same; making Intercession for them; uniting them to him-

(*h*) Rev. 13. 8. (*i*) Heb. 13. 8. (*k*) John 3. 13 Acts 20. 28. (*l*) John 6. 37. Chap. 10, 15, 16. & Ch. 17. 9. Rom. 5. 10.

self

ſelf by his Spirit; (*m*) revealing unto them, in and by the Word, the Myſtery of Salvation; perſwading them to believe, and obey; (*n*) governing their Hearts by his Word and Spirit, and (*o*) overcoming all their Enemies by his Almighty Power, and Wiſdom; in ſuch manner, and ways, as are moſt conſonant to his wonderful, and (*p*) unſearchable diſpenſation; and all of free, and abſolute Grace, without any Condition foreſeen in them, to procure it.

9. This Office of Mediator between God and Man, is proper (*q*) only to Chriſt, who is the Prophet, Prieſt, and King of the Church of God; and may not be either in whole, or any part thereof transferr'd from him to any other.

10. This number and order of Offices is neceſſary; for in reſpect of our (*r*) Ignorance, we ſtand in need of his

---

(*m*) John 17. 6. Eph. 1 9. 1 John 5. 20. (*n*) Rom. 8. 9, 14. Pſalm 110. 1. 1 Cor. 5. 25, 26. (*p*) John 3. 8. Eph. 1. 8. (*q*) 1 Tim. 2. 5. (*r*) John 1. 18.

pro-

prophetical Office; and in reſpect of our alienation from God, (*s*) and imperfection of the beſt of our Services, we need his Prieſtly Office, to reconcile us, and preſent us acceptable unto God: And in reſpect of our averſeneſs, and utter inability to return to God, and for our reſcue, and ſecurity from our ſpiritual Adverſaries, we need his Kingly Office, (*t*) to convince, ſubdue, draw, uphold, deliver, and preſerve us to his Heavenly Kingdom.

CHAP. IX.

Of Free Will.

1. GOD hath indued the Will of Man with that natural liberty and power of acting upon choice, that it is (*a*) neither forced, nor by any ne-

(*s*) Col. 1. 21. Gal. 5. 17. (*t*) John 16. 8. Pſalm 110. 3. Luke 74. 75. (*a*) Matt. 17. 12. Jam. 1. 14. Deut. 30. 10.

ceſſity

ceſſity of nature determined to do good or evil.

2. Man in his ſtate of Innocency, had freedom, and power, to will, and to do, that (*b*) which was good, and well-pleaſing to God; but yet (*c*) was mutable, ſo that he might fall from it.

3. Man by his fall into a ſtate of Sin, hath wholly loſt (*d*) all ability of will, to any ſpiritual good accompanying Salvation; ſo as a natural Man, being altogether averſe from that good, (*e*) and dead in Sin, is not able, by his own ſtrength, to (*f*) convert himſelf, or to prepare himſelf thereunto.

4. When God converts a Sinner, and tranſlates him into the ſtate of Grace, (*g*) he freeth him from his natural Bondage under Sin, and by his Grace alone, enables him (*h*) freely to will, and to do that which is ſpiritually good; yet

(*b*) Eccleſ. 7. 29. (*c*) Gen. 3. 6. (*d*) Rom. 5. 6. Ch. 8. 7. (*e*) Eph. 2. 1, 5. (*f*) Tit. 3. 3, 4, 5. John 6. 44. (*g*) Col. 1. 13. John 8. 36. (*h*) Phi 2. 13.

ſo

ſo as that, by reaſon of his (*i*) remaining Corruptions, he doth not perfectly nor only will that which is good, but doth alſo will that which is evil.

5. The Will of Man is made (*k*) perfectly and immutably free to good alone in the State of Glory only.

CHAP. X.

Of Effectual Calling.

1. THoſe whom God hath predeſtinated unto Life, he is pleaſed in his appointed and accepted time (*a*) effectually to call by his Word and Spirit, out of that ſtate of Sin and Death, in which they are by Nature, to Grace and Salvation (*b*) by Jeſus Chriſt; enlightning their Minds, ſpiritually and ſavingly, to (*c*) underſtand the Things

(*i*) Rom. 7. 15, 18, 19, 22, 23. (*k*) Eph. 4. 13
(*a*) Rom. 8. 30. Rom. 11. 7. Eph. 1 10. 11. 2. Theſſ. 3. 13, 14. (*b*) Eph. 2. 1,--6. (*c*) Acts 26. 18. Eph. 1. 7. 18.

of

of God; taking away their (*d*) Heart of Stone, and giving unto them an Heart of Flesh; renewing their Wills, and by his Almighty Power determining them (*e*) to that which is good, and effectually drawing them to Jesus Christ; yet so, as they come (*f*) most freely, being made willing by his Grace.

2. This Effectual Call is of God's free and special Grace alone, (*g*) not from any thing at all foreseen in Man, nor from any Power or Agency in the Creature, co-working with his special Grace; (*h*) the Creature being wholly passive therein, being dead in Sins and Trespasses, until being quickned and renewed by the Holy Spirit, he is thereby enabled to answer this Call, and to embrace the Grace offered and conveyed in it, and that by no less (*i*) Power

---

(*d*) Ezek 36. 26. (*e*) Deut. 30. 6. Ezek. 36. 27. Eph. 1. 19. (*f*) Psalm 110. 3. Cant. 1. 4. (*g*) 2Tim. 1. 9. Eph 2. 8. (*h*) 1Cor. 2. 14. Eph. 2. 5. John 5. 25. (*i*) Eph. 1. 19, 20.

than

than that which raiſed up Chriſt from the Dead.

3. Elect Infants dying in Infancy, are (*k*) regenerated and ſaved by Chriſt thro' the Spirit, who worketh when, and where, and (*l*) how he pleaſeth: So alſo are all other Elect Perſons, who are uncapable of being outwardly called by the Miniſtry of the Word.

4. Others not elected, altho' they may be called by the Miniſtry of the Word, (*m*) and may have ſome common Operations of the Spirit; yet, not being effectually drawn by the Father, they neither will, nor can truly (*n*) come to Chriſt; and therefore cannot be ſaved: Much leſs can Men that receive not the Chriſtian Religion (*o*) be ſaved, be they never ſo diligent to frame their Lives according to the Light of Nature, and the Law of that Religion they do profeſs.

(*k*) John 3. 3, 5, 6, (*l*) John 3. 8. (*m*) Mat. 22. 4. Ch. 13. 20, 21. Heb. 6. 4, 5. (*n*) John 6. 44. 45, 65. 1 John 2. 24, 25. (*o*) Acts 4. 12. John 4, 22. Ch. 17. 3.

CHAP.

CHAP. XI.

Of Justification.

1. THOSE whom God effectually calleth, he also freely *(a)* justifieth, not by infusing Righteousness into them, but by *(b)* pardoning their Sins, and by accounting and accepting their Persons as *(c)* righteous; not for any thing wrought in them, or done by them, but for Christ's sake alone; not by imputing Faith itself the Act of Believing, or any other *(d)* evangelical Obedience to them, as their Righteousness, but by imputing Christ's active Obedience unto the whole Law, and passive Obedience in his Death, for their whole and sole Righteousness; they *(e)* receiving, and resting on him,

(*a*) Rom. 3. 24. Ch. 8. 30. (*b*)Rom 4. 5, 6, 7, 8. Eph. 1. 7. (*c*) 1 Cor. 1. 30, 31. Rom. 5. 17, 18, 19. (*d*) Phil. 3. 8. 9. Eph. 2. 8, 9, 10. (*e*) John 1. 12. Rom. 5. 17.

and

and his Righteouſneſs by Faith; which they have not of themſelves; it is the Gift of God.

2. Faith thus receiving and reſting on Chriſt and his Righteouſneſs, is the *(f)* alone Inſtrument of Juſtification: Yet it is not alone in the Perſon juſtified, but is ever accompanied with all other ſaving Graces, and is no dead Faith, *(g)* but worketh by Love.

3. Chriſt, by his Obedience and Death, did fully diſcharge the Debt of all thoſe that are juſtified; and did by the Sacrifice of himſelf, in the Blood of his Croſs, undergoing in their ſtead the Penalty due unto them, make a proper, real and full Satiſfaction *(h)* to God's Juſtice in their behalf; yet inaſmuch as he was given by the Father for them, and his Obedience and Satiſfaction accepted in their ſtead, and both *(i)* freely, not for any thing in them, their Juſti-

(f) Rom. 3. 28. *(g)* Gal. 5. 6. James 2. 17, 22, 26. *(h)* Heb. 12. 14. 1 Pet. 1. 18, 19. Iſai. 53. 5, 6. *(i)* Rom 8. 32. 1 Cor. 5. 21.

fication

fication is only of Free Grace, that both the exact Justice and rich Grace of God might be *(k)* glorified in the Justification of Sinners.

4. God did from all Eternity decree to *(l)* justify all the Elect, and Christ did in the Fulness of Time die for their Sins, and *(m)* rise again for their Justification; nevertheless they are not justified personally, until the Holy Spirit doth in due Time *(n)* actually apply Christ unto them.

5. God doth continue to *(o)* forgive the Sins of those that are justified; and although they can never fall from the State of *(p)* Justification, yet they may by their Sins fall under God's (*q*) fatherly Displeasure; and in that Condition, they have not usually the Light of his Countenance restored unto them, until

(*k*) Rom. 3. 26. Eph. 1. 6, 7. Cha. 2. 7. (*l*) Gal. 3. 8. 1 Pet. 1. 2. 1 Tim. 2. 6. (*m*) Rom. 4. 25. (*n*) Col. 1. 21, 22. Tit. 3. 4, 5, 6, 7. (*o*) Mat. 6. 12. 1 John 1. 7, 9. (*p*) John 10. 28 (*q*) Psalm 89. 31, 32, 33.

they

they (*r*) humble themſelves, confeſs their Sins, beg Pardon, and renew their Faith and Repentance.

6. The Juſtification of Believers under the Old Teſtament, was in all theſe Reſpects (*s*) one and the ſame with the Juſtification of Believers under the New Teſtament.

CHAP. XII.

Of Adoption.

ALL thoſe that are juſtified, *God* vouchſafed in and for the Sake of his only *Son Jeſus Chriſt*, to make Partakers of the Grace (*a*) of *Adoption*; by which they are taken into the Number, and enjoy the Liberties and (*b*) Privileges of Children of God; have his (*c*) Name put upon them, (*d*) re-

(*r*) Pſalm 32. 5. & 51 Matt. 26 75. (*s*) Gal. 3. 9. Rom. 4. 22. 23. 24. (*a*) Epheſ. 1. 5. Gal. 4. 4, 5. (*b*) John 1. 12. Rom. 8. 17. (*c*) 2 Cor. 6. 18. Rev. 3. 12. (*d*) Rom. 8. 15.

D ceive

ceive the *Spirit* of *Adoption*, (*e*) have acceſs to the Throne of Grace with boldneſs; are enabled to cry, *Abba*, *Father*; are (*f*) pitied, (*g*) protected, (*i*) provided for, and (*k*) chaſtned by him, as by a Father; yet never (*l*) caſt off, but ſealed (*m*) to the Day of Redemption, and inherit the Promiſes, (*n*) as Heirs of Everlaſting Salvation.

CHAP. XIII.

Of Sanctification.

1. THEY who are united to Chriſt, effectually called, and regenerated, having a new Heart and a new Spirit created in them, through the Vertue of Chriſt's Death and Reſurrection; are alſo (*a*) farther ſanctified,

---

(*e*) Gal. 4. 6. Epheſ. 2. 18 (*f*) Pſalm 103. 13 (*g*) Prov. 14. 26. (*i*) 1 Pet. 5. 7. (*k*) Heb. 12. 6. (*l*) Iſaiah 54. 8, 9. Lam 3. 31. (*m*) Eph. 4. 30. (*n*) Heb. 1. 14. Chap. 6. 12. (*a*) Acts 20. 32. Rom. 6 5, 6.

really,

really and perſonally, through the ſame Vertue, (*b*) by his Word and Spirit dwelling in them ; (*c*) the Dominion of the whole Body of Sin is deſtroyed, (*d*) and the ſeveral Luſts thereof, are more and more weakned, and mortified ; and they more and more quickned, and (*e*) ſtrengthned in all ſaving Graces, to the (*f*) Practice of all true Holineſs, without which no Man ſhall ſee the Lord.

2. This Sanctification is (*g*) throughout in the whole Man, yet imperfect (*h*) in this Life ; there abideth ſtill ſome Remnants of Corruption in every Part, whence ariſeth a (*i*) continual and irreconcilable War ; the Fleſh luſting againſt the Spirit, and the Spirit againſt the Fleſh.

3. In which War, although the remaining Corruption for a Time may much (*k*) prevail, yet through the con-

(*b*) John 17. 17. Eph. 3. 16, 17, 18, 19. 1 Theſſ. 5. 21, 22, 23. (*c*) Rom. 6. 14. (*d*) Gal. 5. 14. 24 (*e*) Col. 1. 11. (*f*) 2 Cor. 7. 1. Heb 12. 14. (*g*) 1 Theſſ. 5. 23. (*h*) Rom. 7. 18, 23. (*i*) Gal. 5. 17. 1 Pet. 2. 11. (*k*) Rom. 7. 23.

D 2. tinual

tinual Supply of Strength, from the *sanctifying Spirit* of *Christ*, (*l*) the regenerate Part doth overcome; and so the Saints grow in Grace, perfecting Holiness in the Fear of God, (*m*) pressing after an Heavenly Life, in Evangelical Obedience to all the Commands which *Christ*, as *Head* and *King*, in his *Word* hath prescribed to them.

CHAP. XIV.

Of Saving Faith.

1. THE Grace of *Faith*, whereby the Elect are enabled to believe to the Saving of their Souls, is the Work of the *Spirit* of *Christ* (*a*) in their Hearts, and is ordinarily wrought by the Ministry of the (*b*) Word; by which also, and by the Administration

---

(*l*) Rom. 6. 4 (*m*) Eph. 4. 15, 16. 2 Cor. 3. 18. Chap. 7. 1. (*a*) 2 Cor. 4. 13. Eph. 2. 8. (*b*) Rom. 10. 14. 17.

of

of *Baptiſm*, and the *Lord's Supper*, *Prayer* and other *Means* appointed of *God*, it is increaſed, (*c*) and ſtrengthned.

2. By this *Faith*, a Chriſtian believeth to be true, * whatſoever is revealed in the *Word*, for the Authority of *God* himſelf; and alſo apprehendeth an Excellency therein (*d*) above all other *Writings*; and all Things in the *World*: As it bears forth the Glory of *God* in his Attributes, the Excellency of *Chriſt* in his Nature and Offices, and the Power and Fulneſs of the *Holy Spirit* in his Workings and Operations; and ſo is enabled to (*e*) caſt his Soul upon the Truth thus believed, and alſo acteth differently upon that which each particular Paſſage thereof containeth; yielding Obedience to the (*f*) Commands, trembling at the (*g*) Threatnings, and embracing the (*h*) Promiſes of *God*, for this Life, and that which is to come: But the principal

(*c*) Luke 17. 5. 1 Pet. 2. 2. Acts 20. 32. * Acts 24. 14. (*d*) Pſalm 19. 7, 8, 9, 10. Pſalm 119. 72. (*e*) 2 Tim. 1. 12. (*f*) John 15. 14. (*g*) Iſa. 66. 2. (*h*) Heb. 11. 13.

pal Acts of *Saving Faith*, hath immediate Relation to *Christ*, accepting, receiving, and resting upon (*i*) him alone, for Justification, Sanctification, and Eternal Life, by vertue of the Covenant of Grace.

3. This *Faith*, although it be different in degrees, and may be weak, (*k*) or strong, yet it is in the least Degree of it, different in the Kind, or Nature of it (as is all other Saving Grace) from the Faith (*l*) and common Grace of temporary Believers ; and therefore, tho' it may be many Times assailed and weakned, yet it gets (*m*) the Victory, growing up in many, to the Attainment of a full (*n*) Assurance through *Christ*, who is both the Author (*o*) and Finisher of our *Faith*.

(*i*) John 1. 12. Acts 16. 31. Gal. 2. 20. Acts 15. 11. (*k*) Heb. 5. 13, 14. Matt. 6. 30. Rom. 4. 19, 20. (*l*) 2 Pet 1. 1. (*m*) Eph. 6. 16. 1 John 5. 4, 5. (*n*) Heb. 6. 11, 12. Col. 2. 2. (*o*) Heb. 12. 2.

CHAP.

CHAP. XV.

Of Repentance unto Life and Salvation.

1. SUCH of the Elect as are converted at riper Years, having (*a*) ſometimes lived in the State of Nature, and therein ſerved divers Luſts and Pleaſures, God in their *Effectual Calling*, giveth them Repentance unto Life.

2. Whereas there is none that doth good, and ſinneth (*b*) not, and the beſt of Men may, through the Power and Deceitfulneſs of their Corruption dwelling in them, with the Prevalency of Temptation, fall into greater Sins and Provocations, God hath in the Covenant of Grace, mercifully provided that Believers ſo Sinning and Falling, (*c*) be renewed through Repentance unto Salvation.

(*a*) Tit. 3. 2, 3, 4, 5. (*b*) Eccl. 7. 20. (*c*) Luke 22. 31, 32.

3. This

3. This Saving Repentance is an (*d*) Evangelical Grace, whereby a Perſon, being by the *Holy Spirit* made ſenſible of the manifold Evils of his Sin, doth, by Faith in Chriſt, humble himſelf for it, with Godly Sorrow, deteſtation of it, and ſelf-abhorrency; (*e*) praying for Pardon and Strength of Grace, with a Purpoſe and Endeavour by Supplies of the *Spirit*, to (*f*) walk before God unto all well-pleaſing in all Things.

4. As Repentance is to be continued through the whole Courſe of our Lives, upon the Account of the Body of Death, and the Motions thereof; ſo it is every Man's Duty to repent of his (*g*) particular known Sins, particularly.

5. Such is the Proviſion which God hath made through Chriſt in the Covenant of Grace, for the Preſervation of Believers unto Salvation, that although there is no Sin ſo ſmall, but it deſerves

(*d*) Zech. 12. 10. Acts 11. 18. (*e*) Ezek. 36. 31. 2 Cor. 7. 11. (*f*) Pſalm 119. 6. Pſalm 119. 128. (*g*) Luke 19. 8. 1 Tim. 13, 15.

(*h*) Dam-

(*b*) Damnation; yet there is no Sin ſo great, that it ſhall bring Damnation on them that (*i*) repent; which makes the conſtant Preaching of Repentance neceſſary.

CHAP. XVI.

Of Good Works.

1. GOOD Works are only ſuch as God hath (*a*) commanded in his Holy Word, and not ſuch as without the Warrant thereof, are deviſed by Men, out of blind Zeal, (*b*) or upon any Pretence of good Intentions.

2. Theſe good Works, done in Obedience to God's Commandments, are the Fruits and Evidences (*c*) of a true and lively Faith; and by them Believers manifeſt their (*d*) Thankfulneſs,

(*h*) Rom 6. 23. (*i*) Iſa. 1. 16, 17. Iſa 55. 7. (*a*) Mic 6. 8. Heb. 13. 21. (*b*) Mat. 15. 9. Iſa. 19. 13. (*c*) Jam. 2. 18. 22. (*d*) Pſalm 116. 12, 13.

ſtrengthen

ſtrengthen their (*e*) Aſſurance, edifie their (*f*) Brethren, adorn the Profeſſion of the Goſpel, ſtop the Mouths of the Adverſaries, and glorifie (*g*) God, whoſe Workmanſhip they are, created in Chriſt Jeſus (*h*) thereunto, that having their Fruit unto Holineſs, they may have the end (*i*) Eternal Life.

3. Their Ability to do good Works, is not at all of themſelves, but wholly from the Spirit (*k*) of Chriſt ; and that they may be enabled thereunto, beſides the Graces they have already received, there is neceſſary an (*l*) actual Influence of the ſame Holy Spirit to work in them to will, and to do of his good Pleaſure ; yet are they not hereupon to grow Negligent, as if they were not bound to perform any Duty, unleſs upon a ſpecial Motion of the Spirit, but they ought to be dilligent in (*m*) ſtir-

(*e*) 1 John 2. 3, 5. 2 Pet. 1. 5---11, (*f*) Mat. 5. 16. (*g*) 1 Tim. 6 1. 1 Pet. 2. 15. Phil. 1. 11. (*h*) Epheſ. 2. 10. (*i*) Rom. 6. 22. (*k*) John 15. 4, 5. (*l*) 2 Cor. 3. 5. Phil. 2. 13. (*m*) Phil. 2. 12. Heb. 6. 11. 1. Iſa 64 7.

ring

ring up the Grace of God that is in them.

4. They who in their Obedience attain to the greateſt Heighth which is poſſible in this Life, are ſo far from being able to ſupererrogate, and to do more than God requires, as that (*n*) they fall ſhort of much which in Duty they are bound to do.

5. We cannot by our beſt Works merit Pardon of Sin, or Eternal Life at the Hand of God, by reaſon of the great Diſproportion that is between them and the Glory to come, and the infinite Diſtance that is between us and God, whom by them we can neither profit, nor ſatisfy, for the Debt of our (*o*) former Sins ; but when we have done all we can, we have done but our Duty, and are unprofitable Servants : and becauſe as they are good, they proceed from his (*p*) Spirit, and as they are wrought

(*n*) Job 9. 2, 3. Gal, 5. 17. Luke 17 10. (*o*) Rom. 3. 20. Eph. 2. 8, 9. Rom. 4. 6. (*p*) Gal. 5. 22, 23.

by

by us, they are defiled, *(q)* and mixed with ſo much Weakneſs and Imperfection, that they cannot endure the Severity of God's Judgment.

6. Yet notwithſtanding the Perſons of Believers being accepted through Chriſt, their Good Works alſo are accepted in *(r)* him; not as though they were in this Life wholly unblameable and unreprovable in God's Sight; but that he looking upon them in his Son, is pleaſed to accept and reward that which is *(s)* ſincere, although accompanied with many Weakneſſes and Imperfections.

7. Works done by unregenerate Men, although for the Matter of them, they may be Things which God commands, and of good Uſe, both to themſelves and *(t)* others; yet becauſe they proceed not from a Heart purified by *(u)* Faith, nor are done in a right Manner

(q) Iſa. 64. 6. Pſalm 143. 2. (r) Eph. 1. 6. 1 Pet. 2. 5. (s) Matt. 25. 21, 23. Heb. 6. 10. (t) 2 Kings 10. 30. 1 Kings 21. 27, 29. (u) Gen. 4. 9. Heb: 11. 4 6.

accord-

according to the *(w)* Word, nor to a right End the *(x)* Glory of God, they are sinful, and cannot please God, nor make a Man meet to receive Grace from *(y)* God; and yet their neglect of them is more sinful, and *(z)* displeasing to God.

CHAP. XVII.

Of Perseverance of the Saints.

1. THose whom God hath accepted in the Beloved, effectually called and sanctified by his Spirit, and given the precious Faith of his Elect unto, can neither totally nor finally fall from the State of Grace, *(a)* but shall certainly persevere therein to the End, and be eternally saved, seeing the Gifts

(*w*) 1 Cor. 13. 1. (*x*) Matt. 6. 2, 5. (*y*) Amos 5. 21, 22. Rom. 9. 16. Tit. 3, 5. (*z*) Job 21. 14, 15. Matt. 25. 41, 42, 43. (*a*) John 10. 28, 29. Phil. 1. 6. 2 Tim, 2, 19. 1 John 2, 19.

and

and Callings of God are without Repentance, (whence he ſtill begets and nouriſheth in them Faith, Repentance, Love, Joy, Hope, and all the Graces of the Spirit unto Immortality) and though many Storms and Floods ariſe and beat againſt them, yet they ſhall never be able to take them off that Foundation and Rock which by Faith they are faſtned upon: Notwithſtanding, through Unbelief and the Temptations of Satan, the ſenſible Sight of the Light and Love of God, may for a Time be clouded, and obſcured from (*b*) them, yet it is ſtill the ſame, (*c*) and they ſhall be ſure to be kept by the Power of God unto Salvation, where they ſhall enjoy their purchaſed Poſſeſſion, they being engraven upon the Palm of his Hands, and their Names having been written in the Book of Life from all Eternity.

2. This Perſeverance of the Saints, depends not upon their own Free Will,

(*b*) Pſalm 89. 31, 32. 1 Cor. 11. 22. (*c*) Mal. 3. 6.

but

but upon the Immutability of the Decree of (*d*) Election, flowing from the free and unchangeable Love of God the Father, upon the Efficacy of the Merit and Intercession of Jesus Christ (*e*) and Union with him, the (*f*) Oath of God, the Abiding of his Spirit, and the (*g*) Seed of God within them, and the Nature of the (*h*) Covenant of Grace; from all which ariseth also the Certainty and Infallibility thereof.

3. And though they may, through the Temptation of Satan, and of the World, the Prevalency of Corruption remaining in them, and the Neglect of Means of their Preservation, fall into grievous (*i*) Sins, and for a Time continue therein; whereby they incur (*k*) God's Displeasure, and grieve his holy Spirit, come to have their Graces and (*l*) Comforts impaired, have their

(*d*) Rom. 8. 30. Chap. 9. 11, 16. (*e*) Rom. 5. 9, 10. John 14. 19. (*f*) Heb. 6. 17, 18. (*g*) 1 John 3. 9. (*h*) Jer. 32. 40. (*i*) Matt. 26. 70, 72, 74. (*k*) Isa. 64. 5. 9. Eph. 4. 30. (*l*) Psa. 51. 10. 12.

Hearts

Hearts hardened, and their Consciences wounded, (*m*) hurt, and scandalize others, and bring temporal Judgments (*n*) upon themselves, yet they shall renew their (*o*) Repentance, and be preserved, through Faith in Christ Jesus, to the End.

CHAP. XVIII.

Of the Assurance of Grace & Salvation.

1. ALthough temporary Believers, and other unregenerate Men, may vainly deceive themselves with false Hopes, and carnal Presumptions, of being in the Favour of God, and State of Salvation, (*a*) which Hope of theirs shall perish; yet such as truly believe in the Lord Jesus, and love him in Sincerity, endeavouring to walk in

(*m*) Psa. 32. 3, 4. (*n*) 2 Sam. 12. 14. (*o*) Luk. 22. 32. and v. 61, 62. (*a*) Job 8. 13, 14. Matt. 7. 22, 23.

all

all good Conſcience before him, may in this Life be certainly aſſured, (*b*) that they are in the State of Grace, and may rejoice in the Hope of the Glory of God, which Hope ſhall never make them (*c*) aſhamed.

2. This Certainty is not a bare conjectural and probable Perſuaſion, grounded upon (*d*) a fallible Hope, but an infallible Aſſurance of Faith, founded on the Blood and Righteouſneſs of Chriſt (*e*) revealed in the Goſpel; and alſo upon the inward (*f*) Evidence of thoſe Graces of the Spirit unto which Promiſes are made, and on the Teſtimony of the (*g*) Spirit of Adoption, witneſſing with our Spirits, that we are the Children of God; and, as a Fruit thereof, keeping the Heart both (*h*) humble and holy.

(*b*) 1 John 2. 3. Ch 3. 14, 18. 19, 21, 24. Ch. 5. 13. (*c*) Rom. 5. 2, 5. (*d*) Heb. 6. 11, 19. (*e*) Heb. 6. 17, 18. (*f*) 2 Pet. 1. 4, 5, 10, 11. (*g*) Rom. 8. 15, 16. (*h*) 1 John 3. 1, 2, 3.

E 3. This

3. This infallible Assurance doth not so belong to the Essence of Faith, but that a true Believer may wait long; and conflict with many Difficulties, before he be (*i*) Partaker of it; yet being enabled by the Spirit, to know the Things which are freely given him of God, he may, without extraordinary Revelation, in the right Use of Means (*k*) attain thereunto; and therefore it is the Duty of every one, to give all diligence to make their Calling and Election sure, that thereby his Heart may be enlarged in Peace and Joy in the Holy Spirit, in love and thankfulness to God, and in strength and chearfulness in the Duties of Obedience, the proper (*l*) Fruits of this Assurance; so far is it (*m*) from inclining Men to looseness.

4. True Believers may have the Assurance of their Salvation divers ways

(*i*) Isa. 50. 10. Psalm 88. & Psalm 77. 1--12. (*k*) 1 John 4. 13. Heb. 6. 11, 12. (*l*) Rom. 5. 1, 2, 5. Ch. 14. 17. Psalm 119. 32. (*m*) Rom. 6. 1, 2. Tit. 2, 11, 12, 14.

shaken

ſhaken, diminiſhed, and intermitted; as (*n*) by negligence in preſerving of it, by (*o*) falling into ſome ſpecial Sin, which woundeth the Conſcience, and grieveth the Spirit; by ſome ſudden, or (*p*) vehement Temptation; by God's withdrawing the (*q*) Light of his Countenance, and ſuffering even ſuch as fear him to walk in Darkneſs, and to have no Light; yet are they never deſtitute of the (*r*) Seed of God, and Life (*s*) of Faith, that Love of Chriſt, and the Brethren, that Sincerity of Heart, and Conſcience of Duty, out of which, by the Operation of the Spirit, this Aſſurance may in due time be (*t*) revived; and by the which, in the mean Time, they are (*u*) preſerved from utter Deſpair.

(*n*) Cant. 5. 2, 3, 6. (*o*) Pſalm 51. 8, 12, 14. (*p*) Pſa. 116. 11. Pſa. 77. 7, 8. Pſalm 31. 22. (*q*) Pſalm 30. 7. (*r*) 1 John 3. 9. (*s*) Luke 22. 32. (*t*) Pſalm 42. 5, 11. (*u*) Lam. 3. 26, 27--31.

E 2 CHAP.

CHAP. XIX.

Of the Law of God.

1. GOD gave to *Adam* a Law of Universal Obedience, (*a*) written in his Heart, and a particular Precept of not eating the Fruit of the Tree of Knowledge of Good and Evil; by which he bound him, and all his Posterity to personal, entire, exact and perpetual (*b*) Obedience; promised Life upon the Fulfilling, and (*c*) threatned Death upon the Breach of it, and indued him with Power and Ability to keep it.

2. The same Law that was first written in the Heart of Man (*d*) continued to be a perfect Rule of Righteousness after the Fall, and was delivered by God upon Mount *Sinai*, in (*e*)

(*a*) Gen. 1. 27. Eccle. 7. 29. (*b*) Rom. 10. 5. (*c*) Gal. 3. 10, 12. (*d*) Rom, 2. 14, 15. (*e*) Deut. 10. 4.

Ten

Ten Commandments, and written in two Tables, the four firſt containing our Duty towards God, and the other ſix our Duty to Man.

3. Beſides this Law, commonly called Moral, God was pleaſed to give to the People of *Iſrael* Ceremonial Laws, containing ſeveral typical Ordinances, partly of Worſhip, (*f*) prefiguring Chriſt, his Graces, Actions, Sufferings, and Benefits; and partly holding forth divers Inſtructions (*g*) of Moral Duties, all which Ceremonial Laws being appointed only to the Time of Reformation, are, by Jeſus Chriſt the true Meſſiah, and only Law-giver, who was furniſhed with Power from the Father for that end, (*h*) abrogated and taken away.

4. To them alſo he gave ſundry Judicial Laws, which expired together with the State of that People, not ob-

(*f*) Heb. 10. 1. Col. 2. 17. (*g*) 1 Cor. 5. 7. (*h*) Col. 2. 14, 16, 17. Eph. 2. 14, 16.

E 3 liging

liging any now by vertue of that Insti-tution; their general (*i*) Equity only being of moral Use.

5. The Moral Law doth for ever bind all, (*k*) as well justified Persons as others, to the Obedience thereof, and that not only in regard of the Matter contained in it, but also in respect of the (*l*) Authority of God the Creator, who gave it; neither doth *Christ* in the Gospel any way dissolve, (*m*) but much strengthen this Obligation.

6. Although true Believers be not under the Law, as a Covenant of Works, (*n*) to be thereby justified or condemned, yet it is of great Use to them, as well as to others, in that, as a Rule of Life, informing them of the Will of God, and their Duty, it directs and binds them to walk accordingly;

(*i*) 1 Cor. 9. 8, 9, 10. (*k*) Rom. 13. 8, 9, 10. James 2. 8, 10, 11, 12. (*l*) James 2. 10, 11. (*m*) Matt. 5. 17, 18, 19. Rom. 3. 31. (*n*) Rom. 6. 14, Gal. 2. 16. Rom. 8. 1. Chap. 10. 4.

(*o*) dif-

(o) diſcovering alſo the ſinful Pollutions of their Natures, Hearts and Lives, ſo as examining themſelves thereby, they may come to further conviction of, humiliation for, and hatred againſt Sin; together with a clearer Sight of the Need they have of Chriſt, and the Perfection of his Obedience: It is likewiſe of Uſe to the Regenerate, to reſtrain their Corruptions, in that it forbids Sin; and the Threatnings of it ſerve to ſhew what even their Sins deſerve, and what Afflictions in this Life they may expect for them, although freed from the Curſe and unallayed Rigour thereof. Theſe Promiſes of it likewiſe ſhew them God's Approbation of Obedience, and what Bleſſings they may expect upon the Performance thereof, though not as due to them by the Law as a Covenant of Works; ſo as Man's doing Good, and refraining from Evil, becauſe the Law incourageth to the

(o) Rom. 3. 20. Chap. 7. &c.

one,

one, and deterreth from the other, is no Evidence of his being *(p)* under the Law, and not under Grace.

7. Neither are the forementioned Uses of the Law *(q)* contrary to the Grace of the Gospel, but do sweetly comply with it, the *Spirit* of *Christ* subduing *(r)* and inabling the Will of Man to do that freely and chearfully, which the Will of God, revealed in the Law, requireth to be done.

CHAP. XX.

Of the Gospel, and of the Extent of the Grace thereof.

1. THE Covenant of Works being broken by Sin, and made unprofitable unto Life, God was pleased to give forth the Promise of *Christ*, *(a)*

(p) Rom. 6. 12, 13, 14. 1 Pet. 3. 8,— 13. *(q)* Gal. 3. 21. *(r)* Ezek. 37. 21. *(a)* Gen. 3. 15.

the

the Seed of the Woman, as the Means of calling the Elect, and begetting in them Faith and Repentance ; in this Promiſe, the *(b)* Goſpel, as to the Subſtance of it, was revealed, and therein effectual, for the Converſion and Salvation of Sinners.

2. This Promiſe of *Chriſt* and Salvation by him, is revealed only by *(c)* the Word of God ; neither do the Works of Creation, or Providence, with the Light of Nature, *(d)* make Diſcovery of Chriſt, or of Grace by him, ſo much as in a general, or obſcure Way ; much leſs, that Men, deſtitute of the Revelation of him by the Promiſe, or Goſpel, *(e)* ſhould be enabled thereby, to attain ſaving Faith, or Repentance.

3. The Revelation of the Goſpel unto Sinners, made in divers Times, and by ſundry Parts, with the Addition of

---

(b) Rev. 13. 8. *(c)* Rom. 1. 17. *(d)* Rom. 10. 14, 15, 17. Prov. 29. 18. Iſa. 25. 7. with Ch. 60. 2, 3.

Promiſes,

Promiſes, and Precepts, for the Obedience required therein, as to the Nations, and Perſons, to whom it is granted, is meerly of the (*f*) Sovereign Will and good Pleaſure of God, not being annexed by vertue of any Promiſe, to the due Improvement of Men's natural Abilities, by vertue of common Light received without it ; which none ever did (*g*) make, or can ſo do : And therefore in all Ages the Preaching of the Goſpel hath been granted unto Perſons and Nations, as to the Extent, or Streightning of it, in great Variety, according to the Counſel of the Will of God.

4. Although the Goſpel be the only outward Means of revealing Chtiſt, and ſaving Grace, and is, as ſuch, abundantly ſufficient thereunto ; yet that Men, who are dead in Treſpaſſes, may be Born again, Quickned or Regenerated, there is moreover neceſſary, an effectual inſuperable (*h*) Work of the

(*f*) Pſalm 147. 10, Acts 16. 7. (*g*) Rom. 1. 18, &c. (*h*) Pſalm 110. 3. 1 Cor. 2. 14. Eph. 1. 19, 20.

the *Holy Spirit*, upon the whole Soul, for the Producing in them a new Spiritual Life; without which no other Means will effect (*e*) their Conversion unto God.

CHAP. XXI.

Of Christian Liberty, and Liberty of Conscience.

1. THE Liberty which *Christ* hath purchased for Believers under the Gospel, consists in their Freedom from the Guilt of Sin, the condemning Wrath of God, the Rigour and (*a*) Curse of the Law, and in their being delivered from this present Evil (*b*) World, Bondage to (*c*) Satan, and Dominion (*d*) of Sin, from the (*e*) Evil of Afflictions, the Fear, and Sting (*f*) of Death,

(*i*) John 6. 44. 2 Cor. 4. 4, 6. (*a*) Gal. 3. 13. (*b*) Gal. 1. 4. (*c*) Acts 26. 18. (*d*) Rom. 8. 3. (*e*) Rom. 8. 28. (*f*) 1 Cor. 15. 54, 55, 56, 57.

Death, the Victory of the Grave, and (*g*) Everlaſting Damnation ; as alſo in their (*h*) free Acceſs to God, and their yielding Obedience unto him, not out of a ſlaviſh Fear, (*i*) but a Child-like Love, and willing Mind.

All which were common alſo to Believers under the Law (*k*) for the Subſtance of them ; but under the New Teſtament, the Liberty of Chriſtians is further enlarged in their Freedom from the Yoke of the Ceremonial Law, to which the *Jewiſh* Church was ſubjected, and in greater Boldneſs of Acceſs to the Throne of Grace, and in fuller Communications of the (*l*) Free Spirit of God, than Believers under the Law did ordinarily partake of.

2. God alone is (*m*) Lord of the Conſcience, and hath left it free from the Doctrines and Commandments of Men (*n*) which are in any Thing con-

(*g*) 2 Theſſ. 1. 10. (*h*) Rom. 8. 15. (*i*) Luke 1. 75. 1 John 4. 18. (*k*) Gal. 3 9, 14. (*l*) John 7. 38, 39. Heb. 10. 19, 20, 21. (*m*) Jam. 4. 12. Rom. 14. 4. (*n*) Acts 4 19. & 5. 29. 1 Cor. 7. 23. Matt. 15. 9.

trary

trary to his Word, or not contained in it. So that to believe fuch Doctrines, or Obey fuch Commands out of Confcience, (*o*) is to betray true Liberty of Confcience ; and the Requiring of an (*p*) implicit Faith, and abfolute and blind Obedience, is to deftroy Liberty of Confcience and Reafon alfo.

3. They who, upon Pretence of Chriftian Liberty, do practice any Sin, or cherifh any finful Luft, as they do thereby pervert the main Defign of the Grace of the Gofpel, (*q*) to their own Deftruction, fo they wholly deftroy (*r*) the End of Chriftian Liberty ; which is, that, being delivered out of the Hands of all our Enemies, we might ferve the Lord without Fear, in Holinefs and Righteoufnefs before him, all the Days of our Lives.

(*o*) Col. 2. 20, 22, 23. (*p*) 1 Cor. 3. 5. 2 Cor. 1. 24. (*q*) Rom. 6. 1, 2. (*r*) Gal. 5. 13. 2 Pet. 2. 18, 21.

CHAP.

CHAP. XXII.

Of Religious Worship, & the Sabbath Day.

1. THE Light of Nature shews that there is a God, who hath Lordship and Sovereignty over all; is Just, Good, and doth Good unto all; and is therefore to be feared, loved, praised, called upon, trusted in, and served, with all the Heart, and all the Soul (*a*) and with all the Might. But the acceptable Way of Worshipping the true God, is (*b*) instituted by himself, and so limited by his own revealed Will, that he may not be worshipped according to the Imaginations and Devices of Men, or the Suggestions of Satan, under any visible Representations, or (*c*) any other Way, not prescribed in the Holy Scriptures.

(*a*) Jer. 10. 7. Mark 12. 33. (*b*) Deut. 12. 32. (*c*) Exod. 20. 4, 5, 6.

2. *Re-*

2. *Religious Worſhip* is to be given to *God* the *Father*, *Son* and *Holy Spirit*, and to him (*d*) alone; not to *Angels*, *Saints*, or any other (*e*) *Creatures*; and ſince the Fall, not without a (*f*) *Mediator*, nor in the *Mediation* of any other but (*g*) Chriſt alone.

3. Prayer, with Thankfulneſs, being one ſpecial Part of Natural Worſhip, is by God required of (*h*) all Men. But that it may be accepted, it is to be made in the (*i*) Name of the Son, by the Help (*k*) of the Spirit, according to (*l*) his Will; with Underſtanding, Reverence, Humility, Fervency, Faith, Love, and Perſeverance; and, with others, in a (*m*) known Tongue.

4. Prayer is to be made for Things lawful, and for all Sorts of Men living, (*n*) or that ſhall live hereafter; but

(*d*) Matt. 4. 9, 10. John 6. 23. Matt. 28. 19. (*e*) Rom. 1 25. Col. 2. 18. Rev. 19. 10 (*f*) John 14. 6. (*g*) 1 Tim. 2. 5. (*h*) Pſalm 95. 1, 7. Pſalm 65. 2, (*i*) John 14. 13, 14. (*k*) Rom. 8. 26. (*l*) 2 John 5. 14. (*m*) 1 Cor. 14. 16, 17. (*n*) 1 Tim. 2. 1, 2. 2 Sam. 7. 29.

not

not (*o*) for the Dead, nor for thoſe of whom it may be known, that they have ſinned (*p*) the Sin unto Death.

5. The (*q*) Reading of the Scriptures, Preaching, and (*r*) Hearing the Word of God, teaching and admoniſhing one another in Pſalms, Hymns, and Spiritual Songs, Singing with Grace in our Hearts to (*s*) the Lord; as alſo the Adminiſtration (*t*) of Baptiſm, and (*u*) the Lord's Supper, are all Parts of Religious Worſhip of God, to be performed in Obedience to him, with Underſtanding, Faith, Reverence, and Godly Fear; moreover, Solemn Humiliation, (*x*) with Faſtings, and Thankſgiving, upon (*y*) ſpecial Occaſions, ought to be uſed in an holy and religious Manner.

6. Neither Prayer, nor any other Part of religious Worſhip, is now, un-

(*o*) 2 Sam. 12. 21, 22, 23. (*p*) 1 John 5. 16. (*q*) 1 Tim. 4 13. (*r*) 2 Tim. 4 2. Luke 8. 18. (*s*) Col. 3. 16. Eph. 5 19 (*t*) Mat. 28. 19, 20. (*u*) 1 Cor. 15. 26. (*x*) Eſth. 4. 16. Joel 2. 12. (*y*) 15. 1. &c. Pſalm 107.

der

der the Goſpel, tied unto, or made more acceptable by any Place in which it is *(z)* performed, or towards which it is directed ; but God is to be worſhipped every where in Spirit, and in Truth ; as in *(a)* private Families *(b)* daily, and *(c)* in ſecret each one by himſelf, ſo more ſolemnly in the Publick Aſſemblies, which are not careleſly, nor wilfully, to be *(d)* neglected or forſaken, when God by his Word or Providence calleth thereunto.

7. As it is of the Law of Nature, that, in general, a Proportion of Time, by God's Appointment be ſet apart for the Worſhip of God, ſo by his Word, in a poſitive, moral, and perpetual Commandment, binding all Men, in all Ages, he hath particularly appointed one Day in Seven for a *(e)* Sabbath to be kept holy unto him, which from the Beginning of the World, to the Reſur-

(z) Joh. 4. 21. Mal. 1. 11. 1 Tim. 2. 8. *(a)* Acts 10. 2. *(b)* Mat. 6. 11. Pſal. 55. 17. *(c)* Mat. 6. 6. *(d)* Heb. 10. 25. Acts 2. 42. *(e)* Exod. 20. 8.

G rection

rection of Chriſt, was the laſt Day of the Week; and from the Reſurrection of Chriſt, was changed into the firſt Day of the Week, (*f*) which is called the Lord's Day; and is to be continued to the End of the World, as the Chriſtian Sabbath; the Obſervation of the laſt Day of the Week being aboliſhed.

8. The Sabbath is then kept holy unto the Lord, when Men, after a due Preparing of their Hearts, and ordering their common Affairs aforehand, do not only obſerve an holy (*g*) Reſt all the Day, from their own Works, Words and Thoughts, about their worldly Employment and Recreations, but alſo are taken up the whole Time in the publick and private Exerciſes of his Worſhip and in the Duties (*h*) of Neceſſity, and Mercy.

(*f*) 1 Cor. 16. 1, 2. Acts 20. 7. Rev. 1. 10. (*g*) Iſa. 58, 13. Neh. 13. 15, 23. (*h*) Mat. 12. 1, 13.

CHAP.

CHAP. XXIII.

Of Singing of Psalms, &c.

WE believe that (*a*) *singing the Praises of God*, is a holy Ordinance of Christ, and not a Part of Natural Religion, or a moral Duty only; but that it is brought under Divine Institution, it being injoined on the Churches of Christ to sing Psalms, Hymns, and Spiritual Songs; and that the whole Church in their Publick Assemblies (as well as private Christians) ought to (*b*) sing God's Praises according to the best Light they have received. Moreover, it was practised in the great Representative Church, by (*c*) our Lord Jesus Christ with his Disciples, after he had instituted and celebrated the Sacred Ordinance of his Holy Supper, as a commemotive Token of Redeeming Love.

(*a*) Acts 16. 25. Eph. 5. 19. Col. 3. 16. (*b*) Heb. 2. 12. Jam. 5. 13. (*c*) Mat. 26. 30. Mar. 14. 26.

G 2 CHAP.

CHAP. XXIV.

Of Lawful Oaths and Vows.

1. A Lawful Oath is a Part of Religious Worſhip, (*a*) wherein the Perſon ſwearing in Truth, Righteouſneſs, and Judgment, ſolemnly calleth God to witneſs what he ſweareth; (*b*) and to judge him according to the Truth or Falſeneſs thereof.

2. The Name of God only is that by which Men ought to ſwear; and therein it is to be uſed with all Holy Fear and Reverence; therefore to ſwear vainly or raſhly by that glorious and dreadful Name, or to ſwear at all by any other Thing, is ſinful and to be (*c*) abhorred; yet as in Matter of Weight and Moment, for Confirmation of Truth, (*d*) and ending all Strife, an Oath is

(*a*) Exod. 20. 7. Deut. 10. 20. Jer. 4. 2. (*b*) 2 Chron. 6. 22. 23. (*c*) Mat. 5. 24, 37. Jam. 5. 12. (*d*) Heb. 6. 16. 2 Cor. 1. 23.

warranted

warranted by the Word of God ; ſo a lawful Oath being impoſed, (*e*) by lawful Authority, in ſuch Matters, ought to be taken.

3. Whoſoever taketh an Oath, warranted by the Word of God, ought duly to conſider the Weightineſs of ſo Solemn an Act, and therein to avouch nothing but what he knoweth to be the Truth ; for that by raſh, falſe, and vain Oaths, the (*f*) Lord is provoked, and for them this Land mourns.

4. An Oath is to be taken in the plain and (*g*) common Senſe of the Words, without Equivocation, or mental Reſervation.

5. A Vow, which is not to be made to any Creature, but to God alone, (*h*) is to be made and performed with all religious Care and Faithfulneſs : But Popiſh Monaſtical Vows, (*i*) of perpetual ſingle Life, profeſſed (*k*) Poverty,

(*e*) Neh. 13. 25. (*f*) Lev. 19. 12. Jer. 23. 10. (*g*) Pſal. 24. 4. (*h*) Pſal. 76. 11. Gen. 28. 20, 21, 22. (*i*) 1 Cor. 7. 2, 9. (*k*) Eph. 4. 28.

G 3 and

and regular Obedience, are ſo far from being Degrees of higher Perfection, that they are ſuperſtitious, (*l*) and ſinful Snares, in which no Chriſtian may intangle himſelf.

CHAP. XXV.

Of the Civil Magiſtrate.

1. GOD, the Supreme Lord, and King of all the World, hath ordained Civil (*a*) Magiſtrates to be under him, over the People, for his own Glory, and the publick Good; and to this End hath armed them with the Power of the Sword, for Defence and Encouragement of them that do Good, and for the Puniſhment of Evil Doers.

2. It is lawful for Chriſtians to accept and execute the Office of a Magiſtrate, when called thereunto; in the Management whereof, as they ought

(*l*) Mat. 19. 11. (*a*) Rom. 13. 1, 2, 3, 4.

eſpecially

eſpecially to maintain (*b*) Juſtice, and Peace, according to the wholeſome Laws of each Kingdom, and Commonwealth: So for that end they may lawfully now under the New Teſtament (*c*) wage War upon juſt and neceſſary Occaſions.

3. *Civil Magiſtrates* being ſet up by God, for the Ends aforeſaid, Subjection in all lawful Things commanded by them, ought to be yielded by us in the Lord, not only for Wrath (*d*) but for Conſcience-ſake; and we ought to make Supplications and Prayers for Kings, and all that are in Authority (*e*) that under them we may live a quiet and peaceable Life, in all Godlineſs and Honeſty.

(*b*) 2 Sam. 23. 3. Pſal. 82. 3, 4. (*c*) Luke 3. 14. (*d*) Rom. 13. 5, 6, 7. 1 Pet. 2. 17. (*e*) 1 Tim. 2. 1, 2.

G 4 CHAP.

CHAP. XXVI.

Of Marriage.

1. MArriage is to be between one *Man* and one *Woman*; (*a*) neither is it lawful for any *Man* to have more than one *Wife*, nor for any *Woman* to have more than one *Huſband* at the ſame Time.

2. Marriage was ordained for the mutual Help (*b*) of *Huſband* and *Wife*, (*c*) for the Increaſe of Mankind with a legitimate Iſſue, and for (*d*) preventing of Uncleanneſs.

3. It is lawful for (*e*) all Sorts of People to *Marry*, who are able with Judgment to give their Conſent; yet it is the Duty of *Chriſtians* (*f*) to *Marry* in the Lord; and therefore ſuch as profeſs the true Religion, ſhould not *Marry*

---

[a] Gen. 2. 24. Mal. 2. 15. Mat. 19. 5, 6. [b] Gen. 2. 18. [c] Gen. 1. 28. [d] 1 Cor. 7. 2, 9. [e] Heb. 13. 4. 1 Tim. 4. 13. [f] 1 Cor. 7. 39.

with

with Infidels, (g) or Idolaters ; neither ſhould ſuch as are godly be unequally yoked, by *Marrying* with ſuch as are wicked in their Life, or maintain damnable Hereſie.

4. *Marriage* ought not to be within the Degrees of Conſanguinity (h) or Affinity, forbidden in the Word ; nor can ſuch inceſtuous *Marriage* ever be made lawful, by any Law of Man or Conſent of Parties, (i) ſo as thoſe Perſons may live together as *Man* and *Wife*.

CHAP. XXVII.

Of the Church.

1. THE Catholick or Univerſal Church, which (with reſpect to the internal Work of the Spirit and Truth of Grace) may be called Inviſible,

---

g Neh 13. 25, 26, 27. h Lev. 18. i Mat. 6. 18. 1 Cor. 5. 1.

conſiſts

consists of the whole (*a*) Number of the Elect, that have been, are, or shall be gathered into one, under Christ, the Head thereof; and is the Spouse, the Body, the Fulness of Him that filleth all in all.

2. All Persons, throughout the World, professing the Faith of the Gospel, and Obedience unto God by Christ, according unto it, not destroying their own Profession by any Errors everting the Foundation, or Unholiness of Conversation, (*b*) are and may be called visible Saints; (*c*) and of such ought all particular Congregations to be constituted.

3. The purest Churches under Heaven are subject (*d*) to Mixture, and Error; and some have so degenerated as to become (*e*) no Churches of Christ, but Synagogues of *Satan*; nevertheless Christ always hath had, and ever shall have

[a] Heb. 12. 23. Col. 1. 18. Eph. 1. 10, 22, 23. *and* chap. 5. 23, 27, 32. [b] 1 Cor. 1. 2. Acts 11. 26. [c] Rom. 1. 7. Eph. 1. 20, 21, 22. [d] 1 Cor. 15. Rev. 2. *and* chap. 3. [e] Rev. 18. 2. 2 Thess. 2. 11, 12.

have a (*f*) Kingdom in this World, to the End thereof, of ſuch as believe in him, and make Profeſſion of his Name.

4. The Lord Jeſus Chriſt is the Head of the Church, in whom, by the Appointment of the Father, (*g*) all Power for the Calling, Inſtitution, Order, or Government of the Church, is inveſted in a ſupreme and ſovereign Manner, neither can the Pope of *Rome* in any ſenſe be Head thereof, but is (*h*) that Antichriſt, that Man of Sin, and Son of *Perdition*, that exalteth himſelf in the Church againſt Chriſt, and all that is called God; whom the Lord ſhall deſtroy with the Brightneſs of his Coming.

5. In the Execution of this Power wherewith he is ſo intruſted, the Lord Jeſus calleth, out of the World unto himſelf, through the Miniſtry of his Word, by his Spirit, (*i*) thoſe that are given

[f] Mat. 16. 18. Pſal. 72. 17. & Pſal. 102. 28. Rev. 12. 17. [g] Col. 1. 18. Matth. 28. 19, 12, 20. Eph. 4. 11, 12. [h] 2 Theſ. 2. 2,---9. [i] John 10. 16. & chap. 12, 32.

given unto him, by his Father, that they may walk before him in all the (*k*) ways of Obedience, which he prefcribeth to them in his Word. Thofe thus called, he commandeth to walk together in particular Societies, or (*l*) Churches, for their mutual Edification and the due Performance of that publick Worfhip, which he requireth of them in the World.

6. The Members of thefe Churches are (*m*) Saints by Calling, vifibly manifefting and evidencing in and by their Profeffion and Walking, their Obedience unto that Call of Chrift; and do willingly confent to walk together according to the Appointment of Chrift, giving up themfelves to the Lord and one to another, by the Will of God, (*n*) in profeffed Subjection to the Ordinances of the Gofpel.

---

[k] Mat. 28. 20. [l] Mat. 18. 15, 20. [m] Rom. 1. 7. 1 Cor. 1. 2. [n] Acts 2. 41, 42. chap. 5. 13, 14. 2 Cor. 9. 13.

7. To

7. To each of these Churches thus gathered according to his Mind, declared in his Word, he hath given all that (*o*) Power and Authority, which is any way needful for their carrying on that Order in Worship and Discipline, which he hath instituted for them to observe, with Commands and Rules, for the due and right exerting and executing of that Power.

8. A particular Church gathered, and compleatly organized according to the Mind of *Christ*, consists of Officers and Members: And the Officers appointed by *Christ* to be chosen and set apart by the Church (so called and gathered) for the peculiar Administration of Ordinances, and Execution of Power, or Duty, which he intrusts them with, or calls them to, to be continued to the End of the World, are (*p*) Bishops, or Elders and Deacons.

---

[o] Matt. 18. 17, 18. 1 Cor. 5. 4, 5. *with* verse 13. 2 Cor. 2. 6, 7, 8. [p] Acts 20. 17, *with* verse 28. Phil. 1. 1.

9. The

9. The Way appointed by *Christ* for the Calling of any Perſon, fitted and gifted by the Holy Spirit, unto the Office of Biſhop, or Elder, in a Church, is, that he be choſen thereunto by the common (*q*) Suffrage of the Church it ſelf; and ſolemnly ſet apart by Faſting and Prayer, with Impoſition of Hands of the (*r*) Elderſhip of the Church, if there be any before conſtituted therein: And of a Deacon (*s*) that he be choſen by the like Suffrage, and ſet apart by Prayer, and the like Impoſition of Hands.

10. The Work of Paſtors being conſtantly to attend the Service of Chriſt, in his Churches, in the Miniſtry of the Word, and Prayer, (*t*) with Watching for their Souls, as they that muſt give an Account to him; it is incumbent on the Churches to whom they miniſter, not only to give them all due reſpect,

[q] Acts 14. 23. See the Original. [r] 1 Tim. 4. 14. [s] Acts 6. 3, 5, 6. [t] Acts 6. 4. Heb. 13. 17.

(*u*) but

(u) but alſo to communicate to them of all their good Things, according to their Ability, ſo as they may have a comfortable Supply, without being themſelves (*x*) entangled in Secular Affairs; and may alſo be capable of exerciſing (*y*) Hoſpitality towards others; and this is required by the (*z*) Law of Nature, and by the expreſs Order of our Lord Jeſus, who hath ordained, that they that preach the Goſpel, ſhould live of the Goſpel.

11. Although it be incumbent on the Biſhops or Paſtors of the Churches, to be Inſtant in Preaching the Word, by Way of Office, yet the Work of Preaching the Word is not ſo peculiarly confined to them, but that others alſo (*a*) gifted, and fitted by the Holy Spirit for it, and approved, and called by the Church, may, and ought to perform it.

---

[u] 1 Tim. 5. 17, 18. Gal. 6. 6, 7. [x] 2 Tim. 2. 4. [y] 1 Tim. 3. 2. [z] 1 Cor. 9. 6, 14. [a] Acts 11. 19, 20, 21. 1 Pet. 4. 10, 11.

12. As

12. As all Believers are bound to join themſelves to particular Churches, when and where they have Opportunity ſo to do ; ſo all that are admitted unto the Privileges of a Church, are alſo (*b*) under the Cenſures and Government thereof, according to the Rule of Chriſt.

13. No Church-members, upon any Offence taken by them, having performed their Duty required of them towards the Perſon they are offended at, ought to diſturb any Church Order, or abſent themſelves from the Aſſemblies of the Church, or Adminiſtration of any Ordinances, upon the Account of ſuch Offence at any of their Fellow-members, but to wait upon *Chriſt*, (*c*) in further Proceeding of the Church.

14. As each Church, and all the Members of it, are bound to (*d*) pray continually, for the Good and Proſperi-

(*b*) 1 Theſſ. 5. 14. 2 Theſſ. 3. 6, 14, 15. (*c*) Matt. 18. 15, 16, 17. Eph. 4. 2, 3. (*d*) Eph. 6. 18. Pſalm 122. 6.

ty

ty of all the Churches of *Christ*, in all Places, and upon all Occasions to further, (every one within the Bounds of their Places and Callings, in the Exercise of their Gifts and Graces) so the Churches (when planted by the Providence of God, so as they may enjoy Opportunity and Advantage for it) ought to hold (*e*) Communion amongst themselves, for their Peace, Increase of Love and mutual Edification.

15. In Cases of Difficulties or Differences, either in Point of Doctrine or Administration; wherein either the Churches in general are concerned, or any one Church, in their Peace, Union, and Edification; or any Member, or Members of any Church are injured, in or by any Proceedings in Censures not agreeable to Truth and Order: It is according to the Mind of Christ, that many Churches holding Communion together, do by their Messengers meet

(*e*) Rom. 16. 1, 2. 3 John 8. 9, 10.

H to

to conſider, (*f*) and give their Advice in or about that Matter in Difference, to be reported to all the Churches concerned; howbeit theſe Meſſengers aſſembled, are not intruſted with any Church-power properly ſo called; or with any Juriſdiction over the Churches themſelves, to exerciſe any Cenſures either over any Churches, or Perſons; or (*g*) to impoſe their Determination on the Churches or Officers.

CHAP. XXVIII.

Of the Communion of Saints.

1. ALL Saints that are united to Jeſus Chriſt their Head, by his Spirit, and Faith, although they are not made thereby one Perſon with him, have (*a*) fellowſhip in his Graces, Suf-

[f] Acts 15. 2, 4, 6. *and* 22, 23, 25. [g] 2 Cor. 1. 24. 1 John 4. 1. [a] 1 John 1. 3. John 1. 16. Phil. 3. 10. Rom. 6. 5, 6.

ferings,

ferings, Death, Resurrection and Glory; and being united to one another in Love, they (*b*) have Communion in each others Gifts and Graces, and are obliged to the Performance of such Duties, publick and private, in an orderly Way, (*c*) as do conduce to their mutual Good, both in the inward and outward Man.

2. Saints by Profession, are bound to maintain an holy Fellowship and Communion in the Worship of God, and in Performing such other Spiritual Services, (*d*) as tend to their mutual Edification; as also in relieving each other in (*e*) outward Things, according to their several Abilities, and Necessities; which Communion, according to the Rule of the Gospel, tho' especially to be exercised by them, in the Relations wherein they stand, whether in

[b] Eph. 4. 15, 16. 1 Cor. 12. 7, 1 Cor. 3. 21, 22, 23. [c] 1 Thess. 5. 11, 14. Rom. 1. 12. 1 John 3. 17, 18. Gal. 6. 10. [d] Heb. 10. 24, 25. with Chap. 3. 12, 13. [e] Acts 12. 29, 30.

H 2 (*f*) Fa-

(*f*) Families, or (*g*) Churches, yet as God offereth Opportunity, is to be extended to all the Houshold of Faith, even all those who in every Place call upon the Name of the Lord Jesus; nevertheless their Communion one with another as Saints, doth not take away, or (*h*) infringe the Title or Property which each Man hath in his Goods and Possessions.

CHAP. XXIX.

Of Baptism and the Lords Supper.

1. BAptism and the Lord's Supper, are Ordinances of positive and sovereign Institution, appointed by the Lord Jesus the only Law-giver, to be continued in his Church (*a*) to the End of the World.

---

[f] Eph. 6. 4. [g] 1 Cor. 12. 14, 27. [h] Acts. 5. 4. Eph. 4. 28. [a] Matth. 28. 19, 20. 1 Cor. 11. 26.

These

2. Theſe holy Appointments are to be adminiſtred by thoſe only, who are qualified, and thereunto called according (*b*) to the Commiſſion of Chriſt.

CHAP. XXX.

Of Baptiſm.

1. BAptiſm is an Ordinance of the New Teſtament, ordained by Jeſus Chriſt, to be unto the Party baptized, a Sign of his Fellowſhip with him in his Death (*a*) and Reſurrection; of his being engrafted into him; of (*b*) Remiſſion of Sins; and of his (*c*) giving up unto God, thro' Jeſus Chriſt, to live and walk in newneſs of Life.

2. Thoſe who do actually profeſs (*d*) Repentance towards God, Faith in, and Obedience to our Lord Jeſus,

[b] Matt. 28. 19. 1 Cor. 4. 1. [a] Rom. 6. 3, 4, 5. Col. 2. 12. Gal. 3. 27. [b] Mark 1. 4. Acts 26. 16. [c] Rom. 6. 24. [d] Mark 16. 16. Acts 8. 37, 38.

H 3 are

are the only proper Subjects of this Ordination.

3. The outward Element, to be u-ſed in this Ordinance, *(e)* is Water, wherein the Party is to be baptized, in the Name of the Father, and of the Son, and of the Holy Spirit.

4. Immerſion, or Dipping of the Perſon *(f)* in Water, is neceſſary to the due Adminiſtration of this Ordinance.

CHAP. XXXI.

Of Laying on of Hands.

WE believe that *(a) laying on of Hands* (with Prayer) *upon baptized Believers, as ſuch*, is an Ordinance of Chriſt, and ought to be ſubmitted unto by all ſuch Perſons that are admitted to partake of the Lord's Supper; and that the End of this Ordinance is

[e] Matt. 28. 19, 20. with Acts 8. 38. [f] Matt. 3. 16. John 3. 23. [a] Heb. 5. 12. and 6. 1, 2. Acts 8. 17, 18, and 19, 6.

not

not for the extraordinary Gifts of the Spirit, but for (*b*) a farther Reception of the Holy Spirit of Promiſe, or for the Addition of the Graces of the Spirit, and the Influences thereof; to confirm, ſtrengthen, and comfort them in Chriſt Jeſus; it being ratified and eſtabliſhed by the (*c*) extraordinary Gifts of the Spirit in the Primitive Times, to abide in the Church, as meeting together on the firſt Day of the Week, was *Acts* 2. 1. that being the Day of Worſhip, or Chriſtian Sabbath, under the Goſpel; and as Preaching the Word was, *Acts* 10. 44. and as Baptiſm was, *Mat.* 3. 16. and Prayer was, *Acts* 4. 31. and ſinging Pſalms, *&c.* was *Acts* 16. 25, 26. ſo this of laying on of Hands was, *Acts* 8. & *ch.* 19, For as the whole Goſpel *was confirmed by (d) Signs and Wonders, and divers Miracles and Gifts of the Holy Ghoſt* in general, ſo was every Ordinance in like manner confirmed in particular.

[b] Eph. 1. 13, 14. [c] Acts 8. and 19. 6. [d] Heb. 2. 3, 4.

CHAP.

CHAP. XXXII.

Of the Lord's Supper.

1. THE Supper of the Lord Jesus, was instituted by him, the same Night wherein he was betrayed, to be observed in his Churches unto the end of the World, for the perpetual Remembrance, and shewing forth the Sacrifice of himself in his Death, (*a*) Confirmation of the Faith of Believers in all the Benefits thereof, their spiritual Nourishment, and Growth in him, their further Ingagement in and to all Duties which they owe unto him; (*b*) and to be a Bond and Pledge of their Communion with him, and with each other.

2. In this Ordinance Christ is not offered up to his Father, nor any real Sacrifice made at all for Remission of Sin, of the Quick or Dead, but only a Memorial of that (*c*) one offering up

[a] 1 Cor. 11. 23, 24, 25, 26. [b] 1 Cor. 10. 16, 17, 21. [c] Heb. 9. 25, 26, 28.

of

of himſelf, by himſelf, upon the Croſs, once for all ; and a Spiritual Oblation of all (*d*) poſſible Praiſe unto God for the ſame. So that the *Popiſh* Sacrifice of the Maſs (as they call it) is moſt abominable, injurious to Chriſt's own only Sacrifice, the alone Propitiation for all the Sins of the Elect.

3. The Lord Jeſus hath in this Ordinance, appointed his Miniſters to Pray, and Bleſs the Elements of Bread and Wine, and thereby to ſet them apart from a common to an holy Uſe, and to take and break the Bread ; to take the Cup (*e*) and (they communcating alſo themſelves) to give both to the Communicants.

4. The Denial of the Cup to the People, worſhipping the Elements, the lifting them up, or carrying them about for Adoration, and reſerving them for any pretended Religious Uſe, (*f*)

[d] 1 Cor. 11. 24. Matt. 26. 26, 27. [e] 1 Cor. 11. 23. 24, 25, 26, &c. [f] Matt. 26. 26, 27, 28. Matt. 15, 9. Exod. 20. 4, 5.

are

are all contrary to the Nature of this Ordinance, and to the Inſtitution of Chriſt.

5. The outward Elements in this Ordinance, duly ſet apart to the Uſes ordained by Chriſt, have ſuch Relation to him crucified, as that truly, although in Terms uſed figuratively, they are ſometimes called by the Name of the Things they repreſent, to wit, the *(g)* Body and Blood of Chriſt, albeit in Subſtance and Nature, they ſtill remain truly and only *(h)* Bread and Wine, as they were before.

6. The Doctrine which maintains a Change of the Subſtance of Bread and Wine, into the Subſtance of Chriſt's Body and Blood (commonly called Tranſubſtantiation) by Conſecration of a Prieſt, or by any other Way, is repugnant not to Scripture *(i)* alone, but even to common Senſe and Reaſon, overthroweth the *(k)* Nature of the

---

[g] 1 Cor. 11, 27. [h] 1 Cor. 11. 26. & Ver. 28. [i] Acts 3. 21. Luke 24. 6. & Ver. 39. [k] 1 Cor. 11. 24, 25.

Ordinance,

Ordinance, and hath been, and is the Cause of manifold Superstitions, yea, of gross Idolatries.

7. Worthy Receivers, outwardly partaking of the visible Elements in this Ordinance, do then also inwardly, by Faith, really and indeed, yet not carnally and corporally, but spiritually receive, and feed upon Christ crucified, *(l)* and all the Benefits of his Death; the Body and Blood of Christ being then not corporally or carnally, but spiritually present to the Faith of Believers in that Ordinance, as the Elements themselves are to their outward Senses.

8. All ignorant and ungodly Persons, as they are unfit to enjoy Communion (*m*) with Christ, so are they unworthy of the Lord's Table, and cannot, without great Sin against him, while they remain such, partake of these Holy Mysteries *(n)* or be admitted there-

[l] 1 Cor. 10. 16. ch. 11. 23,----26. [m] 2 Cor. 6. 14 15. [n] 1 Cor. 11. 29. Matt. 7. 6.

unto:

unto: Yea, whoſoever ſhall receive unworthily, are guilty of the Body and Blood of the Lord, eating and drinking Judgment to themſelves.

CHAP. XXXIII.

Of the State of Man after Death, and of the Reſurrection of the Dead.

1. THE Bodies of Men after Death return to Duſt, (*a*) and ſee Corruption; but their Souls (which neither die or ſleep) having an immortal Subſiſtence, immediately (*b*) return to God who gave them: The Souls of the Righteous being then made perfect in Holineſs, are received into Paradiſe, where they are with *Chriſt*, and behold the Face of *God*, in Light and (*c*) Glory, waiting for the full Redemption of their Bodies; and the Souls of the Wicked

[a] Gen. 3. 19. Acts 13. 36. [b] Eccl. 12. 7. [c] Luke 23. 43. 2 Cor. 5. 1, 6, 8. Phil. 1. 23. Heb. 12. 23.

Wicked are caſt into Hell, where they remain in Torment and utter Darkneſs, reſerved to (*d*) the Judgment of the Great Day; beſides theſe two Places, for Souls ſeparated from their Bodies, the Scripture acknowledgeth none.

2. At the Laſt Day, ſuch of the Saints as are found alive, ſhall not ſleep, but be (*e*) changed; and all the Dead ſhall be raiſed up with the ſelf-ſame Bodies, and (*f*) none other; although with different (*g*) Qualities, which ſhall be united again to their Souls for ever.

3. The Bodies of the Unjuſt ſhall, by the Power of Chriſt, be raiſed to diſhonour; the Bodies of the Juſt, by his Spirit, unto Honour, (*h*) and be made conformable to his own glorious Body.

---

[d] Jude 6. 7. 1 Pet. 3. 9. Luke 16. 23, 24. [e] 1 Cor. 15. 51, 52. 1 Theſſ. 4. 17. [f] Job 19. 29, 27. [g] 1 Cor. 15. 42, 43. [h] Acts 24. 15. John 5. 28, 29. Phil. 3. 21.

CHAP.

CHAP. XXXIV.

Of the Laſt Judgment.

1. GOD hath appointed a Day wherein he will judge the World in Righteouſneſs, by (*a*) Jeſus Chriſt; to whom all Power and Judgment is given of the Father; in which Day not only the (*b*) Apoſtate Angels ſhall be judged, but likewiſe all Perſons that have lived upon the Earth, ſhall appear before the Tribunal of Chriſt, (*c*) to give an Account of their Thoughts, Words and Deeds, and to receive according to what they have done in the Body, whether Good or Evil.

2. The End of God's appointing this Day, is, for the Manifeſtation of the Glory of his Mercy, in the Eternal Sal-

---

[a] Acts 17. 31. John 5. 22, 27. [b] 1 Cor. 6. 3. Jude 6. [c] 2 Cor. 5. 10. Eccl. 12. 14. Matt 12. 36. Rom. 14. 10, 12. Matt. 25. 32, &c.

vation

vation of the Elect; (*d*) and of his Juſtice, in the Eternal Damnation of the Reprobate, who are wicked and diſobedient; for then ſhall the Righteous go into Everlaſting Life, and receive that Fulneſs of Joy and Glory, with Everlaſting Reward, in the Preſence (*e*) of the Lord: But the Wicked who know not God, and obey not the Goſpel of Jeſus Chriſt, ſhall be caſt into Eternal Torments, and (*f*) puniſhed with Everlaſting Deſtruction, from the Preſence of the Lord, and from the Glory of his Power.

3. As Chriſt would have us to be certainly perſwaded, that there ſhall be a Day of Judgment, both (*g*) to deter all Men from Sin, and for the greater (*h*) Conſolation of the Godly, in their Adverſity, ſo will he have that Day unknown to Men, that they may ſhake off all carnal Security, and be

---

[d] Rom. 9. 22, 23. [e] Matt. 25. 21, 34. 2 Tim. 4. 8. [f] Matt. 25. 26. Mark 9. 48. 2 Theſſ. 1. 7, 8, 9, 10. [g] 2 Cor. 5. 10, 11. [h] 2 Theſſ. 1. 5, 6, 7.

always

always watchful, because they know not at what Hour the *(i)* Lord will come, and may ever be prepared to say *(k) Come, Lord Jesus, Come quickly.* Amen.

---

[i] Mark 13. 35, 36, 37. Luke 13, 35, 36. [k] Rev. 22. 20.

THE

THE
CONTENTS.

I 16. *Of*

The CONTENTS.

A

"...TO SET THEM IN ORDER :"

A SHORT

TREATISE

OF

Church-Difcipline.

PHILADELPHIA:
Printed by B. FRANKLIN, 1743.

(iii)

To all Those into whose Hands the foregoing Confession of Faith, unto which the following Abstract concerning our Discipline is now annexed, shall come.

OUR last Association, met at Philadelphia, Sept. 25. 1742. *taking into Consideration the general Interest of the Gospel, and especially the Interest of the Churches they were related unto and did then represent, judged it expedient to reprint the* Confession of Faith, *put forth by the Elders and Brethren of upwards of* 100 *Congregations, baptised upon Profession of Faith in* England & Wales, *met*

(iv)

met in London, Sept. 3. 1689. *with the Additions concerning* Impoſition of Hands, *and* Singing of Pſalms in the Worſhip of God.

The Aſſociation likewiſe thought it proper to annex an Abſtract, or brief Treatiſe concerning our Diſcipline, but not having (for ſome Reaſons) fixed on any particular Piece extant, they left it to Mr. Jenkin Jones *and myſelf to prepare a ſhort Narrative, in the moſt compendious Manner we could; but Mr.* Jones, *by reaſon of his other Avocations, not being able to prepare any thing in due Time, requeſted me to take it upon myſelf, which, after we had conſulted on ſome Particulars (tho' many other Things at this Juncture requiring my Time and employing my Thoughts, I could wiſh ſome other Perſon had undertaken) I accepted that I might prevent any Diſappointment, and have endeavoured to perform as my ſmall Leiſure would permit. And we having a ſmall Tract publiſhed by Mr.*

Mr. Elias Keach, *and having alſo found a Manuſcript left by my Brother* Abel Morgan, *deceaſed, which he intended (had he longer lived) to have reviſed and put in Print for the Benefit of our Churches; I have tranſcribed ſome Things out of ſaid Manuſcript, and ſome other Things out of Mr.* Keach, *ſome Things without Variation, and ſome Things with Variation; beſides which I have in ſome Caſes conſulted Dr.* Owen *and Dr.* Goodwin, *and in ſome Things I have followed the Agreement that our Aſſociation came to ſome Years ago, eſpecially concerning the Admiſſion and Diſmiſſion of Members. I have endeavoured to include the moſt material Things in Diſcipline (tho' very briefly) in the few following Pages; and I deſire the Reader may be pleaſed to take the pains to peruſe the Scriptures referred to in every Particular, that the Grounds of our Practice may be better underſtood.*

That

That this impartial Account of our Principles and Practice may be accompanied with the Blessing of God, to be beneficial unto Men, is the hearty Prayer of

Your Well-wisher,

and Servant,

in all Gospel-Service,

BENJA. GRIFFITH.

A SHORT

A SHORT TREATISE, &c.

Concerning a true and orderly Goſpel CHURCH.

BEFORE there can be any orderly Diſcipline among a chriſtian Aſſembly, they muſt be orderly conſtituted into a Church-State, according to the Inſtitution of Chriſt in the Goſpel.

1. A viſible Goſpel Church is made by gathering divers ſelect Perſons unto Jeſus Chriſt, in a Spiritual Body, and Relation

Relation to him as their political Head, *Ezek.* 34. 11. 2 *Theſſ.* 2. 1. himſelf being the great Shepherd, that firſt ſeeks them, and prepares them by the Work of renewing Grace, for ſuch ſpiritual Building.

2. Chriſt as the Mediator of the new Covenant, ordereth the everlaſting Goſpel to be preached, and accompanying it with his holy Spirit, bleſſeth it to the turning of Men from Darkneſs to Light, working Faith and Love in them. *Epheſ.* 2. 17. *Acts* 26. 1 .

3. When Sinners are thus wrought upon effectually, to ſuch a ſuitable Number, as may be an eſſential Church, *i. e.* ſo many as may act properly and orderly as a Church, *Math.* 18. 15,—17. that then it will be proper for them by their mutual Conſent, to propoſe to be conſtituted a Church, or that others ſeeing the Expediency thereof may encourage the ſame. *Acts* 11.

4. For the Accompliſhment of ſo glorious a Work, it is neceſſary that a

Day

Day of Fafting and Prayer be appointed by and among fuch Believers, and that fuch procure fuch neighbouring Helps as they can, efpecially of the Miniftry. *Acts* 8. 14. 1 *Theff.* 3. 2.

5. The Perfons being firft orderly Baptifed, according to the Command of Chrift in *Math.* 28. 19. and being all fatisfied of the Graces and Qualifications of each other, and being willing in the Fear of God to take the Laws of Chrift upon them, and do by one mutual Confent give up themfelves to the Lord, and to one another in the Lord, 2 *Cor.* 8. 5. folemnly fubmitting to the Government of Chrift in his Church, and being united, they are to be declared a Gofpel-Church of Jefus Chrift, *Phil.* 2. 2, 3, 4. *Rom.* 15. 7. *Chap.* 12. 1. *Acts.* 2. 41, 42.

6. A Number of Believers thus united under Chrift their myftical Head, are become a Church effential; and as fuch is the firft and proper Subject of the Keys, and have Power and Privilege

ledge to govern themſelves, and to chooſe out their. own miniſterial Officers. *Acts* 14. 23. *Chap.* 6. 3.

Concerning Miniſters, &c.

A CHURCH thus conſtituted, is not yet compleated, while wanting ſuch miniſterial Helps, as Chriſt hath appointed for its Growth and well being; and wanting Elders and Deacons to officiate among them. Men, they muſt be, that are qualified for the Work; their Qualifications are plainly and fully ſet down in holy Scripture, 1 *Tim.* 3. 2—7. *Tit.* 4. 5—10. all which muſt be found in them, in ſome good Degree, and it is the Duty of the Church to try the Perſons, by the Rule of the Word.

Objection. But what ſhall a Church do, in caſe they can have none among them fit to bear Office according to the Rule of the Word?

Anſw.

Answ. (1.) That to expect to have Officers perfect in the highest Degrees of those Qualifications, were to expect apostolical and extraordinary ceased Gifts in ordinary Times. (2.) If none among the Members of a Church be found fit in some Measure for the Ministry, a neighbouring Church may and ought, if possible, to supply them, *Cant.* 8. 8. (3.) Let such as they have, if they have any that seem hopeful, be a while upon Tryal; and the Person that the Lord shall chuse, will flourish in some good Measure with *Aaron*'s Rod among the Rods of the Tribes.

2. A Church being destitute of ministerial Helps, may, after mature and often deliberate Consultation, and serious Prayers to God, pitch upon some Person or Persons in particular, giving him or them a solemn Invitation to the Work of the Ministry upon Tryal; and if such accept of the Church's Call, let such be upon Tryal, to see if such fear God, make Godliness their Business, and

and be addicted to the Work of the Miniſtry, ſeeking to further the Intereſt of Chriſt, and the Edification of his People in ſound and wholeſome Doctrine; and to ſee if any Vices or Immorality appear in their Advances, 1 *Cor.* 16. *Phil.* 2. 20, 21. Read the Qualifications in 1 *Tim.* 3. And in caſe a Church ſhould call a Perſon to be their Miniſter, who is a Member of ſome Siſter-Church, and he accept their Call to be their Miniſter, he muſt in the firſt Place give himſelf a Member with the Church ſo calling him, that ſo they may chuſe him among themſelves, as *Acts* 6. 3.

After having taken all due Care to chuſe One for the Work of the Miniſtry, they are, by and with the unanimous Conſent or Suffrage of the Church, to proceed to his Ordination; which is a ſolemn Setting-apart of ſuch a Perſon for the ſacred Function (in this wiſe) By ſetting apart a Day of Faſting and Prayer, *Acts* 13. 2, 3. the whole

Church

Church being present, he is to have the Hands of the Presbytery of that Church (or of neighbouring Elders called and authorized by that Church) whereof such a Person is a Member, solemnly laid upon him, 1 *Tim.* 5. 22. *Tit.* 1. 5. *Acts* 14. 23. 1 *Tim.* 4. 14. and thus such a Person is to be recommended into the Work of the Lord, and to take particular Care of the Flock of whom he is thus chosen, *Acts* 20. 28.

4. The Minister being thus put upon his Work, proceeds (1) to preach the Word of God unto them, thereby to feed the Flock, and therein ought to be faithful and laborious, studying to show himself a Workman that needeth not to be ashamed, rightly dividing the Word of Truth, 2 *Tim.* 2. 15. as he is a Steward of God in the Mysteries of the Gospel, 1 *Cor.* 4. 1, 2. and therefore ought to be a Man of good Understanding and Experience, being sound in the Faith, not a Novice, or a double-minded unstable Man, nor such as is light-spirited or

or of a shallow Understanding, but one that is Learned in the Mysteries of the Kingdom, because he is to feed the People with Knowledge and Understanding, *Jer.* 3. 15. he must be faithful in declaring the whole Counsel of God, *Acts* 20. 20. he is to instruct them in all practical Godliness, Laying before them their manifold Duties, and to urge them upon their Consciences, *Tit.* 2. 1—15. 1 *Tim.* 4. 6. (2) he must watch over them, as one that must give an Account to God, *Heb.* 13. 17. such must have an Eye upon every Member to see how they behave in the House of God, where the Presence of the Lord is more eminently, and where also the Angels do always attend; and also their Behaviour in the Families they belong to, and their Conversation abroad: According to their Capacities, they are not to sleep under their Charge. (3) He is to visit his Flock, to know their State, in order to minister suitable doctrinal Relief unto them, and that he may

may know what Diſorders there may be amongſt them, that the Unruly may be reproved, *Pro.* 27. 23. 1 *Theſſ.* 5. 14, 15. (4) He is to adminiſter all the Ordinances of Chriſt amongſt them : as Baptiſm, and the Lord's Supper, and herein he muſt be careful to follow the primitive Pattern, thereby to hold forth the great End, wherefore they were ordained. (5) He muſt be inſtant with God, in his Prayers for and with them, as Opportunity may ſerve. (6) He muſt ſhow them a good Example in all Reſpects, in Converſation, Sobriety, Charity, Faith and Purity, 1 *Tim.* 4. 12. behaving himſelf impartial unto all, not preferring the Rich before the Poor, nor lording it over God's Heritage, nor aſſume greater Power than God hath given him, *James* 2. 4. 1 *Tim.* 5. 21. 1 *Pet.* 5. 3, 5.

K *Of*

Of Ruling Elders.

RULING Elders are ſuch Perſons as are endued with Gifts, to aſſiſt the Paſtor or Teacher in the Government of the Church; it was as a Statute in Iſrael, *Exod.* 18. *Deut.* 1. 9-13. The Works of Teaching and Ruling belong both to the Paſtor; but in caſe he be unable, or the Work of Ruling too great for him, God hath provided ſuch for his Aſſiſtance, and they are called Ruling Elders, 1 *Tim.* 5. 17. Helps, 1 *Cor.* 12. 28. Governments. or he that ruleth, *Rom.* 12. 8. They are qualified for, and called unto, one Part of the Work: And Experience teacheth us the Uſe and Benefit of ſuch Rulers in the Church, in eaſing the Paſtor or Teacher, and keeping up the Honour of the Miniſtry. Their Qualifications are ſuch as are requiſite to Rule, as Knowledge,

Knowledge, Judgment, Prudence, *&c.* and as to the Manner of their Ordination, it is like Ordination unto other Offices in the Church, with Faſting and Prayer, with Impoſition of Hands. Their Office only relateth to Rule and Order, in the Church of God, and doth not include Teaching; yet if the Church findeth they have Gifts and Abilities to be uſeful in Teaching, they may be put upon Tryal, and if approved, they may be called and ſolemnly ſet apart by Ordination, it being wholly a diſtinct Office from the former, which was only to rule well, and not to labour in Word and Doctrine.

Of Deacons.

DEACONS are Men called forth by the Church, to ſerve in the outward Concerns thereof; whoſe Office is to ſerve Tables. *Acts* 6. 2—7. they are to be entruſted with the Stock

K 2 of

of the Church, out of which Stock they are to aſſiſt the poor Members of the Church, and to provide Bread and Wine for the Lord's Table, and alſo to have Regard to the Miniſter's Table; and moreover they ſhould ſee that all the Members of the Church do contribute towards the proper Uſes of the Church, (that therefrom all neceſſary Occaſions may be ſupplied,) as God hath given them, they to the Poor, ſo that none be neglected, 1 *Cor*. 16. 2. by the faithful Diſcharge of which Office they ſhall purchaſe to themſelves a good Degree and great Boldneſs in the Faith, 1 *Tim*. 3 13. The Qualifications of theſe Officers are laid down 1 *Tim*. 3. 8—13. *Acts* 6. 2—8.

Of the Admiſſion of Church Members.

THE Lord Jeſus Chriſt hath committed the Uſe and Power of the Keys, in in Matters of Government, to every visible congregational Church, to be used, according to the Rules and Directions that he hath given in his Word, in his Name and to his Glory: The Keys are the Power of Christ, which he hath given to every particular Congregation, to open and shut itself by; and to do all Things in order to the great Things proposed, *viz.* his Glory and his Peoples spiritual Benefit, in Peace and Purity, *Isa.* 9. 7. *Chap.* 22. 22. *Revel.* 3. 7. *Hebr.* 3. 6. *Eph.* 2. 19—22. *Math.* 16. 19. *John* 20. 23.

By Virtue of the Charter and Power aforesaid, which Christ hath given to his Church, his spiritual Corporation, they are enabled to receive Members in, and to exclude unworthy Members as Occasion may require, as may appear by divers Examples, *Rom.* 14. 1 *Acts* 2. 41. 1 *Cor.* 5. 4, 5. *Mat.* 18. 18. 2 *Thess.* 2. 6, 14.

In this Case, a Church hath to do, either with Nonmembers, or those that

K 3 are

are Members of other Churches ; as to Nonmembers proposing for Admission into the Church, the Pastor, Teacher and Elders of the Church are to be acquainted therewith, and the Body of the Church also, in order that they may know the Intent of such Person or Persons. A convenient Meeting is necessary. When the Church is come together, and the Person proposing being present, after Prayer to God for Direction, the Minister or Pastor of the Church, is to put several Questions to the Person proposing. (1) Concerning the Ground and Reason of his Hope, 1 *Pet.* 3. 15 wherein is to be enquired, what Experience he hath of the manifold Graces of the holy Spirit, working in him Repentance from dead Works as *Acts* 2. 38. *Heb.* 6. 2: and Faith towards our Lord Jesus Christ in whom alone is Salvation hoped for, *Acts* 20. 21. *Philem.* 5. for without there be some good Grounds, in the Judgment of Charity, that such an one is a new Creature,

Creature, the Door of Admiffion is not to be opened, for that would be Abufing the Privileges of the Houfe of God. Therefore all due and regular Care, is to be taken, *Pfal.* 66. 16. *Acts* 9. 27.

Secondly. What competency of Knowledge, in the principal Doctrines of Faith and Order, fuch hath acquired, 1 *Tim.* 2. 4—6. whether fuch Perfon be well inftructed in the Knowledge of God, in his glorious Attributes, in the Doctrine of the Trinity, or one God in three Perfons, the Perfon, Natures and Offices of Chrift; the Nature of the Law; of original Sin; of the Pollution of Man, by Reafon of Sin, and loft and undone Eftate thereby, and of his being a Child of Wrath by Nature; of the Nature of the Redemption wrought by Chrift, his Sufficiency to fatisfie Divine Juftice; of theReconciliation of Sinners to God, by the Death of his Son; of our Sins being imputed to Chrift, and his Righteoufnefs imputed to us for Juftification,

K 4 being

being received by Faith alone; of the Resurrection of Christ's Body, and his Ascension into Heaven, and of his coming thence the second Time, to Judge the Quick and the Dead; and of the Resurrection of the dead Bodies of Men, and of the Eternal Judgment; and of such proposing Person's Resolution to persevere in the Profession of these Truths unto the End. Such Things are needful to be enquired into, by Reason that too many in our Day do build their Conversion upon their Convictions, and some General Notions of the Christian Religion, when indeed they are utter Strangers unto, and very ignorant of the great Mysteries of the Gospel. Yet great Care is to be taken that the Weak be not discouraged, for the smoaking Flax is not to be quenched, nor the bruised Reed to be broken, but such ignorant Persons are to be taught by gentle Instructions, and Means ought to be used for their Furtherance in the Knowlege of divine Truths,

Truths, *Math.* 28. 19. and where there is the Beginnings of true and faving Grace in the Heart, fuch will with a fpiritual Appetite, receive the fincere Milk of the Word, that they may grow thereby, 1 *Pet.* 2. 2. and a Church ought to be careful not to reject thofe, whom they judge to have the leaft Degree of the Work of faving Grace, wrought in them, *Rom.* 14. 1.

Thirdly, Enquiry muft be made whether fuch a Perfon's Life and Converfation is anfwerable to fuch a Profeffion, that he be likely to adorn the Gofpel with a holy Converfation, *Tit.* 2. 11—15. *Chap.* 3. 8. This regular Carefulnefs is an indifpenfible Duty of all regular Churches, to ufe in the Admiffion of Members; and tho' all due Care be ufed, yet fome unfound and rotten Profeffors will creep in unawares, and have crept into the pureft Churches, *Jude* ver. 4. 1 *John* 2. 19. *Acts* 5. *Acts* 20. 29, 30. *Galat.* 2. 4. and the fallibility of Churches in this Matter, is not

not to be urged, as an Argument or Ground to neglect the Duty incumbent on the Churches, according to the Rule of the Word.

And after ſuch Examination, the Queſtion is to be put to the Church, whether they are all ſatisfied with the Party's Confeſſion and Converſation; and if the Anſwer be in the Affirmative, then the Paſtor or Miniſter is to proceed, to aſk the Party propoſing, if he be willingly reſolved (as God ſhall give Ability) to walk in a profeſſed Subjection to the Commands and Inſtitutions of Chriſt revealed in the Goſpel, and to give himſelf a Member of that Church in particular, *Rom.* 12. 1. *Chap.* 15. 7, 8, 9. 2 *Cor.* 8. 5 and to continue in the Communion, Faith, and Order thereof, according to the Goſpel-Rules and Directions, and after the Perſon is baptiſed according to the Inſtitution and Command of Chriſt, and come under the Impoſition of the Hands of the Elders of the Church, according to to the Practice of the Apoftles, *Acts* 8. 14—17. *Hebr.* 6. 2. the Paftor, Minifter or Elders, as prefiding in the Acts of the Church's Power, do receive fuch an one into the Communion and Fellowfhip of that Church in particular. But if the Church is not fatisfied with the Perfon's Confeffion or Converfation, it is proper (if the Objections be of any Weight) to defer the Party's Admiffion untill a more ample Satisfacton can be given, that all, if poffible, may receive fuch with Freedom in Love, and fo as to difcharge all Gofpel Duties towards him, as may promote his Edification in the Faith and his Increafe in Grace, 2 *Cor.* 1. 24. *Chap.* 10. 8.

And concerning thofe that are Members of Sifter Churches, their Admiffion is either tranfient and occafional Admiffion; or when any Perfon is difmiffed wholly from one Church, and tranfmitted or recommended to another Church of the fame Faith, Order and Practice. (1) Such as are and continue Members

Members of other regular Churches, may (where they are well known) be admitted into tranſient Communion, without a Letter of Recommendation from the Church they belong unto: But from thoſe that a Church hath no Knowledge of, a teſtimonial Letter is neceſſary, that a Church may not be impoſed on by any looſe or diſorderly Perſons. (2) Thoſe whoſe Reſidence is removed, or Place of Abode is more convenient to be with another Congregation than that of which they are Members, are, upon their Requeſt made to the Church whereof ſuch are Members, to be diſmiſſed, and to have a Letter from that Church they were Members of, ſubſcribed by the Officers and Members, and directed to the Church that the Perſon is diſmiſſed unto; whereby the Party is diſcharged from his or her original Relation of particular Memberſhip to that Church, and is transferred to the conſtant Communion, Watch, and Care of the other Church: Such Perſons

Perfons are to be received upon their Propofal, according to the Credentials they bring; except the Church they apply unto, hath a fpecial Reafon to defer or refufe.

As it appears to be the Practice of Believers, in the Primitive Times, to give themfelves Members of particular Churches, *Acts* 2. 41. *Chap.* 5. 13, 14. it appears alfo that in the Apoftles Days, there were many diftinct and diftant particular Churches, as 1 *Cor.* 1. 2. *Gal.* 1. 2. 1 *Cor.* 16. 1. *Phil.* 1. 1. which Churches are feveral Corporations of Men profeffing Repentance from dead Works, and Faith in our Lord Jefus Chrift, and incorporated by mutual Confent (as before mentioned) whofe End is to glorifie God by Obedience to his revealed Will, and to their own Edification in the Faith, and the Good of others; fo it is the Duty of Believers to give themfelves in particular Memberfhip, in fuch a particular Church as fhall appear by the Word of God to be Orthodox

dox in the fundamental Articles of the Christian Religion, and to practice according to the Mind of Christ declared in the New Testament, in all Gospel Institutions and Worship.

From which Considerations, it appears the reasonable Duty of every Believer to give himself a Member to such an orderly Church, as is most conveniently situated (that is, meeting nighest the Place of his or her Residence) for which there are these apparent Reasons. (1) For Men to give themselves Members of a distant Church, when another of the same Faith and Gospel-Order is nigher, is for such a Person, to put himself under a Necessity of neglecting the ordinary appointed Meetings of that Church, whereof he is Member, and whereof the Particular Charge is given, *Heb.* 10. 25. that he might attend and wait in the Use of God's appointed Means, for his Edification by the Ministry of that Church. (2) Such puts himself under a wilful Necessity

ceſſity to neglect his Duty of Care over, and conſtant Communion with his fellow Members, and wilfully deprives himſelf of their Care over him, Advice, chriſtian Converſing, and brotherly loving Inſtructions and Counſels, that by the Bleſſing of God might increaſe his Knowlege, Grace and Comfort. (3) Such cannot be aſſiſtant to the Church in Diſcipline, Contribution, and the like Duties, nor cannot be taken Care of, and be aſſiſted (without much unneceſſary Trouble) by the Church, in caſe of Need. (4) Such a Practice tends directly to the Confuſion of Churches, and all Church Order, and ſuits well with the Humour of noiſy, lifeleſs, looſe, or covetous niggardly Perſons. (5) It is a way that the Church cannot find what uſeful Talents ſuch Perſons may have, to the Benefit of the Body of the Church. (6) It is caſting great Contempt upon the nearer Church, in her Miniſtry and Order, and the like.

And

And here it is further to be conſidered, that as it is expedient for Perſons to give themſelves Members of ſuch regular Churches, with which they may keep the moſt intimate Fellowſhip and Communion in all the Parts of Religious Worſhip. So it is highly reaſonable that they, that are Members of ſuch regular Churches, where the Word is purely preached, the Ordinances of the Goſpel duly adminiſtred, and Goſpel Diſcipline is impartially practiſed; ſhould continue their Memberſhip with ſuch Chuch; altho' there be Weakneſs, Imperfection and Frailty, in the particular practical Acts thereof; which while the Affairs of the Church are managed by Men, even their holy Things will have Iniquity as of old, *Exod.* 28. 38. it is thefore unreaſonable to diſmiſs any Member, from a Church that is near to any one's Reſidence, to a Church more remote, upon Diſguſt taken at the management of ſome particular Caſe, wherewith ſuch is not well pleaſed, and for

for ſuch Cauſe demands Diſmiſſion; and it is unreaſonable alſo to grant a Diſmiſſion to ſuch a Member, who ſhould demand a Diſmiſſion in peremptory Manner, without giving a Reaſon for ſuch a Demand; in either of which Caſes, ſuch a Diſmiſſion is not to be granted. (1) Becauſe by ſo doing the greateſt Confuſion would be introduced: For one Member would thus be diſmiſſed to one diſtant Church, and another to another diſtant Church, and the other Churches doing the like, it can end in nothing leſs than the Confuſion of every Church. (2) The ſame Liberty that Members have, Paſtors, Minſters, ruling Elders, and Deacons have alſo, whereby any Church may diſmiſs her Members until ſhe is unable to maintain Worſhip and Communion: For thoſe that reſide near, are become Members of a remote Body, and ſo unconcern'd; and thoſe that are Members live remote and ſo under an impoſſibility to occupy their Place. (3) This in the Tendency of

L it,

it, is to remove the Bounds of Churches, which is to consist of such Members, as can, with the utmost Conveniency, meet together in one Place, for both Worship and Government, 1 *Cor*. 11.20. *Chap*. 14. 33. (4) This hath a Tendency to alter the Constitution of particular Churches, from being congregational Corporations, into the national or universal Notion of the Church; which universal Church we believe to be the mystical Body of Jesus Christ, which as such is not the Seat of instituted Worship and Ordinances. Also it is not reasonable to dismiss to the World at large, nor to dismiss a Member to a Church, with which the Church dismissing, cannot hold Communion.

Of

Of the Duties of Church-Members.

THE Members of Churches, owe all their Duties in a Way of Obedience to the Will of God revealed in his Word, and their Duties are to be performed, in Love to our Lord Jefus Chrift; *John* 14. 15. who is the great Prophet, Prieft and King of his Church, which he hath purchafed with his own Blood; *Acts* 20. 28. *Rev.* 1. 5. 2 *Cor.* 5. 15. unto whom all Power in Heaven and Earth is given; *Math.* 28. 18. and is therefore our Lord and Lawgiver, *Ifai.* 33. 22. who alone is Head of his Church, *Ephef.* 1. 22. his Perfon is to be honoured, and all his Commands are to be obferved, *Heb.* 1. 2. *John* 5. 23. all Worfhip is to be afcribed unto him, as God bleffed for ever, *Rom.* 9. 5. all Church Members, therefore, are under the ftricteft Obligations to do and obferve whatfoever Chrift enjoyn-

L 2 eth

eth on them, as mutual Duties towards one another.

The Officers of the Church, whom Chriſt hath appointed, are to be reſpected. (1) TheDeacons of the Church (tho' they officiate but in the outward Concerns of the Church, as in the Section about Deacons is noted) if they are faithful, do purchaſe unto themſelves a good Degree, 1 *Tim.* 3. 13. are therefore to be reſpected. (2) Ruling Elders alſo are to be reſpected, ſeeing they are fitted of God, and called by the Church to go before the Church, or to preſide in Acts of Government and Rule, 1 *Tim.* 5. 17. (3) Miniſters, who are the Stewards of the Myſteries of the Goſpel, are in an eminent Manner to be regarded, as being the Ambaſſadors of Peace, 2 *Cor.* 5. 20. tho' they are not to hunt for it, as the Phariſees of old, *Math* 23. 5. 6, 7. The Duties of Church Members, towards their Elders, Teachers, Miniſters and Paſtors, may be included in their

(1) pray-

(1) praying for them, that God would open a Door of Utterance unto them, to unfold the Myfteries, *Eph.* 6. 18, 19, 20. (2) To obey them in the Lord, in whatfoever they admonifh them, according to the Word of God, *Heb.* 13. 17, 22. (3) In following their Example and Footfteps, as far as warranted by the Word, 1 *Cor.* 4. 16. *Chap.* 11. 1. *Phil.* 3. 17. *Heb.* 13. 7. (4) In ftanding by them, in all their Tryals and Afflictions, and in defending them in all good Caufes, as far as in them lies; in 2 *Tim.* 1. 15. thofe of *Afia* are blamed, for turning away, or not ftanding by the Apoftle. (5) In not expofing their Perfons for their Infirmities, as far as may be, confidering the Profperity of the Gofpel much depends on their good Report, *Acts* 23. 5. (6) In contributing towards their Maintenance, that they may attend wholly on Teaching and give themfelves to the Miniftry of the Word and to Prayer,

L 2 *Acts*

Acts 6. 4. the Reaſon thereof is evident, by a threefold Law. (1.) The Law of Nature, from whence the Apoſtle argues, 1 *Cor*. 9. 7—11. (2.) The Levitical Law, 1 *Cor*. 9.13. (3) The Goſpel enjoyneth and requireth the ſame, *Gal*. 6. 6. 1 *Cor*. 9. 14. Let theſe above-cited Places of Scripture, be conſidered, with many other of like Importance; and the Nature and Tendency of the Work of the Miniſtry be well weighed, and it will be clear that it is a Duty required of God himſelf; and that not in a Way of Alms, as to the Poor, which is another ſtanding Ordinance of Chriſt, but is to be performed in Love to Chriſt, and Obedience to his Laws, in order to ſupport and carry the Intereſt of the Goſpel. Yet this is not to be given to any one that may pretend to be a Miniſter, or thruſt himſelf upon a Church, or to ſuch as run without a Miſſion for filthy Lucres ſake; but Churches ought to take a ſpecial Care who to call forth to the Work of the

the Miniftry, according to the Rule of Inftruction given by Infpiration of God, be they learned or unlearned as to human Learning, be they Rich or Poor, as to worldly Wealth.

The Liberality of the People (if they be able) fhould furmount the Neceffity of the Minifter, fo as that he may exercife thofe Acts of Love and Hofpitality, as is required of fuch, that therein he may be exemplary in good Works, *&c.* Moreover it is a Duty on all thofe that attend on their Miniftry, to affift herein, *Gal.* 6. 6. and as People do fow, fo fhall they reap, *Gal.* 6. 7, and 8. vide *Confeffion of Faith, Chap.* 26. §. 10. When People neglect their Duty towards their Minifters, fuch Minifters muft of Neceffity neglect their Studies, and betake to other fecular Employments to fupport themfelves and Families, or be worfe than Infidels; then fuch People muft be great fpiritual Lofers in their Edification: Yet when and where a Church is not able to raife

L 4 a coma comfortable Maintenance for to support their Minister, there it is not only lawful, but the Duty of such Ministers to labour with their Hands; for to leave such a Congregation destitute, to languish without the Ministry, would be very uncharitable, and smell very much of filthy Lucre; and to expect from a People, more than they are able, would be Oppression or Extortion.

Of the manifold Duties of Christians, especially to the Houshold of Faith.

SOME of them are these. (1) Love unfeigned and without Dissimulation, for all their Things ought to be done in Love, *John* 13. 34, 35. *Rom.* 12. 9, 10. *Chap.* 13. 8, 9, 10. (2) To labour to keep the Unity of the Spirit in the Bond of Peace, *Ephes.* 4. 3. (3) Endeavour for the Edification, and spiritual Benefit of the whole Body, that they

they all may grow up to be a holy Temple in and for the Lord 1 *Cor*. 14. 12, 26. *Ephef*. 4. 12, 16, 29. *Chap*. 2. 21, 22. (4) That they all watch over one another for Good, *Phil*. 2. 3, 4. (5) That they do pray with and for one another, *James* 5. 16. (6) That they neglect not the Affembling of themfelves together, for the celebrating of divine Worfhip, and fo promote one anothers fpiritual Benefit, *Heb*. 10. 25. *Acts* 2. 42. (7) That they ufe all Means to keep the Houfe of God in due Order and Cleannefs, walking unoffenfive towards one another, and all others, with confcientious Diligence, and fo unanimoufly to contend for the Faith and Truth once delivered to the Saints, in the Purity thereof, according to the holy Scripture, *Pfal*. 93. 5. *Zech*. 14. 20, 21, 1 *Cor*. 14. 33, 40. *Chap*. 11. 2.

Of

Of Church Cenſures.

HAVING ſpoken of the gathering together of a particular goſpel Church, and it's Officers, and the Rules whereby we are to be guided in chooſing and ordaining of them, and of the Admiſſion of Members, *&c.* it is meet to give a ſhort View of a Church's Duties and Authority, in reſpect of Cenſures upon Offenders.

Firſt, of Admonition.

(1) Admonition is a holy, tender and wiſe Endeavour, to convince a Brother, that hath offended in Matter of Fact, or elſe is fallen into a way, wherein to continue is like to be prejudicial to the Party himſelf or ſome others; where the Matter, whatever it be, and the Sinfulneſs thereof, with the aggravating Circumſtances attending it, is to be charged on his Conſcience, in the Sight of God,

God, with due Application of the Word of God, which concerns his Condition; thereby leading him to his Duty and true Reformation. (2) Admonition is private by one or more of the Brethren, or more Publick by the whole Church. (1) When one Brother trefpaffes againft another, the offended Brother is not to divulge the Offence, but to go in a gofpel Way to the Offender, and to ufe his Endeavour to reclaim his Brother; and if he repents, the offended Brother ought to forgive him, *Math.* 18. 15. *Luke* 17. 3. but if the offending Brother will not hear, then the offended Brother ought to take two or three other Brethren, and them fuch as may be moft likely to gain upon the Offender; but if this Admonition alfo takes no Effect, it is to be brought before the Church, *Math.* 18. 16, 17. (2) The Church when Matters come thus before them, fhall admonifh and endeavour to reclaim the Offender, in the Spirit of Meeknefs; and if the Brother that offended conti-

nues

nues obstinate and impenitent, the Church is directed to exclude him, *Math.* 18. 17.

(1) From whence it follows, every Church-Member has somewhat to do in his Place, *Heb.* 12. 15. (2.) In case of private Offences it is prepoſterous to publiſh them or acquaint the Church or the Elders thereof therewith, before the two lower Degrees of Admonition are duly accompliſhed, and the Offender has neglected to hear. (3.) That when Matters are thus regularly brought to the Church, then private Proceedings may ceaſe. (4.) That when private Offences are brought to the Church without ſuch proper private Proceedure, that the Church may and ought to refuſe it, as not coming according to Goſpel-Rule aforeſaid, in *Mat.* 18. (5) But when thoſe things that begin in private are thus regularly brought into the Church, they muſt be received and adjudged according to the ſaid Rule, *Mat.* 18. So that it may and

and doth oftentimes fall out, that those Things that begin with private Admonition, do end in publick Excommunication,

Secondly, of Suspension.

(1) A Suspension may be, when the Church is informed that a Member hath acted amiss, either in Matters of Faith or Practice, and not having satisfactory Proof whether the Information is true or false, and the Case requiring Time to enquire therein, it is expedient to suspend such a Person from Communion at the Lord's Table, until the Elders of the Church can make suitable Enquiry; as might be signified by the Law in the Case of Leprosy, *Lev.* 13th and 14th chapters.

(2.) Suspension is rather to be looked upon to be, when a Church doth debar a Member from Communion for some Irregularity that he may be guilty of, which yet doth not amount so high as to be ripe for the great Sentence of Excommunication; but that the Person

for

(for such Irregularity) ought to be debarred of the Privilege of special Communion and Exercise of Office, in order to his Humiliation, 2 *Thess.* 3. 6, 7, 10, 11, 14, 15. such is not to be accounted as an Enemy, but to be exhorted as a Brother in Union tho' not in Communion; but if such an one remain impenitent and incorrigible, the Church (after due waiting for his Reformation) is to proceed to Excommunication, *Math.* 18. 17. for that would be a not hearing the Church in the highest Degree.

Thirdly, of Excommunication.

Excommunication is a judicial Act or Censure of the Church, upon an Offender, by the Authority of Jesus Christ, and by his Direction, delivered to his Church by himself or his Apostles, in the New Testament, which a gospel-Church ought to put in Practice, when Matters of Fact require, according to gospel Rule: as first, when a Member (after all due Admonition) continues obstinate, and will hear no Reproof, *Math.*

Mat. 18.17. *Secondly*, When a Member hath committed a groſs Sin, which is directly againſt the moral Law, and being notorious and ſcandalous, and proved beyond Diſpute, 1 *Cor*. 5. 4, 5. 1 *Tim*. 5. 24. 2 *Cor*. 10. 6. then a Church is immediately to proceed unto Cenſure (notwithſtanding any preſent Signs of Conviction or Remorſe) for the neceſſary Vindication of the Glory of God, the Vindication of the Church alſo, and their holy Profeſſion : And to manifeſt their juſt Indignation and Abhorrence againſt ſuch Wickedneſs, 1 *Cor*. 5. 1—13. *Thirdly*, When a Member is found to be erroneous, defective, or heretical in ſome fundamental Point, or to ſwerve from the right Faith, in the Principles of the Chriſtian Religion, 1 *Tim*. 1. 19, 20.

The Manner of Proceeding unto this great and awful inſtituted Ordinance, is : The Church being gathered together ; the Offender alſo having Notice to come to make his Anſwer and Defence

Defence (if he comes not, he aggravates his Offence by deſpiſing the Authority of Chriſt in his Church) the Body of the Church is to have Knowledge of the Offender's Crime fully, and the full Proof thereof as of plain Matter of Fact; and after mature deliberate Conſideration and conſulting the Rules of Direction given in the Word of God (whether the Offender be preſent or abſent) the Miniſter or Elder puts the Queſtion to the whole Church, Whether they judge the Perſon guilty of ſuch Crime now proved upon him, is worthy of the Cenſure of the Church for the ſame? to which the Members in general give their Judgment; which if it be in the Affirmative, then the Judgment of the Members in general being had, or the Majority of them, the Paſtor, Miniſter, or Elder ſums up the Sentence of the Church, opens the Nature of the Crime, with the ſuitableneſs of the Cenſure, according to Goſpel Rule; and having thus proceeded, a proper Time

Time is fixed to put the Sentence in Execution, at which Time the Paftor, Minifter or Elder of the Church (as his Place and Duty requires) is to lay open the Heinoufnefs of fuch a Sin, with all the aggravating Circumftances thereof, and fhewing what an abominable Scandal, fuch an Offender is become to Religion, what Difhonour it is to God, *&c.* applying the particular Places of Scripture that are proper to the Cafe, in order to charge the Offence home upon the Confcience of the Offender if prefent, that others alfo may fear; fhewing alfo the awful Nature of this great Cenfure, and the main End thereof, for the Salvation and not the Deftruction of the Soul, and with much Solemnity in the whole Society, calling upon God for his gracious Prefence, and his Bleffing upon this his Sacred Ordinance; that the great End thereof may be obtained. Still expreffing the deep Senfe the Church hath, of the Fall of this Brother, with the great Humiliation of the Church, and great Sorrow for, and Deteftation of the Sin

M committe

committed. The ſaid Paſtor, Miniſter, or Elder in the Name of the Lord Jeſus Chriſt, in the Preſence of the Congregation, and by and with the Conſent and according to the Judicial Sentence of the Church, cuts off, & ſecludes ſuch an Offender by Name, from the Union & Communion of the Church, becauſe of his Offences: So that ſuch a Perſon is not thenceforth to be looked on, deemed or accounted as a Brother or Member of ſuch a Church, until God ſhall reſtore him again by Repentance.

Which Excluſion carries in it the full Senſe of our Lord's Words, *Mat.* 18. 17. *Let him be unto thee as an Heathen Man and a Publican*; or of the Apoſtle, 1 *Cor.* 5. 5. *to deliver ſuch an one to Satan*; which is an authoritative putting of ſuch a Perſon out of the Communion of the Church, the Kingdom of Heaven; into the World, the Kingdom of Satan, the Prince of the Power of the Air, the Spirit that now worketh in the Children of Diſobedience, in order to his being humbled and broken under

under a Sight and Senfe of his Sins, which is meant by the Deftruction of the Flefh, and to the End that the Spirit may be faved in the Day of the Lord.

Amongft the many Diforders, which Church-Members may be guilty of, and for the obftinate Continuance therein a Church may and ought to ufe the Power that Chrift hath given to exclude them from her Communion, that is one, which is when a Member doth feclude himfelf, and that not in any regular Way, but contrary to all Rule and Order : For when a Church-Member, by reafon of fome Offence he hath taken at the Church or fome of the Members thereof, and hath not done his Duty according to the Rule of the Word, or elfe is a dying away in Religion, by one Means or another, as by the Love of the World, Change of Condition in Marriage, not having his expected Preferment in the Church, or the like, doth as it were excommunicate himfelf, the Church according to their Duty ought to ufe their Endeavours to reclaim fuch ; which Endeavours,

M 2

deavours, if they prove fruitleſs, and the Party obſtinate, the Church ought not to acquieſce in his irregular Departure from them, as if all their Bonds of Relation and Duty were over, and no more was to be done, ſeeing the Party hath uſurped the Power of the Keys to himſelf: The Church therefore muſt maintain the Power that Chriſt hath committed unto it, tho' it cannot hinder the inordinate and unruly Paſſions of ſuch an one, if God leaves him to it. He will run away from the Church, renting himſelf ſchiſmatically off, breaking thro' all Order and Covenant Obligations, in Oppoſition to brotherly Endeavours to hinder him, and to ſtay him in his Place; the Church is to proceed judicially to turn the Key upon ſuch a ſinful diſorderly Departer; and publickly to declare, that as ſuch an one by Name hath been guilty of ſuch a Thing (naming his Diſorders) he is no longer in their Communion, nor under their Watch and Care, *&c.* and that ſuch a Perſon is not to return to their Communion, until he hath given Satisfaction to the Church,

Church, *Rom.* 16. 17. Such a Separation or Departure is very finful, for thefe and the like Reafons. (1) Becaufe the Church is a Corporation privileged with Laws and Rules for Admittance and Dimittance, which ought to be obferved, *Matth.* 18. *Rom.* 12. 4, 5. (2) Such a Departure is rude & indecent, therefore difhonourable, 1 *Cor.* 14.40. (3) Becaufe if Members may take this Liberty, all the Officers of the Church, Minifters, Ruling Elders & Deacons may take the fame Liberty, which would foon un-church any Church, or at leaft be deftructive to its Beauty, Comfort & Edification, *Joh.* 6. 67. (4) All Members do covenant the contrary, *Ifai.* 44. 5. and therefore it is a Breach of Covenant, which is a black Character, 2 *Tim.* 3. 3. (5) It deftroys totally the Relation between Elders and People, which God hath ordained, *Matth.* 9. 36. (6) It is an Ufurping of the Keys, or rather ftealing of them, *Amos* 6. 13. (7) It is Schifm: If there is fuch a Thing in the World, it is of particular Churches, 1 *Cor.* 11. 18. ch. 12. 25. (8) It is a high Contempt of Chrift in the

M 3 Government,

Government of his Church, *Jude* 18. 19. 2 *Pet*. 2. 10, 11. (9) It is to break the Staff of Beauty [*Covenant*] and of Bands and Brotherhood too, *Zech*. 11. 10, 14. (10) It argues either some great undiscovered Guilt lying on the Party, or some By-Ends in his first seeking Admission into such a Church. All which put together, it declares the great Unity of a congregational Gospel-Church, and the Sinfulness of such disorderly Persons in Breaking off without a just Cause: But if any Church becomes heretical in Principles, or idolatrous in Worship, or immoral in Life, it is lawful for Persons, after they have discharged their Conscience and Duty in Reproving and bearing Witness against such gross Defections, to depart, 2 *Cor*. 6. 17, 18.

Other Disorders and Causes of Discords in Churches are these, and many of the like; (1) When Members of Churches, by their Ignorance of the Rules of Discipline & right Government of the Church of Christ, do not act according to their Duty; particularly when that Rule, *Mat*. 18.

18. 15, 16. is not obſerved; and that is, either (1) When offended Members, inſtead of going to the Offender, to tell him his Fault, will be divulging it diſorderly to others whether Members or Nonmembers. (2) When offended Members inſtead of acting according to the ſaid Rule, do conceal the Matter from the Offender and everybody elſe, leſt they ſhould be looked upon as contentious Perſons; and there by they ſuffer Sin upon their Brother, and are become guilty of other Men's Sins, and thereby they ſuffer the Name of God, their holy Profeſſion, and the Church, to lie under a Reproach by their Neglect; either of which Ways is very ſinful, as being contrary to the expreſs Rule given by our Lord Chriſt; and ſuch ought (as being thereby become Offenders themſelves) to be in a Goſpel-Way dealt with.

(2) When an Elder or a Church do know that ſome of the Members are immoral and ſcandalous in Life, or heretical in Matters of Faith and Judgment, and yet bear with them, or connive at them.

M 4 (3) When

(3) When Members of Churches take Liberty to go to hear to other Places, when the Church is assembled to worship God, which is directly contrary to *Heb.* 10. 25. and is no less than breaking Covenant with the Church they belong unto, and may soon dissolve and unchurch any particular Church; for, by the same Rule that one Member takes such Liberty, another may, yea, all the Members may, until their Assembling entirely cease. And moreover it is casting great Contempt on the Ministry of such a Church, and may cause others to be disaffected to the Doctrine taught in such, tho' sound and orthodox. Yet no Restraint ought to be laid on Members going to hear at other Places, where sound Doctrine is taught, at other Times.

(4) When Members take Liberty to go to hear Men that are corrupt in Doctrine, and so suck in some unsound Notions of Religion, and endeavour to corrupt others with what they have imbibed themselves. And alas! how many in our unhappy Days are corrupted with *Arminianism*, *Socinianism*,

anifm, and what not? Such caufe Trouble and great Diforders.

(5) Another Diforder that may caufe Difcord, is, when Members are received without the general and unanimous Confent of the Church; or when any are admitted, with whofe Confeffion or Life & Converfation, the Generality of the Members are not fatisfied: Or when Elders and Minifters or Leaders of the Church, are remifs and carelefs in the Reception of Members.

(6) When a Church fhall receive a Charge againft a Member (it being an Offence given by one Brother to another Brother) before an orderly Procedure has been made by the offended Brother, according to the Rule, *Matth.* 18.

(7) When Judgment paffes with Partiality, or fome are connived at out of Favour or Affection, and others cenfured out of Envy or without due Conviction. *Levi* was not to know his Father, Mother or Children in Judgment, *Deut.* 33. 8.

(8) When the Charges of a Church are not

not equally born by the Members according to their ſeveral Abilities, but ſome are burthened when others do little or nothing.

(9) When Accuſations are received againſt an Elder, contrary to the Rule, 1 *Tim.* 5. 16. which requires two or three Witneſſes as to Matter of Fact.

(10) When any Member ſhall divulge to Perſons not of the Congregation, nor concerned in thoſe Matters, what is done in the Church-Meetings: The Church in this reſpect, as well as in others, is to be a Garden encloſed, a Spring ſhut up, a Fountain ſealed, *Cant.* 4. 12. This often occaſions great Grief & Trouble, and therefore ſuch diſorderly Perſons ſhould be detected. Is it not a Shame to any to divulge the Secrets of a Family? but far greater Shame do ſuch Perſons expoſe themſelves unto.

(11) When Days of Prayer, Faſting or Thankſgiving, or Days of Diſcipline appointed by the Church, are not carefully obſerved and kept.

In all theſe and many other Things of like Nature, the Members of particular Churches,

Churches ought to give all Diligence to walk worthy of their Vocation, and according to the Rule & Direction of the Word of God, that Diforders may be prevented, & that Church Communion may be maintain'd in Peace & Purity, to the Edifying of the Body of the Church of Chrift in Love.

Of the Communion of Churches.

EVERY particular congregational Church incorporated by and according to the Inftitution of Chrift in the Gofpel, and duly organized according to the Pattern of the primitive Churches, hath fufficient Power from Chrift to call and ordain its own Officers; fo that no Man or Set of Men have Authority to chufe Officers for them, or impofe any Officers on them, without their previous Knowledge and voluntary Confent, *Acts* 6. 3. Deacons are to be chofen by the Multitude, *Acts* 14. 23. Elders were ordained in every Church by Election or Suffrage of the Church; and every particular Church, as fuch, affembled with her proper Elders, hath fufficient Power to receive

ceive Members, *Acts* 2. 41. *Rom.* 14. 7. And in the Exercise of any Acts of Discipline, such a Church being convened with her own Officers or Elders in the Name of Christ may act according to Gospel-Rule in any Case, even to excommunicate such Members as are found to be obstinate in Disorders, or heretical in Principles, after due Admonition ; or such as are guilty of gross and scandalous Immoralities in Conversation, *&c.* independant on any other Church-Power superior to itself, or higher Judicatory lodged in any Man or any Set of Men, by any Institution of Christ : And therefore the Elders of a Church, meeting in the Absence of the Members, or convened with the Elders of other Churches, are not entrusted with a Power to act for a Church in Admission of Members, Ordination, or Censures, *&c.* and it is the Duty of such a Church to admonish any of her Members or Officers, their Teacher or Pastor, *Col.* 4. 17. & exclude any too, when their Crimes require, according to the Rule of the Gospel.

And such particular congregational Churches,

ches, conſtituted and organized according to the Mind of Chriſt revealed in the New Teſtament, are all equal in Power and Dignity, and we read of no Diſparity between them, or Subordination among them, that ſhould make a Difference between the Acts of their mutual Communion, ſo as the Acts of one Church ſhould be Acts of Authority, and the Acts of others ſhould be Acts of Obedience or Subjection, altho' they may vaſtly differ in Gifts, Abilities and Uſefulneſs.

Such particular diſtinct Churches, agreeing in Goſpel-Doctrine and Practice, may and ought to maintain Communion together in many Duties, which may tend to the mutual Benefit and Edification of the Whole ; and thereby one Church that hath Plenty of Gifts, may and ought, if poſſible, to ſupply another that lacketh, *Cant.* 8. 8. they may have mutual Giving & Receiving, *Phil.* 4. 15. and mutual Tranſlation, Recommendation or Diſmiſſion of Members from one Church to another as Occaſion may require. It is to be noted, that Perſons called to Office are not to be diſmiſſed

miſſed as Officers, but as Members ; tho' another Church may call ſuch to the ſame Office again.

By Virtue alſo of ſuch Communion, the Members of one ſuch Church may, where they are known, occaſionally partake at the Lord's Table with a Siſter-Church. Yet notwithſtanding ſuch Communion of Churches, by voluntary Conſent and Confederation, the Officers of one particular Church may not act as Officers in another Church, in any Act of Government, without a particular Call thereunto from the other Church where they occaſionally come.

It is expedient that particular Churches, conſtituted in the Way and Manner, and for the Ends declared in the former Part of this Narrative (when they are planted by the Providence of God, ſo as they may have Opportunity and Advantage ſo to do) ſhould by their mutual Agreement appoint proper Times and Places, to meet by their reſpective Meſſengers or Delegates, to conſider of ſuch Things as may be for the common Benefit of all ſuch Churches, for their

their Peace, Prosperity, and mutual Edification, and what may be for the Furtherance of the Gospel, and the Interest of Christ in the World.

And forasmuch as it falls out many times that particular Churches have to do with doubtful and difficult Matters, or Differences in Point of Doctrine or Administration (like the Church of *Antioch* of old) wherein either the Churches in general are concerned, or any one Church, in their Peace, Union or Edification; or any Member or Members of a Church are injured, in or by any Proceeding in Censures not agreeable to Gospel-Rule and Order; it is according to the Mind of Christ, that many Churches holding Communion together, should meet by their Messengers and Delegates to consider of, and to give Advice in or about such Matters in Difference; and their Sentiments to be reported to all the Churches concerned: And such Messengers and Delegates, convened in the Name of Christ, by the voluntary Consent of the several Churches in such mutual Communion may declare & determine of the Mind of the Holy Ghoſt, revealed in Scripture, concerning Things in Difference; and may decree the Obſervation of Things that are true and neceſſary, becauſe revealed and appointed in the Scripture. And the Churches will do well to receive, own and obſerve ſuch Determinations, on the Evidence and Authority of the Mind of the Holy Ghoſt in them, as in *Acts* 15. 29. Yet ſuch Delegates thus aſſembled, are not intruſted or armed with any coercive Power, or any ſuperior Juriſdiction over the Churches concerned, ſo as to impoſe their Determinations on them or their Officers, under the Penalty of Excommunication, or the like. See the *Confeſſion*, *Chap*. 26. §. 14, 15. See alſo Dr. *Owen*, *On the Nature of the Goſpel Church*, chap. 11. and Dr. *Goodwin*, Vol. 4. Bo. 5. chap. 8, 9, 10, 11, *&c. of the Government of the Churches of Chriſt*.

THE END.

II. THE BAPTIST CATECHISM OF 1786

The Catechism of 1786 and Subsequent Efforts Made to Revise It.

by Terry Wolever

On October 13, 1774, at the fall session[1] held in Philadelphia,

> The Association considering that the catechising or instructing youth in the principles of the Christian religion, though so plain and important a duty, is yet too generally neglected, have thought it expedient to recommend to the churches, seriously to consider and promote the same.[2]

Due to the Revolutionary War, it was not until 1786 that Robert Aitken, famed printer of the first complete English Bible in America, published on behalf of "the General Association of Philadelphia"[3] the standard edition of what was commonly known as Keach's catechism.

Eight years later, at the 1794 session of the association, the members present,

> Resolved, That it be recommended to the different churches in this Association, to institute the chatechising of children in their respective congregations, at stated seasons.[4]

This resolution prompted the pastor of the First Baptist church of Philadelphia, Thomas Ustick, and fellow ministers present from that church, William Rogers and Morgan Edwards to raise concerns they had over some of the terminology used in the catechism, proposing the following question to the membership,

> Whether the word *exhibited* would not be

---

[1] The Philadelphia Association had also previously met together in New York on May 25th.

[2] *Ibid.*, p. 141.

[3] *A Baptist Catechism* (Philadelphia: Robert Aitken, 1786), title.

[4] *Ibid.* [6] *Ibid.* [7] *Ibid.* [8] *Ibid.* [9] *Ibid.*, pp. 305-306.

> preferable to the word *offered,* in question 34th of the Catechism, and in other places where it is used in the *same sense?* [6]

The Associational members, "determined, that the word *offered* be expunged, and the words *held forth* be inserted in the place thereof."[7] A committee was of both Ustick and Rogers, and Samuel Jones of the Lower Dublin church, was "appointed to revise the whole of the Catechism, and to recommend such alterations to the next Association as to them may seem proper."[8]

The Association received the committee's report of recommended revisions the following year at the second day's session on October 7, 1795, and voted to insert those recommended changes in the minutes for that year to be printed shortly thereafter, "for the inspection of the churches," who were then "desired to manifest their approbation, or disapprobation," at the next Associational meeting in 1796.[9] In all, the committee recommended changes in the wording of sixteen of the questions and eight of the answers.[10] Clearly the Pennsylvanians were not satisfied with the catechism in its present form.

Interestingly, that same year of 1795 a second edition of the catechism, in its original form, was published—not in Philadelphia however, but in Boston, by the printing firm of Manning and Loring. Was this an attempt to forestall the revision effort by the Pennsylvanians, knowing that changes in the catechism would also have led to changes in the wording of the Confession of 1742? We may never know. But the reprinting by the New England concern may in part have led members of the Association at the meetings in October of 1796 to "for the present set aside" the proposed amendments to the catechism, after their having been "brought under consideration."[11]

Presented in the following pages is a facsimile reprint of the Baptist Catechism of 1786, from a copy in the Library of Congress.

---

[10] *Ibid.*, pp. 307-309. For the full lest of the recommended changes, see A. D. Gillette, editor. *Minutes of the Philadelphia Baptist Association.* pp. 307-309.

[11] *Ibid.*, p. 317.

"...TO SET THEM IN ORDER :"

THE

BAPTIST *CATECHISM;*

OR, A

BRIEF INSTRUCTION,

IN THE

PRINCIPLES

OF THE

CHRISTIAN RELIGION,

AGREEABLY TO THE

CONFESSION OF FAITH

Put forth by upwards of an Hundred Congregations in Great-Britain July the 3d, 1689; adopted by the General Association of Philadelphia, September the 22d, 1742; and now received by Churches of the same Denomination in most of the United States.

To which are added, the

PROOFS FROM SCRIPTURES.

PHILADELPHIA:
Printed and Sold by ROBERT AITKEN, at *Pope's Head* in Market-Street.

M.DCC.LXXXVI.

To the READER.

HAVING a desire to shew our near agreement with many other Christians, of whom we have great esteem; we some years since put forth a Confession of our Faith, almost in all points the same with that of the Assembly and Savoy, which was subscribed by the Elders and Messengers of many Churches, baptized on profession of their faith; And do now put forth a short account of Christian Principles, for the instruction of our families, in most things agreeing with the Shorter Catechism of the Assembly. And this we were the rather induced to, because we have commonly made use of that catechism in our families, and the difference being not much, it will be more easily committed to memory.

THE

BAPTIST CATECHISM.

QUESTION I.

WHO is the first and chiefest being?

Ans. God is the first (*a*), and chiefest being. (*b*)

Q. 2. *Ought every one to believe there is a God?*

A. Every one ought to believe there is a God (*c*), and it is their great sin and folly who do not. (*d*)

Q. 3. *How may we know there is a God?*

A. The light of nature in man, and the works of God, plainly declare there is a God (*e*), but his Word and Spirit only do it fully and effectually for the salvation of sinners. (*f*)

Q. 4. *What is the word of God?*

A. The holy scriptures of the Old and New Testament are the word of God (*g*), and the only certain rule of faith and obedience. (*h*).

Q. 5. *May all men make use of the holy scriptures?*

A. All men are not only permitted (*i*), but commanded and exhorted, to read (*k*), hear, and understand the holy scriptures. (*l*)

Q. 6. *What things are chiefly contained in the holy scriptures?*

A. The holy scriptures chiefly contain what man ought to believe concerning God (*m*), and what duty God requireth of man. (*n*)

Q. 7. *What is God?*

A. God is a spirit (*o*), infinite (*p*), eternal (*q*), and unchangeable (*r*), in his being (*s*), wisdom (*t*), power (*u*), holiness (*w*), justice (*x*), goodness and truth. (*y*)

A 2 Q. 8.

(*a*) Isa. xliv. 6. *b* Psal. xcvii. 9. *c* Heb. xii. 6. *d* Psal. xiv. 1. *e* Rom. i. 19, 20. Psal. xix. 1, 2. *f* 1 Cor. ii. 10. 2 Tim. iii. 15. *g* John x. 34, 35. 2 Tim. iii. 16. *h* Eph. ii. 20. Isa. viii. 20. Luke xvi. 29. *k* Job v. 39. *l* Acts viii. 30. Matth. xv. 10. *m* 2 Tim. i. 13. Acts xxiv. 14. *n* Micah vi. 8. Eccles. xii. 13. *o* John iv. 24. *p* Job xi. 7. *q* Psal. xc. 2. *r* James i. 17. *s* Exod. iii. 14. 1 Tim. i. 17. *u* Psal. cxlvii. 5. *w* Rev. iv. 8. *x* Psal. lxxxix. [illegible]

Q. 8. *Are there more gods than one?*

A. There is but one only, the living and true God. (z)

Q. 9. *How many persons are there in the Godhead?*

A. There are three persons in the Godhead, the Father, the Son, and the Holy Spirit, and these three are One God, the same in essence, equal in power and glory. (*a*)

Q. 10. *What are the decrees of God?*

A. The decrees of God are his eternal purpose, according to the counsel of his will, whereby, for his own glory he hath fore-ordained whatsoever comes to pass. (*b*)

Q. 11. *How doth God execute his decrees?*

A. God executeth his decrees in the works of creation and providence. (*c*)

Q. 12. *What is the work of creation?*

A. The work of creation is God's making all things of nothing, by the word of his power, in the space of six days, and all very good. (*d*)

Q. 13. *How did God create man?*

A. God created man, male and female, after his own image, in knowledge, righteousness, and holiness, with dominion over the creatures. (*e*)

Q. 14. *What are God's works of providence?*

A. God's works of providence are, his most holy (*f*), wise (*g*), and powerful preserving (*h*) and governing all his creatures, and all their actions. (*i*)

Q. 15. *What special act of providence did God exercise towards man, in the estate wherein he was created?*

A. When God had created man, he entered into a covenant of life with him, upon condition of perfect obedience, forbidding him to eat of the tree of knowledge, of good and evil, upon pain of death. (*k*)

Q. 16. *Did our first parents continue in that estate wherein they were created?*

A. Our first parents being left to the freedom of their own will, fell from the estate wherein they were created, by sinning against God. (*l*)

Q. 17

(z) Deut. vi. 4. Jerem. x. 10. *a* 1 John v. 7. Matth. xxviii. 19 *b* Eph. i. 4, 11. Rom. ix. 22, 23. *c* Rev. iv. 11. Dan. iv. 35 *d* Gen. i. 1. Heb. xi. 3. Gen. i. 31. *e* Gen. i. 27, 28. Col. iii. 10 Eph. iv. 24. *f* Psal. cxlv. 17. *g* Isa. xxviii. 29. *h* Heb. i. 3 *i* Psal. ciii. 19. Mat. x. 29. *k* Gal. iii. 12. Gen. ii. 17. *l* Eccl. vii. 29. Rom. iii. 23.

Q. 17. *What is ſin?*

A. Sin is any want of conformity unto, or tranſgreſſion of the law of God. (*m*)

Q. 18. *What was the ſin whereby our firſt parents fell from the eſtate wherein they were created?*

A. The ſin whereby our firſt parents fell from the eſtate wherein they were created, was their eating the forbidden fruit. (*n*)

Q. 19. *Did all mankind fall in Adam's firſt tranſgreſſion?*

A. The covenant being made with Adam, not only for himſelf, but for his poſterity, all mankind deſcending from him by ordinary generation, ſinned in him and fell with him in his firſt tranſgreſſion. (*o*)

Q. 20. *Into what eſtate did the fall bring mankind?*

A. The fall brought mankind into an eſtate of ſin and miſery. (*p*)

Q. 21. *Wherein conſiſts the ſinfulneſs of that eſtate whereinto man fell?*

A. The ſinfulneſs of that eſtate whereinto man fell, conſiſts in the guilt of Adam's firſt ſin (*q*), the want of original righteouſneſs (*r*), and the corruption of his whole nature, which is commonly called original ſin (*ſ*), together with all actual tranſgreſſions which proceed from it. (*t*)

Q. 22. *What is the miſery of that eſtate whereinto man fell?*

A. All mankind, by their fall, loſt communion with God (*u*), are under his wrath (*w*) and curſe (*x*), and ſo made liable to all the miſeries in this life (*y*), to death itſelf (*z*), and to the pains of hell for ever. (*a*)

Q. 23. *Did God leave all mankind to periſh in the eſtate of ſin and miſery?*

A. God having out of his mere good pleaſure, from all eternity, elected ſome to everlaſting life (*b*), did enter into a covenant of grace, to deliver them out of the eſtate of ſin and miſery, and to bring them into an eſtate of ſalvation by a redeemer. (*c*).

Q. 24. *Who is the Redeemer of God's elect?*

A 3 A. The

(*m*) 1 John iii. 4. *n* Gen. iii. 6, 12, 13. *o* Gen. ii. 16, 17. 1 Cor. xv. 21, 22. Rom. v. 12. *p* Pſal. li. 5. Rom. v. 17, 18. *q* Rom. v. 19. *r* Rom. iii. 10. *ſ* Job xiv. 4. *t* Iſa. lxiv. 6. Jam. i. 14. Mat. xv. 19. *u* Gen. iii. 8, 24. *w* Eph. ii. 3. *x* Gal. iii. 10. *y* Job xiv. 1. *z* Rom. vi. 23. *a* Mat. xxv. 46. Pſal. ix. 17. *b* 2 Theſſ. ii. 13. *c* Iſa. xlix. 8. Rom. v. 21.

A. The only Redeemer of God's elect is the Lord Jesus Christ (*d*), who being the eternal son of God (*e*), became man (*f*), and so was and continueth to be God and man, in two distinct natures (*g*), and one person, for ever. (*h*)

Q. 25. *How did Christ, being the son of God, become man?*

A. Christ, the Son of God, became man, by taking to himself a true body (*i*), and a reasonable soul (*k*), being conceived by the power of the Holy Spirit, in the womb of the virgin Mary, and born of her (*l*,) yet without sin. (*m*)

Q. 26. *What offices doth Christ execute as our Redeemer?*

A. Christ as our Redeemer executeth the offices of a prophet (*n*), of a priest (*o*), and of a king (*p*), both in his estate of humiliation and exaltation.

Q. 27. *How doth Christ execute the office of a prophet?*

A. Christ executeth the office of a prophet, in revealing to us (*q*), by his Word (*r*) and Spirit (*s*), the will of God for our salvation.

Q. 28. *How doth Christ execute the office of a priest?*

A. Christ executeth the office of a priest, in his once offering up of himself a sacrifice to satisfy divine justice (*t*), and reconcile us to God (*u*), and in making continual intercession for us. (*w*).

Q. 29. *How doth Christ execute the office of a king?*

A. Christ executeth the office of a king, in subduing us to himself (*x*), in ruling (*y*) and defending us (*z*), and in restraining (*a*) and conquering all his and our enemies. (*b*)

Q. 30. *Wherein did Christ's humiliation consist?*

A. Christ's humiliation consisted in his being born, and that in a low condition (*c*), made under the law (*d*), undergoing the miseries of this life (*e*), the wrath of God (*f*), and the cursed death of the cross (*g*), in being buried (*h*), and continuing under the power of death for a time. (*i*)

Q. 31. *Wherein consisteth Christ's exaltation?*

A. Christ's exaltation consisteth in his rising again from the

(*d*) Gal. iii. 13. 1 Tim. ii. v. *e* 2 John 3. *f* John i. 14. *g* 1 Tim. vi. 16. Rom. ix. 5. *h* Col. ii. 9. Heb. vii. 24. *i* Heb. ii. 14. Heb. x. 5. *k* John xii. 27. *l* Luke i. 31, 35. *m* Heb. iv. 15. Heb. vii. 20. *n* Acts iii. 22. *o* Heb. v. 6. *p* Psal. ii. 6. *q* John i. 18. *r* John xv. 15. *s* John xiv. 26. *t* Heb. ix. 28. Eph. v. 2. *u* Heb. ii. 17. *w* Heb. vii. 25. *x* Psal. cx. 3. *y* Matth. ii. 6. *z* Zech. ix. 15. *a* Psal. lxxvi. 10. *b* 1 Cor. xv. 25. *c* Luke ii 7. *d* Gal. iv. 4. *e* Isa. liii. 3. *f* Luke xvii. 44. Mat. xxvii. 46. *g* Phil. ii. 8. *h* 1 Cor. xv. 4. *i* Matth. xii. 40.

the dead on the third day (*k*), in aſcending up into heaven (*l*), in ſitting at the right hand of God the Father (*m*), and in coming to judge the world at the laſt day. (*n*)

Q. 32. *How are we made partakers of the redemption purchaſed by Chriſt?*

A. We are made partakers of the redemption purchaſed by Chriſt, by the effectual application of it to us (*o*) by his holy Spirit. (*p*)

Q. 33. *How doth the Spirit apply to us the redemption purchaſed by Chriſt?*

A. The Spirit applieth to us the redemption purchaſed by Chriſt, by working faith in us (*q*), and thereby uniting us to Chriſt (*r*) in our effectual calling. (*ſ*)

Q. 34. *What is effectual calling?*

A. Effectual calling is the work of God's Spirit (*t*), whereby convincing us of our ſin (*u*) and miſery (*w*), enlightening our minds in the knowledge of Chriſt (*x*), and renewing our wills (*y*), he doth perſuade and enable us to embrace Jeſus Chriſt, freely offered to us in the goſpel. (*z*)

Q. 35. *What benefits do they that are effectually called partake of in this life?*

A. They that are effectually called do in this life partake of juſtification (*a*), adoption (*b*), and ſanctification (*c*), and the ſeveral benefits which in this life do either accompany or flow from them. (*d*)

Q. 36. *What is juſtification?*

A. Juſtification is an act of God's free grace (*e*), wherein he pardoneth all our ſins (*ſ*), and accepteth us as righteous in his ſight (*g*), only for the righteouſneſs of Chriſt imputed to us (*h*), and received by faith alone. (*i*)

Q. 37. *What is adoption?*

A. Adoption is an act of God's free grace (*k*), whereby we are received into the number, and have a right to all the privileges of the ſons of God. (*l*)

Q. 38. *What is ſanctification?*

A 4 A. Sancti-

(*k*) 1 Cor. xv. 4. *l* Acts i. 11. *m* Eph. i. 20. Mark xvi. 19. *n* Acts xvii. 31. *o* Gal. iv. 5. *p* Tit. iii. 5, 6. *q* Eph. ii. 8. *r* Eph. iii. 17. *ſ* 1 Cor. i. 9. *t* 2 Tim. i. 9. *u* John xvi. 8. *w* Acts ii. 37. *x* Acts xxvi. 18. *y* Ezek. xxxvi. 26. *z* John vi. 44, 45. *a* Rom. viii. 30. *b* Gal. iii. 26. *c* 1 Cor. vi. 11. *d* 1 Cor. i. 30. *e* Rom. iii. 24. *ſ* Eph. i. 7. *g* 2 Cor. v. 21. *h* Rom. iv. 6. *i* Rom. iii. 22. Phil. iii. 9. *k* 1 John iii. 1. *l* John i. xii. Rom. viii. 17.

A. Sanctification is the work of God's free grace (*m*), whereby we are renewed in the whole man after the image of God (*n*), and are enabled more and more to die unto ſin and live unto righteouſneſs. (*o*)

Q. 39. *What are the benefits which in this life do accompany or flow from juſtification, adoption and ſanctification?*

A. The benefits which in this life do accompany or flow from juſtification, adoption and ſanctification, are aſſurance of God's love, peace of conſcience (*p*), joy in the holy Spirit (*q*), increaſe of grace (*r*), and perſeverance therein to the end. (*ſ*)

Q. 40. *What benefits do believers receive from Chriſt at their death?*

A. The ſouls of believers are at their death made perfect in holineſs (*t*), and do immediately paſs into glory (*u*), and their bodies being ſtill united to Chriſt (*w*), do reſt in their graves (*x*) till the reſurrection. (*y*)

Q. 41. *What benefits do believers receive from Chriſt at the reſurrection?*

A. At the reſurrection, believers being raiſed up in glory (*z*), ſhall be openly acknowledged and acquitted in the day of judgment (*a*), and made perfectly bleſſed both in ſoul and body, in the full enjoyment of God (*b*) to all eternity. (*c*)

Q. 42. *But what ſhall be done to the wicked at their death?*

A. The ſouls of the wicked ſhall at their death be caſt into the torments of hell (*d*), and their bodies lie in their graves till the reſurrection and judgment of the great day [*e*]

Q. 43. *What ſhall be done to the wicked at the day of judgment?*

A. At the day of judgment the bodies of the wicked being raiſed out of their graves, ſhall be ſentenced together with their ſouls to unſpeakable torments, with the devil and his angels for ever. [*ſ*]

Q. 44.

(*m*) 2 Theſſ. ii. 13. *n* Eph. iv. 23, 24. *o* Rom. vi. 11. *p* Rom. v. 1, 2, 5. *q* Rom. xiv. 7. *r* Prov. iv. 18. *ſ* 1 Pet. i. 5. *t* Heb. xii. 23. *u* Phil. i. 23. 2 Cor. v. 8. *w* 1 Theſſ. iv. 14. *x* Iſa. lvii. 2. *y* Job xix. 26. *z* 1 Cor. xv. 43. *a* Mat. x. 32. Acts iii. 19. *b* 1 John iii. 2. *c* 1 Theſſ. iv. 17. *d* Luke xvi. 22, 23, 24. *e* Pſal. xlix. 14 *ſ* Dan. xii. 2. John v. 28, 29. 2 Theſſ. i. 9. Mat. xxv. 41.

Q. 44. *What is the duty which God requireth of man?*

A. The duty which God requireth of man, is obedience to his revealed will. [*g*]

Q. 45. *What did God at first reveal to man for the rule of his obedience?*

A. The rule which God at first revealed to man for his obedience, was the moral law. [*h*]

Q. 46. *Where is the moral law summarily comprehended?*

A. The moral law is summarily comprehended in the ten commandments. [*i*]

Q. 47. *What is the sum of the ten commandments?*

A. The sum of the ten commandments is, to love the Lord our God with all our heart, with all our soul, with all our strength, and with all our mind; and our neighbour as ourselves. [*k*]

Q. 48. *What is the preface to the ten commandments?*

A. The preface to the ten commandments is in these words, *I am the Lord thy God, which have brought thee out of the land of Egypt, out of the house of bondage.* [*m*]

Q. 49. *What doth the preface to the ten commandments teach us?*

A. The preface to the ten commandments teacheth us, that because God is the Lord, and our God, and Redeemer, therefore we are bound to keep all his commandments. [*n*]

Q. 50. *Which is the first commandment?*

A. The first commandment is, *thou shalt have no other Gods before me.* [*o*]

Q. 51. *What is required in the first commandment?*

A. The first commandment requireth us to know and acknowledge God to be the only true God, and our God [*p*], and to worship and glorify him accordingly. [*q*]

Q. 52. *What is forbidden in the first commandment?*

A. The first commandment forbiddeth the denying (*r*) or not worshipping the true God, as God (*s*), and our God (*t*), and the giving that worship and glory to any other, which is due unto him alone. (*u*).

A 5 Q. 53.

(*g*) Micah vi. 8. Psal. cxix. 4 *h* Rom. ii. 14, 15. *i* Deut. x. 4. Mat. xix. 17. *k* Mat. xxii. 37, 38, 39, 40. *m* Exod. xx. 2. *n* Deut. xi. 1. Luke i. 74, 75. *o* Exod. xx. 3. *p* 1 Chron. xxviii. 9. Deut. xxvi. 17. *q* Psal. xxix. 2. Mat. iv. 10. *r* Josh. xxiv. 27. *s* Rom. i. 20, 21. *t* Isa. lix. 13. *u* Rom. i. 25.

Q. 53. *What are we especially taught by these words* [before me] *in the first commandment?*

A. These words [*before me*] in the first commandment, teach us, that God, who seeth all things, taketh notice of, and is much displeased with the sin of having any other God. (*w*)

Q. 54. *Which is the second commandment?*

A. The second commandment is, *thou shalt not make unto thee any graven image, or any likeness of any thing that is in Heaven above, or that is in the earth beneath, or that is in the water under the earth. Thou shalt not bow down thyself to them, nor serve them: for I the Lord thy God am a jealous God, visiting the iniquity of the fathers upon the children, unto the third and fourth generation of them that hate me; and shewing mercy unto thousands of them that love me, and keep my commandments.* (*x*)

Q. 55. *What is required in the second commandment?*

A. The second commandment requireth the receiving, observing, keeping pure and entire, all such religious worship and ordinances, as God hath appointed in his word. (*y*)

Q. 56. *What is forbidden in the second commandment?*

A. The second commandment forbiddeth the worshipping of God by images (*z*), or any other way not appointed in his word. (*a*)

Q. 57. *What are the reasons annexed to the second commandment?*

A. The reasons annexed to the second commandment, are God's sovereignty over us (*b*), his propriety in us (*c*), and the zeal he hath to his own worship. (*d*).

Q. 58. *Which is the third commandment?*

A. The third commandment is, *thou shalt not take the name of the Lord thy God in vain; for the Lord will not hold him guiltless that taketh his name in vain.* (*e*).

Q. 59. *What is required in the third commandment?*

A. The third commandment requireth the holy and reverent use of God's name (*f*), titles (*g*), attributes (*h*), ordinances (*i*), word (*k*), and works. (*l*)

Q 60.

(*w*) Psal. xliv. 20, 21. (*x*) Exod. xx. 4, 5, 6. (*y*) Deut. xxxii. 46. Mat. xxviii. 20. Deut. xii. 32. (*z*) Deut. iv. 15, 16. (*a* Col. ii. 21, 22. *b* Psal. xcv. 2, 3. *c* Psal. xiv. 11. *d* Exod. xxxiv. 14. *e* Exod. xx. 7. *f* Mat. vi. 9. Psal. cxi. 9. *g* Deut. xxviii. 58. Psal. lxviii. 4. *h* Deut. xxxii. 3, 4. *i* Eccl. v. 1. *k* Psal. cxxxviii. 2. *l* Job xxxvi. 24.

Q. 60. *What is forbidden in the third commandment?*

A. The third commandment forbiddeth all prophaning or abuſing of any thing whereby God maketh himſelf known. (*m*)

Q. 61. *What is the reaſon annexed to the third commandment?*

A. The reaſon annexed to the third commandment is, that however the breakers of this commandment may eſcape puniſhment from men, yet the Lord our God will not ſuffer them to eſcape his righteous judgment. (*n*).

Q. 62. *Which is the fourth commandment?*

A. The fourth commandment is, *remember the ſabbath day to keep it holy. Six days ſhalt thou labour and do all thy work, but the ſeventh day is the ſabbath of the Lord thy God: in it thou ſhalt not do any work, thou, nor thy ſon, nor thy daughter, thy man ſervant, nor thy maid ſervant, nor thy cattle, nor the ſtranger that is within thy gates; for in ſix days the Lord made heaven and earth, the ſea, and all that in them is, and reſted the ſeventh day: wherefore the Lord bleſſed the ſabbath day, and hallowed it* (*o*)

Q. 63. *What is required in the fourth commandment?*

A. The fourth commandment requireth the keeping holy to God one whole day in ſeven to be a ſabbath to himſelf. (*p*)

Q. 64. *Which day of the ſeven hath God appointed to be the weekly ſabbath?*

A. Before the reſurrection of Chriſt, God appointed the ſeventh day of the week to be the weekly ſabbath (*q*), and the firſt day of the week ever ſince, to continue to the end of the world, which is the chriſtian ſabbath. (*r*)

Q. 65. *How is the ſabbath to be ſanctified?*

A. The ſabbath is to be ſanctified by a holy reſting all that day, even from ſuch worldly employments and recreations as are lawful on other days (*ſ*), and ſpending the whole time in the public and private exerciſes of God's worſhip (*t*), except ſo much as is to be taken up in the works of neceſſity and mercy. (*u*)

Q. 66.

(*m*) Mal. i. 6, 7. *n* Deut. lviii. 59. Mal. ii. 2. *o* Exod. xx. 8, 9, 10, 11. *p* Lev. xix. 30. Deut. v. 12. *q* Exod. xxxi. 15. *r* John xx. 19. Acts xx. 7. 1 Cor. xvi. 1, 2. Rev. I. 10. *ſ* Lev. xxii. 3. Iſa. lviii. 13. *t* Pſal. xcii. Iſa. lxvi. 23. *u* Mat. xii. 11, 12.

Q. 66. *What is forbidden in the fourth commandment.*

A. The fourth commandment forbiddeth the omiſſion or careleſs performance of the duties required (*w*), and the prophaning the day by idleneſs, (*x*) or doing that which is in itſelf ſinful, (*y*) or by unneceſſary thoughts, words, or works, about worldly employments or recreations. (*z*)

Q. 67. *What are the reaſons annexed to the fourth commandment?*

A. The reaſons annexed to the fourth commandment, are, God's allowing us ſix days of the week for our own lawful employments, (*a*) his challenging ſpecial property in a ſeventh, (*b*) his own example, (*c*) and his bleſſing the ſabbath day. (*d*)

Q. 68. *Which is the fifth commandment?*

A. The fifth commandment is, *honour thy father and thy mother, that thy days may be long upon the land which the Lord thy God giveth thee.* (*e*)

Q. 69. *What is required in the fifth commandment?*

A. The fifth commandment requireth the preſerving the honour, and performing the duties belonging to every one in their ſeveral places and relations, as ſuperiors, (*f*) inferiors, (*g*) or equals. (*h*)

Q. 70. *What is forbidden in the fifth commandment?*

A. The fifth commandment forbiddeth the neglecting of, (*i*) or doing any thing againſt the honour and duty which belongeth to every one in their ſeveral places and relations. (*k*)

Q. 71. *What is the reaſon annexed to the fifth commandment?*

A. The reaſon annexed to the fifth commandment, is, a promiſe of long life and proſperity, (ſo far as it ſhall ſerve for God's glory, and their own good) to all ſuch as keep this commandment. (*l*)

Q. 72. *Which is the ſixth commandment?*

A. The ſixth commandment is, *thou ſhalt not kill.* (*m*)

Q. 73. *What is required in the ſixth commandment?*

A. The

(*w*) Ezek. xxii. 26. *x* Acts xx. 9. *y* Ezek. xxiii. 38. *z* Neh. xiii. 15, 17. Amos viii. 5. *a* Exod. xxxiv. 21. *b* Exod. xxxv. 2. *c* Exod. xxi. 16, 17. *d* Gen. ii. 3. *e* Exod. xx. 12. *f* 1 Pet. ii. 17. Rom. xiii. 1. *g* Eph. v. 21, 22. Eph. vi. 1, 5, 9. Col. iii. 19. *h* Rom. xii. 10. *i* 1 Deut. xxi. 18, 19, 20, 21. Prov. xxx. 17. *k* Rom. xiii. 7, 8. *l* Eph. vi. 2, 3. *m* Exod. xx. 13.

A. The ſixth commandment requireth all lawful endeavours to preſerve our own life, (*n*) and the life of others. (*o*)

Q. 74. *What is forbidden in the ſixth commandment?*

A. The ſixth commandment abſolutely forbiddeth the taking away our own life, (*p*) or the life of our neighbour unjuſtly, or whatſoever tendeth thereto. (*q*)

Q. 75. *Which is the ſeventh commandment?*

A. The ſeventh commandment is, *thou ſhalt not commit adultery.* (*r*)

Q. 76. *What is required in the ſeventh commandment?*

A. The ſeventh commandment requireth the preſervation of our own (*s*) and our neighbour's chaſtity, (*t*) in heart, (*u*) ſpeech (*w*) and behaviour. (*x*)

Q. 77. *What is forbidden in the ſeventh commandment?*

A. The ſeventh commandment forbiddeth all unchaſte thoughts, (*y*) words (*z*) and actions. (*a*)

Q. 78. *Which is the eighth commandment?*

A. The eighth commandment is, *thou ſhalt not ſteal.* (*b*)

Q. 79. *What is required in the eighth commandment?*

A. The eighth commandment requireth the lawful procuring and furthering the wealth and outward eſtate of ourſelves (*c*) and others. (*d*)

Q. 80. *What is forbidden in the eighth commandment?*

A. The eighth commandment forbiddeth whatſoever doth or may unjuſtly hinder our own (*e*) or our neighbour's wealth or outward eſtate. (*f*)

Q. 81. *Which is the ninth commandment?*

A. The ninth commandment is, *thou ſhalt not bear falſe witneſs againſt thy neighbour.* (*g*)

Q. 82. *What is required in the ninth commandment?*

A. The ninth commandment requireth the maintaining and promoting of truth between man and man, (*h*) and of our own (*i*) and our neighbour's good name, (*k*) eſpecially in witneſs bearing. (*l*)

Q. 38.

(*n*) Eph. v. 28, 29. Job ii. 4. *o* Pſal. lxxxii. 3, 4. Prov. xxiv. 11. *p* Acts xvi. 28. *q* Gen. ix. 6. *r* Exod. xx. 14. *ſ* 1 Cor. vii. 2. *t* 1 Cor. vi. 18. *u* 2 Tim. ii. 22. Mat. v. 28. *w* Col. iv. 6. *x* 1 Pet. iii. 2. *y* Job xxxi. 1. *z* Eph. v. 4. *a* Rom. xiii. 13. Eph. v. 3. *b* Exod. xx. 15. *c* Gen. xxx. 30. Prov. xxvii. 23. *d* Lev. xxv. 35. Deut. xxii. 1, 3, 4. *e* 1 Tim. v. 8. Prov. xxviii. 19. *f* Prov. xxiii. 20, 21. Eph. iv. 28. *g* Exod. xx. 16. *h* Zch. viii. 16. *i* Eccl. vii. 1. *k* 3 John xii. *l* Prov. xiv. 25.

Q. 83. *What is forbidden in the ninth commandment?*

A. The ninth commandment forbiddeth whatsoever is prejudicial to truth, (*m*) or injurious to our own, (*n*) or our neighbour's good name. (*o*)

Q. 84. *Which is the tenth commandment?*

A. The tenth commandment is, *thou shalt not covet thy neighbour's house, thou shalt not covet thy neighbour's wife, nor his man servant, nor his maid servant, nor his ox, nor his ass, nor any thing that is thy neighbour's.* (*p*)

Q. 85. *What is required in the tenth commandment?*

A. The tenth commandment requireth full contentment with our own condition, (*q*) with a right and charitable frame of spirit towards our neighbour and all that is his. (*r*)

Q. 86. *What is forbidden in the tenth commandment?*

A. The tenth commandment forbiddeth all discontentment with our own estate, (*s*) envying or grieving at the good of our neighbour, (*t*) and all inordinate motions and affections to any thing that is his. (*u*)

Q. 87. *Is any man able perfectly to keep the commandments of God?*

A. No mere man since the fall, is able in this life perfectly to keep the commandments of God (*w*), but doth daily break them, in thought (*x*), word (*y*), or deed. (*z*)

Q. 88. *Are all transgressions of the law equally heinous?*

A. Some sins in themselves, and by reason of several aggravations, are more heinous in the sight of God than others. (*a*)

Q. 89. *What doth every sin deserve?*

A. Every sin deserveth God's wrath and curse, both in this life, and that which is to come. (*b*)

Q. 90. *What doth God require of us, that we may escape his wrath and curse due to us for sin?*

A. To escape the wrath and curse of God, due to us for sin, God requireth of us faith in Jesus Christ (*c*), repentance unto life (*d*), with the diligent use of all the outward means whereby Christ communicateth to us the benefits of redemption. (*e*)

Q. 91.

(*m*) Eph. iv. 25. *n* Prov. x. 7. Prov. xxii. 1. *o* Psal. xv. 3. *p* Exod. xx. 17. *q* Heb. xiii. 5. 1 Tim. vi. 6. *r* Rom. xii. 15. 1 Cor. xiii. 4, 7. *s* 1 Cor. x. 10. *t* Mat. xx. 15. James v. 9. *u* 1 Kings xxi. 4. Col. iii. 5. *w* Eccles. vii. 20. 1 John i. 8. *x* Gen. vi. 5. *y* James iii. 8. *z* James iii. 2. *a* Ezek. viii. 13. John xix. 11. 1 John v. 16. *b* Eph. v. 6. Prov. iii. 33. Psal. xi. 6. Rev. xxi. 8. *c* Acts xvi. 30, 31. *d* Acts xvii. 30. *e* Prov. ii. 3, 4, 5. Prov. viii. 34, 35.

Q. 91. *What is faith in Jesus Christ?*

A. Faith in Jesus Christ is a saving grace (*f*), whereby we receive (*g*) and rest upon him alone for salvation, as he is offered to us in the gospel. (*h*)

Q. 92. *What is repentance unto life?*

A. Repentance unto life is a saving grace (*i*), whereby a sinner, out of a true sense of his sins (*k*), and apprehension of the mercy of God in Christ (*l*), doth, with grief and hatred of his sin, turn from it unto God (*m*), with full purpose of, and endeavour after new obedience. (*n*)

Q. 93. *What are the outward means whereby Christ communicateth to us the benefits of redemption?*

A. The outward and ordinary means whereby Christ communicateth to us the benefits of redemption, are his ordinances, especially the word, baptism, the Lord's supper and prayer; all which means are made effectual to the elect for salvation. (*o*)

Q. 94. *How is the word made effectual to salvation?*

A. The Spirit of God maketh the reading (*p*), but especially the preaching of the word, an effectual means of convincing and converting sinners (*q*,) and of building them up in holiness and comfort (*r*), through faith unto salvation. (*s*)

Q. 95. *How is the word to be read and heard, that it may become effectual to salvation?*

A. That the word may become effectual to salvation, we must attend thereunto with diligence (*t*), preparation (*u*), and prayer (*w*), receive it with faith (*x*) and love (*y*), lay it up in our hearts (*z*), and practise it in our lives. (*a*)

Q. 96. *How do baptism and the Lord's supper become effectual means of salvation?*

A. Baptism and the Lord's supper, become effectual means of salvation, not from any virtue in them, or in him that doth administer them (*b*), but only by the blessing of Christ (*c*), and the working of his Spirit, in those who by faith receive them. (*d*)

Q. 97.

(*f*) Heb. x. 39. *g* John i. 12. *h* Phil. iii. 9. *i* Acts xi. 18. *k* Acts ii. 37. *l* Joel ii. 13. *m* Jer. xxxi. 18, 19. *n* Psal. cxix. 59, 60. *o* Acts ii. 41, 42. Psal. xcii. 13, 14. *p* Neh. viii. 8. Psal. xix. 7. *q* Psal. li. 13. Rom. x. 14, 17. *r* Acts xx. 32. 1 Cor. xiv. 3. *s* Rom. i. 16. *t* 1 Tim. iv. 13. Heb. ii. 1. *u* 1 Pet. ii. 1, 2. *w* Psal. cxix. 18. *x* Heb. iv. 2. *y* 2 Thess. ii. 10. *z* Psal. cxix. 11. *a* James i. 25. *b* 1 Cor. iii. 7. 1 Pet. iii. 21. *c* 1 Cor. iii. 6. *d* 1 Cor. xii. 13.

Q. 97. *What is baptiſm?*

A. Baptiſm is an ordinance of the New Teſtament, inſtituted by Jeſus Chriſt (*e*), to be unto the party baptized a ſign of his fellowſhip with him, in his death, and burial, and reſurrection (*f*), of his being ingrafted into him (*g*), of remiſſion of ſins (*h*), and of his giving up himſelf unto God, through Jeſus Chriſt, to live and walk in newneſs of life. (*i*)

Q. 98. *To whom is baptiſm to be adminiſtered?*

A. Baptiſm is to be adminiſtered to all thoſe who actually profeſs repentance toward God (*k*), faith in, and obedience to our Lord Jeſus Chriſt; and to none other. (*l*)

Q. 99. *Are the infants of ſuch as are profeſſing believers to be baptized?*

A. The infants of ſuch as are profeſſing believers, are not to be baptized; becauſe there is neither command nor example in the holy ſcriptures, or certain conſequence from them, to baptize ſuch. (*m*)

Q. 100. *How is baptiſm rightly adminiſtered?*

A. Baptiſm is rightly adminiſtered by immerſion, or dipping the whole body of the party in water (*n*), into the name of the Father, and of the Son, and of the Holy Spirit, according to Chriſt's inſtitution (*o*), and the practice of the apoſtles (*p*), and not by ſprinkling or pouring of water, or dipping ſome parts of the body, after the tradition of men. (*q*)

Q. 101. *What is the duty of ſuch who are rightly baptized?*

A. It is the duty of ſuch who are rightly baptized, to give up themſelves to ſome particular and orderly church of Jeſus Chriſt (*r*), that they may walk in all the commandments and ordinances of the Lord blameleſs. (*s*)

Q. 102. *What is the Lord's ſupper?*

A. The Lord's ſupper is an ordinance of the New Teſtament, inſtituted by Jeſus Chriſt, wherein by giving and receiving bread and wine, according to his appointment, his death is ſhewed forth (*t*), and the worthy receivers are,

(*e*) Mat. xxviii. 19. *f* Rom. vi. 3. Col. ii. 12. *g* Gal. iii. 27. *h* Mark i. 4. Acts xxii. 16. *i* Rom. vi. 4, 5. *k* Acts ii. 38. Mat. iii. 6. *l* Mark xvi. 16. Acts viii. 12, 36, 37. Acts x. 47, 48. *m* Exod. xxiii. 13. Prov. xxx. 6. Luke iii. 7, 8. *n* Mat. iii. 16. John iii. 23. *o* Mat. xxviii. 19, 20. *p* John iv. 1, 2. *q* Acts viii. 38, 39. *r* Acts ii. 47. Acts ix. 26. *s* 1 Pet. ii. 5. Luke i. 6. *t* 1 Cor. xi. 23, 24, 25, 26.

are, not after a corporal and carnal manner, but by faith made partakers of his body and blood, with all his benefits, to their spiritual nourishment, and growth in grace. *(u)*

Q. 103. *Who are the proper subjects of this ordinance?*

A. They who have been baptized upon a personal profession of their faith in Jesus Christ, and repentance from dead works. *(w)*

Q. 104. *What is required to the worthy receiving of the Lord's supper?*

A. It is required of them that would worthily partake of the Lord's supper, that they examine themselves of their knowledge to discern the Lord's body *(x)*, of their faith to feed upon him *(y)*, of their repentance (z), love (*a*), and new obedience *(b)*; lest coming unworthily, they eat and drink judgment to themselves. *(c)*

Q. 105. *What is prayer?*

A. Prayer is an offering up our desires to God, (*d*) by he assistance of the holy spirit, (*e*) for things agreeable to is will, (*f*) in the name of Christ, (*g*) believing, (*h*) with onfession of our sins, (*i*) and thankful acknowledgment of his mercies. (*k*)

Q. 106. *What rule hath God given for our direction in prayer?*

A. The whole word of God is of use to direct us in prayer, (*l*) but the special rule of direction is that prayer, which Christ taught his disciples, commonly called, *The Lord's prayer.* (*m*)

Q. 107. *What doth the preface to the Lord's prayer teach us?*

A. The preface of the Lord's prayer, which is, *our father which art in Heaven,* (*n*) teacheth us to draw near to God, with all holy reverence and confidence, as children to a father able and ready to help us, (*o*) and that we should pray with and for others. (*p*)

Q. 108. *What do we pray for in the first petition?*

A. In

(u) 1 Cor. x. 16. *w* Acts ii. 41, 42. *x* 1 Cor. xi. 28. *y* 2 Cor. xiii. 5. *z* 1 Cor. xi. 31. *a* 1 Cor. xi. 18, 20. *b* 1 Cor. v. 8. *c* 1 Cor. xi. 29. *d* Psal. lxii. 8. *e* Rom. viii. 26. *f* Rom. viii. 27. *g* John xvi. 23. *h* Mat. xxi. 22. *i* Dan. ix. 4. *k* Phil. iv. 6. *l* Luke xi. 1. 2 Tim. iii. 16, 17. 1 John v. 14. *m* Mat. vi. 9. *n* Mat. vi. 9. *o* Rom. viii. 15. Mat. vii. 11. Isa. lxiv. 8. *p* Acts xii. 5. 1 Tim. ii. 1, 2.

A. In the first petition, which is, *hallowed be thy name,* (*q*) we pray that God would enable us and others to glorify him in all that whereby he maketh himself known, (*r*) and that he would dispose all things to his own glory. (*s*)

Q. 109. *What do we pray for in the second petition.*

A. In the second petition, which is, *thy kingdom come,* (*t*) we pray that satan's kingdom may be destroyed, (*u*) and that the kingdom of grace may be advanced, (*w*) ourselves and others brought into it, and kept in it, (*x*) and that the kingdom of glory may be hastened. (*y*)

Q. 110. *What do we pray for in the third petition?*

A. In the third petition, which is, *thy will be done on earth as it is in Heaven,* (z) we pray that God, by his grace, would make us able and willing to know, obey, (*a*) and submit to his will in all things, (*b*) as the angels do in Heaven. (*c*)

Q. 111. *What do we pray for in the fourth petition?*

A. In the fourth petition, which is, *give us this day our daily bread,* (*d*) we pray, that of God's free gift, we may receive a competent portion of the good things of this life, (*e*) and enjoy his blessing with them. (*f*)

Q. 112. *What do we pray for in the fifth petition?*

A. In the fifth petition, which is, *and forgive us our debts as we forgive our debtors,* (*g*) we pray that God for Christ's sake would freely pardon all our sins, (*h*) which we are the rather encouraged to ask, because by his grace we are enabled from the heart to forgive others. (*i*)

Q. 113. *What do we pray for in the sixth petition?*

A. In the sixth petition, which is, *and lead us not into temptation, but deliver us from evil,* (*k*) we pray, that God would either keep us from being tempted to sin, (*l*) or support and deliver us when we are tempted. (*m*

Q. 114. *What doth the conclusion of the Lord's prayer teach us?*

A. The

(*q*) Mat. vi. 9. *r* Psal. lxvii. 1, 2. *s* Psal. lxxxiii. 18. Rom. xi. 36. *t* Mat. vi. 10. *u* Psal. lxviii. 1, 18. *w* Psal. li. 18. Rom. x. 1. *x* 2 Thess. iii. 1. John xvii. 20, 21. *y* Rev. xxii. 20. *z* Mat. vi. 10. *a* Psal. cxix. 34, 36. *b* Luke xxii. 42. Acts xxi. 14. *c* Psal. ciii. 20, 21. *d* Mat. vi. 11. *e* Prov. xxx. 8. *f* Exod. xxiii. 25. 1 Tim. iv. 4, 5. *g* Mat. vi. 12. *h* Psal. li. 1, 2, 7. *i* Mat. vi. 14. Luke xi. 4. *k* Mat. vi. 13. *l* Mat. xxvi. 41. Psal. xix. 13. *m* 2 Cor. xii. 7, 8. 1 Cor. x. 13.

A. The conclufion of the Lord's prayer, which is, *for thine is the kingdom, and the power, and the glory, for ever, Amen,* (n) teacheth us to take our encouragement in prayer from God only, (o) and in our prayers to praife him, afcribing kingdom, power and glory to him; (p) and in teftimony of our defire and affurance to be heard we fay, *Amen.* (q)

(n) Mat. vi. 13. o Dan. ix. 4, 9, 18, 19. p 1 Chron. xxix. 11, 13. q 1 Cor. xiv. 16. Rev. xxii. 20.

FINIS.

The TEN COMMANDMENTS, Exodus xx.

GOD ſpake all theſe words, ſaying, I am the Lord thy God, which have brought thee out of the land of Egypt, out of the houſe of bondage.

I. Thou ſhalt have no other Gods before me.

II. Thou ſhalt not make unto thee any graven image, or any likeneſs of any thing, that is in heaven above, or that is in the earth beneath, or that is in the water under the earth; thou ſhalt not bow down thyſelf to them, nor ſerve them; for I the Lord thy God am a jealous God, viſiting the iniquity of the fathers upon the children unto the third and fourth generation of them that hate me; and ſhewing mercy unto thouſands of them that love me, and keep my commandments.

III. Thou ſhalt not take the name of the Lord thy God in vain; for the Lord will not hold him guiltleſs that taketh his name in vain.

IV. Remember the ſabbath day to keep it holy. Six days ſhalt thou labour, and do all thy work; but the ſeventh day is the ſabbath of the Lord thy God; in it thou ſhalt not do any work, thou, nor thy ſon, nor thy daughter, thy man-ſervant, nor thy maid-ſervant, nor thy cattle, nor thy ſtranger that is within thy gates; for in ſix days the Lord made heaven and earth, the ſea, and all that in them is, and reſted the ſeventh day; wherefore the Lord bleſſed the ſabbath day, and hallowed it.

V. Honour thy father and thy mother, that thy days may be long upon the land, which the Lord thy God giveth thee.

VI. Thou ſhalt not kill.

VII. Thou ſhalt not commit adultery.

VIII. Thou ſhalt not ſteal.

IX. Thou ſhalt not bear falſe witneſs againſt thy neighbour.

X. Thou ſhalt not covet thy neighbour's houſe, thou ſhalt not covet thy neighbour's wife, nor his man-ſervant, nor his maid-ſervant, nor his ox, nor his aſs, nor any thing that is thy neighbour's.

The LORD's PRAYER, Matthew vi.

OUR Father which art in heaven, hallowed be thy name. Thy kingdom come. Thy will be done on earth, as it is in heaven. Give us this day our daily bread. And forgive us our debts, as we forgive our debtors. And lead us not into temptation, but deliver us from evil: For thine is the kingdom, and the power, and the glory, for ever. AMEN.

The CREED.

I BELIEVE in God the Father Almighty, Maker of heaven and earth, and in Jeſus Chriſt his only Son our Lord, who was conceived by the Holy Ghoſt, born of the Virgin Mary, ſuffered under Pontius Pilate, was crucified, dead, and buried: He deſcended into hell *, the third day he roſe again from the dead, he aſcended into heaven, and ſitteth on the right hand of God the Father Almighty; from thence he ſhall come to judge the quick and the dead. I believe in the Holy Ghoſt, the holy catholic church, the communion of ſaints, the forgiveneſs of ſins, the reſurrection of the body, and the life everlaſting. AMEN.

* i. e. *Continued in the ſtate of the dead, and under the power of death, till the third day.*

DIVINE SONGS FOR CHILDREN.

PRAISE *to* GOD *for learning to* READ.

1 THE praiſes of my tongue
  I offer to the Lord,
That I was taught, and learnt ſo young
  To read his holy word.
2 That I am brought to know
  The danger I was in,
By nature and by practice too,
  A wretched ſlave to ſin.
3 That I am led to ſee
  I can do nothing well;
And whither ſhall a ſinner flee
  To ſave himſelf from hell.
4 Dear Lord, this book of thine
  Informs me where to go,
For grace to pardon all my ſin,
  And make me holy too
5 Here I can read and learn,
  How Chriſt the Son of God
Has undertook our great concern,
  Our ranſom coſt his blood.
6 And now he reigns above,
  He ſends his Spirit down,
To ſhew the wonders of his love,
  And make his goſpel known.
7 O may that Spirit teach,
  And make my heart receive
Thoſe truths which all thy ſervants preach,
  And all thy ſaints believe !
8 Then ſhall I praiſe the Lord
  In a more chearful ſtrain,
That I was taught to read his word,
  And have not learnt in vain.

Againſt IDLENESS *and* MISCHIEF.

1 HOW doth the little buſy bee
  Improve each ſhining hour,
And gather honey all the day,
  From every opening flower !

2 How

2 How ſkilfully ſhe builds her cell?
  How neat ſhe ſpreads the wax?
And labours hard to ſtore it well,
  With the ſweet food ſhe makes.
3 In works of labour or of ſkill,
  I would be buſy too:
For Satan finds ſome miſchief ſtill,
  For idle hands to do.
4 In books, or work, or healthful play,
  Let my firſt years be paſt,
That I may give for every day,
  Some good account at laſt.

THE DANGER OF DELAY.

1 WHY ſhould I ſay, 'tis yet too ſoon
  To ſeek for heaven, or think of death?
A flower may fade before 'tis noon,
  And I this day may loſe my breath.
2 If this rebellious heart of mine,
  Deſpiſe the gracious calls of heaven;
I may be hardened in my ſin,
  And never have repentance given.
3 What if the Lord grow wroth and ſwear,
  While I refuſe to read and pray,
That he'll refuſe to lend an ear
  To all my groans another day.
4 What if his dreadful anger burn,
  While I refuſe his offer'd grace,
And all his love to fury turn,
  And ſtrike me dead upon the place?
5 'Tis dangerous to provoke a God,
  His pow'r and vengeance none can tell;
One ſtroke of his almighty rod
  Shall ſend young ſinners quick to hell.
6 Then 'twill for ever be in vain
  To cry for pardon and for grace,
To wiſh I had my time again,
  Or hope to ſee my Maker's face.

I Du

[23]

I Die Daily, *an* Hymn.

GREAT God! thy energy impart,
And write thy leffon on my heart:
Roufe every folemn thought, that I
May ponder what it is to die.
To die—and quit this houfe of clay,
And unembody'd pafs away,
From all things mortal; and have done
With all concerns beneath the fun!
When all my days fhall be fulfill'd,
My character and ftate be feal'd;
My naked fpirit borne to God,
And fentenc'd to its long abode!—
My change is fure, and may be foon,
Each haft'ning minute leads it on:
The fhafts of Death around me fly,
And every day I live—I die.
This, this my ftate, to die, I'd learn;
And make it every day's concern:
Then let which will be laft—(this may)
I'm not unpractis'd in the way.
O may I daily live above
This flefh, this world, and wean my love:
And every day abftract my cares,
From mortals, and their mean affairs.
Spend every day as 'twere the laft,
And time redeem, e'er time is paft;
And all it's precious portions o'er,
Redeemable alas!—no more.
Examine oft the ftate I'm in,
(Whether a ftate of grace or fin,)
If Chrift has mark'd me for his own,
He'll meet me at his Father's throne.
Rejoice my foul in fuch a ftay,
Jefus, the life, the truth, the way:
And trace the footfteps of thy head,
Up where thy heavenly hopes are laid.
He'll guide me to my dying day,
And guide it with a chearful ray,
And to my foul a manfion give,
Where bright Immortals ever live.

BOOKS Printed and Sold, Wholefale and Retail, by R. AITKEN, at Pope's Head, Market-Street.

A NEAT Edition of the Bible, fingle, by the dozen or hundred.

Ditto, Beautifully bound in 2 volumes, in Calf and Morocco bindings.

Dr. Blair's Lectures on Rhetoric and Belles Lettres.

Dr. Croxall's Fables with Cuts.

Dr. Lowth's Englifh Grammar.

Cheap Copy of the Schoolmafter's Affiftant, newly corrected by an experienced Accomptant of Philadelphia.

Dr. Watts's Pfalms.

Watts's Lyric Poems.

A Beautiful Edition of the Scots Verfion of the Pfalms of David, large print with Henry's Notes.

Mourner, or the Afflicted Relieved.

Janneway's Token for Children,

Oeconomy of Human Life.

Dr. Gregory's Legacy to his daughters.

Ladies Friend.

Chefterfield's Principles of Politenefs.

Effay on the Character, Manners and Genius of Women in different ages.

Baptift Confeffion of Faith.

Ditto, Catechifms.

Larger and Shorter Affembly's Catechifms.

Muckarfie's Catechifms *for Children.*

New England and Manfon's Primers.

Dilworth's Spelling Book, by the thoufand, hundred, dozen, or fingle one.

Several hundreds of Newberry's pretty little books for Children.

Writing Paper, Quills, Ink-Powder, Wax and Wafers.

The higheft Price given for

LINEN RAGS.

III. LIST OF DOCTRINAL SERMONS

In 1759 it was, "Agreed and concluded upon, that one of our ministering brethren yearly, and from year to year, who is esteemed qualified in some competent measure, is to preach, at the opening of the Association, upon one of the fundamental articles of the Christian faith, and his subject to be given him by the association the year before."*

Preacher and Alternate	*Subject*	*Date*	*Minutes pages*
Isaac Taylor Abel Morgan	The Being and Attributes of God	1760	79
Abel Morgan Benjamin Griffith	The Divinity and Authority of the Holy Scriptures	1761	81
Benjamin Griffith Morgan Edwards	Doctrine of the Trinity	1762	83
Morgan Edwards David Davis	The State of Man Before and After the Fall	1763	89
John Gano Samuel Jones	The Recovery of Man	1764	91
Samuel Jones Isaac Stellè	Effectual Calling	1765	92
Isaac Stellè Peter P. VanHorne	The Incarnation of the Son of God	1766	95
Peter P. VanHorne Benjamin Miller	Final Perseverance	1767	99
Benjamin Miller John Davis	Imputed Righteousness	1768	102

* A. D. Gillette, editor, *Minutes of the Philadelphia Baptist Association*, p. 79.

IV. LIST OF DOCTRINAL LETTERS

Minister	*Subject treated*	*Date*	*Page*
Abel Morgan	The Scriptures	1774	137
Samuel Jones	The Trinity	1774	146
Abel Morgan	God's Decree (one appointed not given)	1775	153
Robert Kelsay	General Letter	1776	157
Samuel Jones	General Exhortations	1778	162
Samuel Jones	Divine Providence		167
Abel Morgan	Fasting	1779	168
Abel Morgan	Fall of Man	1780	172
Samuel Jones	God's Covenant	1781	178
Oliver Hart	Christ the Mediator	1782	191
Samuel Jones	The Freedom of Man's Will	1783	197
John Gano	Effectual Calling	1784	203
William Rogers	Justification	1785	214
Thomas Ustick	Adoption	1786	224
Peter P. VanHorne	Sanctification	1787	233
David Jones	Saving Faith	1788	242
Burgiss Allison	Repentance unto Life and Salvation	1789	250

"...TO SET THEM IN ORDER :"

Minister	*Subject treated*	*Date*	*Page*
William White	The Office-work of the Holy Spirit	1803	391
Burgiss Allison	Prayer	1804	406
Silas Hough	Brotherly Love	1805	417
William Rogers	Christian Missions	1806	433
William Staughton	What are the Qualifications of a Gospel Minister	1807	440

A. D. Gillette, editor. *Minutes of the Philadelphia Baptist Association,* pp. 135 ff.

V. LETTER TO THE WARREN ASSOCIATION

"The Elders and Messengers of the several Baptist churches met in association at Philadelphia, the 14th, 15th and 16th days of October, 1766. To the Elders and Messengers of the several Baptist Churches of the same faith and order, to meet in Association at Warren, in the Colony of Rhode Island, the 6th day of September, 1767, send greeting.

DEARLY BELOVED BRETHREN:—When we under-stood that you had concluded to meet at the time and place above mentioned, with a view to lay the foundation-stone of an associational building, it gave us peculiar joy, in that it opened to our view a prospect of much good being done. You will perhaps judge this our address to you premature, because as yet you have only an ideal being, as a body by appointment. But if you should call this our forwardness blind zeal, we are still in hopes you will not forget that our embracing the first opportunity of commencing Christian fellowship and acquaintance with you, affords the strongest evidence of our approbation of your present meeting, and how fond we should be of mutual correspondence between us in this way.

A long course of experience and observation has taught us to have the highest sense of the advantages which accrue from associations; nor indeed does the nature or thing speak any other language. For, as particular members are collected together and united in one body, which we call a particular church, to answer those ends and purposes which could not be accomplished by any single member, so a collection and union of churches into one associational body may easily be conceived capable of answering those still greater purposes which any particular church could not be equal to. And by the same reason, a union of associations will still increase the body in weight and strength, and make it good that a threefold cord is not easily broken.

Great, dear brethren, is the design of you meeting; great is the work which lies before you. You will need the guidance and influence of the Divine Spirit, as well as the exertion of all prudence and wisdom. It is therefore our most ardent prayer that you may meet in love, that peace and unanimity may subsist among you during your consultations, that you may be animated with zeal for the glory of God, and directed to advise and determine what may most conduce to promote the Redeemer's kingdom.

From considering the divided state of our Baptist churches in your quarter, we foresee that difficulties may arise, such as may call for the exercise of the greatest tenderness and moderation, that if haply, through the blessing of God on your endeavors, those lesser differences may subside, and a more general union commence.

As touching our consultations at this our meeting, the minutes of our proceedings (a printed copy whereof we shall herewith enclose) will inform you; and if in anything further you should be desirous of information with regard to us, we refer you to our reverend and beloved brethren Morgan Edwards, John Gano, and Samuel Jones, who, as our representative delegates, will present you with this our letter, and whom we recommend to Christian fellowship with you.

And now, dear brethren, farewell. May the Lord bless and direct you in all things, and grant that we may all hereafter form one general assembly at his right hand, through infinite riches of free grace in Christ Jesus our Lord.

Signed by order and in behalf of the Association, by

BENJAMIN MILLER, Moderator.
SAMUEL JONES, Clerk."*

---

* Spencer, David. The Early Baptists of Philadelphia. (Philadelphia: William Syckelmoore, 1877). pp. 95-96.

VI. MORGAN EDWARDS' PLAN OF UNION

"By the said union is meant, an union of individuals into churches so that no baptized believers abide loose and scattered (like the stones of the sanctuary in the book of Lamentation) as is now the case in some places; also, an union of those churches (and of other churches which have hitherto stood by themselves) into associations in proper vicinities, which associations may be multiplied so as to have one in every province; and likewise, an union of those associations (like that of Ketokton and Warren) to the association. of Philadelphia, which, from its situation, must ever be central to the whole—By the forementioned means of intercourse are to be understood, letters and messengers from the churches to their respective associations, and from those associations to their common center; and from the center back to the associations, and thence to the churches, and so to individuals. These means will not only be useful for receiving and returning intelligence, mutual advice, help but also for "knitting together" the several parts of the visible Baptist church on this continent, as the parts of the natural body are by "joints and bands." Gal. ii:19. This project is not a new one, but was begun in the year 1765 when the churches to the west of Philadelphia formed themselves into an association at Ketokton in Virginia; and was furthered in 1767 when the churches to the east of Philadelphia did the same at Warren in Rhode Island government, both adopting the Philadelphian plan and engaging to use the means of union and intercourse before described. The thing is practicable, as appears by five years trial; and withal, most beneficial, as might be proved by variety of examples. What remains is only to perfect what has been begun. In order to which the following things have been judged requisite.

1. That the association of Philadelphia be embodied by charter: and that one person from every provincial association be made a member of that enchartered body;

2. Then an able preacher be appointed to visit all the churches in the character and office of any EVANGELIST; and a sufficient fund raised to defray his expenses. Such a fund was set on foot in Philadelphia in 1766, and is increasing every year;

3. That the nature of associations among the Baptists be made public. Something of the kind was attempted in 1769 under the title of THE SENTIMENTS AND PLAN OF THE WARREN ASSOCIATION; wherein is shown that they are only ADVISORY COUNCILS, disclaiming all jurisdiction and power and every thing else which may clash with the rights of particular churches or those of private judgment; and herein they differ from all assemblies of the kind known by the same or other names;

4. That all the baptist churches from Nova Scotia to Georgia be made sufficiently known one to another; for it hath been found by experience that a want of this kind of knowledge hath much retarded the proposed design. To remedy which (as hinted before) is the end of publishing the following little volumes.* And it is presumed the publication will be found adequate to the design; and will also preserve some anecdotes, chronologies and facts which otherwise would have perished with the loose papers from which many were taken, or with the death of ancient people who communicated others from memory. The publisher well knows that the work wants all the apologies he can make both for it, and the price. As to the last he only takes leave to observe that he has not struck off many copies, but just enow [sic] to furnish every Baptist church with [a] few. Had he intended to sell to every one that [would] buy he would have enlarged the edition and so would have reduced the price. If the books should not be valuable they will be scarce. As to apologies for the work itself he will not attempt any, being firmly of opinion that if he should lose any reputation by it he cannot lose it in a better way than in endeavoring to promote the baptist interest; which, in his judgment, is the interest of Christ above any in christendom. Whoever finds fault with the performance will thereby intimate that he is able to supply its defects and correct its errors; and if he will do both or either the author would be well pleased should every reader be a fault-finder.

5. Lastly, that the terms of the proposed union should be so general as not to preclude any baptist church of fair character, though differing from others in unessential points of faith or order. Practising believer's -baptism is our denominating article. If this be

---

* his *Materials Towards a History of the American Baptists.*

taken away we shall differ from the Independents in no point whatsoever. And the one thing which distinguishes us from every sect of christians, and made, and keeps us a separate and distinct body of people is, one would think, a sufficient ground of union among ourselves, excepting only where this 'truth is held in unrighteousness'."*

* Morgan Edwards. *Materials Towards History of the Baptists In Pennsylvania, Both British and German.* (Philadelphia: Joseph Crukshank and Isaac Collins, 1770). Facsimile reprint by the Regular Baptist Publishing, 1998.

VII. THE POWER AND DUTY OF AN ASSOCIATION

"The Association unanimously approved and agreed to an essay of Benjamin Griffith, respecting the power and duty of an Association, to be inserted in the Association book.

* * * * * * * *

At our annual Association, met September the 19th, 1749, an essay on the power and duty of an Association of churches, was proposed, as above hinted, to the consideration of the Association; and the same, upon mature deliberation, was approved and subscribed by the whole house; and the contents of the same was ordered to be transcribed as the judgment of the Association, in order to be inserted in the Association book, to the end and purpose that is may appear what power an Association of churches hath, and what duty is incumbent on an Association; and prevent the contempt with which some are ready to treat such an assembly, and also to prevent any future generation from claiming more power than they ought—lording over the churches."[1]

"An Essay on the Power and Duty of an Association, originally drawn up by the Rev. Mr. Benjamin Griffith, of Montgomery, Pennsylvania: afterward, by the advice and consent of the Association meeting in Philadelphia, inserted in their Association Book—And by the Association, met for the first time in Charleston, October 21st, 1751, concluded to be inserted in their Book, as judging it most expressive of the Power and Duty of an Association; and worthy to be adhered to by all our future Associations."[2]

---

[1] A. D. Gillette, editor. *Minutes of the Philadelphia Baptist Association.* (Philadelphia: American Baptist Publication Society, 1851), p. 60.

[2] Written by Basil Manly, Sr. in the margin of the original Minute Book of the Charleston Association. Furman University Collections.

"...TO SET THEM IN ORDER :"

An Essay On The

Power And Duty Of An Association (1744)

by Benjamin Griffith

"That an Association is not a superior judicature, having such superior power over the churches concerned; but that each particular church hath a complete power and authority from Jesus Christ, to administer all gospel ordinances, provided they have sufficiency of officers duly qualified, or that they be supplied by the officers of another sister church or churches, as baptism, and the Lord's supper, &c.; and to receive in and cast out, and also to try and ordain their own officers, and to exercise every part of gospel discipline and church government, independent of any other church or assembly whatever.

And that several such independent churches, where Providence gives them their situation convenient, may, and ought, for their mutual strength, counsel, and other valuable advantages, by their voluntary and free consent, to enter into an agreement and confederation, as is hinted in our printed Narrative of discipline, page 59, 60, 61.

Such churches there must be agreeing in doctrine and practice, and independent in their authority and church power, before they can enter into a confederation, as aforesaid, and choose delegates or representative, to associate together; and thus the several independent churches being the constituents, the association, council or assembly of their delegates, when assembled, is not to be deemed a superior judicature, as having a superintendency over the churches, but subservient to the churches, in what may concern all the churches in general, or any one church in particular; and, though no power can regularly arise above its fountain from where it rises, yet we are of opinion, that an Association of the delegates of associate churches have a very considerable power in their hands, respecting those churches in their confederation; for if the agreement of several distinct churches, in sound doctrine and regular practice, be the first motive, ground, and foundation or basis of their confederation, then it must naturally follow, that a defection in doctrine or practice in any church, in such confederation, or any party in any such church, is ground sufficient for an Association to withdraw from such a church or party so deviating or making defection, and to exclude such from them in some formal manner, and to advertise all the churches in confederation thereof, in order that every church in confederation may withdraw from such in all acts of church communion, to the end they may be ashamed, and that all the churches may discountenance such, and bear testimony against the defection.

Such withdrawing from a defective or disorderly church, or that ought to be towards a delinquent church, is such as ariseth from their voluntary confederation aforesaid, and not only from the general duty that is incumbent on all orthodox persons, and churches to do, where no such confederation is entered into, as 2 Cor. vi. 16, 17. Now from that general duty to withdraw from defective persons or churches, there can no more be done, than to desist from such acts of fellowship as subsisted before the withdrawing, which is merely negative, and in no wise any thing positive. Churches, as they are pillars of truth, may, and ought to endeavor to promote truth among others also; which endeavors, if they prove fruitless, as they are but *mystico modo,* they may be withdrawn; the withdrawing, therefore, must be accordingly; which is only to cease from future endeavors, leaving the objects as they were or are. But if there be a confederation and incorporation, by mutual and voluntary consent, as the Association of churches must and ought to be, then something positive may and ought to be done; and, though an Association ought not to assume a power to excommunicate or deliver a defective or disorderly church to Satan, as some do claim, yet it is a power sufficient to exclude the delegates of a defective or disorderly church from an Association, and to refuse their presence a their consultations, and to advise all the churches in confederation to do so too. A godly man may, and ought to withdraw, not only from a heathen, but from such as have the form of godliness, if they appear to want the power of it, 2 Timothy iii:5, by the same parity of reason the saints, in what capacity soever they may be considered, may withdraw from defective or disorderly churches or persons; but excommunicate they cannot, there being no institution to authorize them so to do. But in the capacity of a congregational church, dealing with her own members, an Association, then, of the delegates of associate churches, may exclude and withdraw from defective and unsound or disorderly churches or persons, in manner abovesaid; and this will appear regular and justifiable by the light and law of nature, as is apparent in the conduct and practice of all regular civil and political corporations and confederations whatsoever; who all of them have certain rules to exclude delinquents from their societies, as well as for others to accede thereunto.

We judge those things in the 15th chapter of the Acts of the Apostles to be imitable by an Association, viz.: 1st, their disowning of the erroneous and judaising teachers, saying, to whom we gave no such commandments, verse 24; 2dly, the sending delegated persons of their own number, with Paul and Barnabas, to support their sentence in the place where the debate sprung up, verse 25; and a third thing followed in consequence thereof, viz., a delivering of the decrees to the other churches, to be observed as well as the church of Antioch, Chap. xvi.4. Consistent therewith, the practice of after ages is found to be; when, because they had no council, synod, or association to convene, of course they called a council, in order to make head against any error or disorders, when in a particular church, such things grew too big for a particular church peaceably to determine, as the case about circumcision was at Antioch. In such cases all the churches were looked upon as one church, and all the bishops as universal, because of the unity of the faith and conformity of practice which ought to be in the churches of Christ; though in all other cases, the several distinct churches acted independent of each other, as Cyprian relates the practice of his time, viz.: That the bishops were so united in one body, that if any one of the body broached any heresy, or began to waste and tear the flock of Christ, all the rest came immediately to its rescue. Cyprian, cited by Bingham, book 2, page 101. And the same author observes, that they disowned the faulty, and advertised all the churches of the same. And Mr. Crosby relates, that an Association in London did disown a certain disorderly church in London, and did caution all the churches they were related to, not to countenance them in any way, nor to suffer their members to frequent their meetings; and thus an Association may disown and withdraw from a defective or disorderly church, and advise the churches related to them to withdraw from, and to discountenance such as aforesaid, without exceeding the bounds of their power.

And further, that an Association of the delegates of confederate churches may doctrinally declare any person or party in a church, who are defective in principles or disorderly in practice, to be censurable, when the affair comes under their cognizance, and without exceeding the bounds of their power and duty, to advise the church that such belong unto, how to deal with such, according to the rule of gospel discipline; and also to strengthen such a church, and assist her, if need be, by sending able men of their own number to help the church in executing the power vested in her by the ordinance of Jesus Christ, and to stand by her, and to defend her against the insults of such offending persons or parties."*

---

* A. D. Gillette, editor. *Minutes of the Philadelphia Baptist Association,* pp. 60-63.

VIII. SENTIMENTS TOUCHING AN ASSOCIATION

Sentiments of the churches seeking to Form the Warren Asso-iation, as Modified by James Manning, and adopted in 1769.

"1. That such a combination of churches is not only prudent, but useful, as has appeared even in America by the experience of upwards of sixty years. Some of the uses of it are, union and communion among themselves; maintaining more effectually the order and faith once delivered to the saints; having advice in cases of doubt, and help in distress; being more able to promote the good of the cause, and becoming important in the eye of the civil powers, as has already appeared in many instances on this continent.

2. That such an association is consistent with the independency and power of particular churches, because it pretends to be no other than an *advisory council,* utterly disclaiming superiority, jurisdiction, coercive right, and infallibility.

3. That any association should consist of men knowing and judicious, particularly in the Scriptures. The reasons are obvious: such men are the fittest to represent communities who profess the Scriptures to be the only rule of faith and practice in religious matters, and who expect that every advice, opinion, or direction they receive from an association be Scriptural. They should be skilled and expert in the laws of their God, as counselors are in the laws of the land; for that is the ground of the church's application to them."*

---

* Reuben A. Guild, *Early History of Brown University, Including the Life, Times, and correspondence of President Manning, 1756-1791.* (Providence, R. I.: Snow & Farnham, 1897), p. 76. [For the full text of thc *Plan of the [Warren] Association,* as adapted and modified by James Manning from the Philadelphia model, see Guild, pp. 77-78.—Editor]

Horatio Gates Jones, Jr. (1822-1893), author of the following church histories, was elected clerk for the Philadelphia Baptist Association in 1858, retaining the office for 15 years, when he was then chosen as moderator. He was a member of the Lower Merion Baptist Church and was very active in the various historical societies with which he was connected. Portrait from *Centennial Memorial of the Roxborough Baptist Church, 1789-1899*. (Philadelphia: National Baptist, 1890), p. 8.

"...TO SET THEM IN ORDER :"

HISTORICAL SKETCH

OF THE

LOWER DUBLIN

(OR PENNEPEK)

BAPTIST CHURCH,

Philadelphia, Pa.,

WITH NOTICES OF THE PASTORS, &c.

BY

HORATIO GATES JONES,

Of Philadelphia.

—o—

MORRISANIA, N. Y.
1869.

PREFATORY NOTE.

This brief historical Sketch of the Lower Dublin Baptist Church was prepared, several years since, at the special request of the Church, by which I was furnished with their ancient records. It was designed, at the time. for publication in the Minutes of the Philadelphia Baptist Association, and hence was more of a sketch than a history. When desired to edit the August number (1868) of THE HISTORICAL MAGAZINE, by Mr. Henry B. Dawson, I availed myself of the opportunity thus presented to give to the public the sketch referred to, with considerable corrections and additions. I regret that want of time has prevented a fuller and more complete history of this venerable Church of God.

For the Portrait of Dr. SAMUEL JONES, which accompanies this, I am indebted to the liberality of Mr. William P. Wilstach, of Philadelphia, who married a grand-daughter of Doctor Jones. H. G. J.

PHILADELPHIA, July, 1869.

To the

VENERABLE AND REVEREND

DAVID BENEDICT, D. D.,

Of Pawtucket, Rhode Island,

THE LABORIOUS AND SELF-SACRIFICING
HISTORIAN OF THE BAPTISTS OF AMERICA,

whoſe earlier writings were the ſtudies of my youthful days, and whoſe friendſhip in later life is moſt highly cheriſhed, this brief ſketch of the Oldeſt Baptiſt Church in Pennyſlvania, is reſpectfully dedicated, in token of admiration for his many virtues and his great hiſtorical acquirements,

By his friend,

THE AUTHOR.

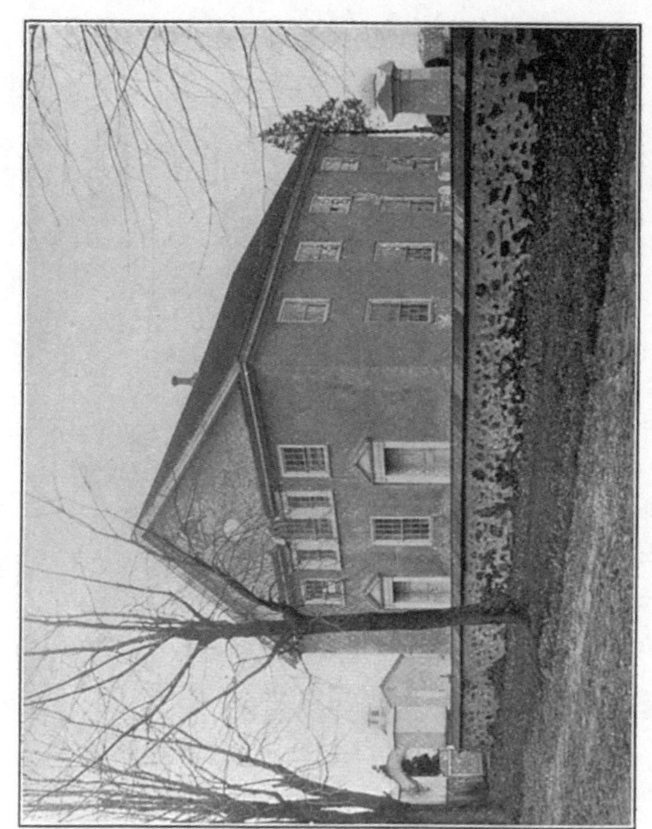

The Lower Dublin Baptist Church as it appeared in 1898. Built in 1805 this structure is still standing and with the exception of electricity for lighting, remains very much as it was originally. *See also page 9*. The Pennepek congregation was the mother church for Baptists in the Middle Atlantic States of Pennsylvania, New Jersey, New York and Delaware much like the First Baptist Church of Providence, Rhode Island was in the New England States.

"...TO SET THEM IN ORDER :"

CONTENTS.

The Barbados Storehouse, which was located at the northwest corner of Second and Chestnut streets in Philadelphia, was the scene of early Baptist preaching in the city. Beginning in April of 1695 John Watts, pastor of the Lower Dublin Church, preached twice a month here, and on December 11, 1698 what later became the First Baptist Church was organized.

PENNEPEK CHURCH.

I.—SKETCH OF THE CHURCH.

The religious Freedom which William Penn, the Founder of Pennsylvania, proclaimed as one of the organic Laws of his Colony, attracted, at the very outset, from Great Britain and also from the Continent—chiefly from Germany—persons of every religious faith. They were assured, from the well-known character of that disinterested philanthropist, who had been imprisoned for his adhesion to the doctrines of the Quakers, that they would find in his Colony protection from all persecution. Hence, we find Quakers and Church-men, Baptists and Presbyterians, and Roman Catholics, and even the strange ascetic Pietists of Germany, among the earliest settlers of Pennsylvania, and all living together in harmony.

This same plan had been tested nearly half a century before, by Roger Williams, in his Colony of Rhode Island, under far more disadvantageous circumstances, and where he had advocated the grand doctrine of "soul-liberty," at a time when such a principle was regarded as one of the worst forms of heresy, and the maintenance of which was one cause of his expulsion by the authorities of Massachusetts.

Both Williams and Penn had been sorely persecuted for conscience sake; and both were, therefore, the better able to appreciate the importance of allowing every one to think and act as he thought right in matters relating to religious concerns. Penn, at the beginning of his legislation in Pennsylvania, had passed by the Assembly, the "Great Law," the first Section of which had regard to religious matters; and, among other things, provided that no person then or thereafter living in the Province, shall "at any time be compelled to frequent or maintain any religious worship, place, or ministry, "whatever, contrary to his or her mind, but shall "freely and fully enjoy his or her Christian liberty in that respect, without any interruption "or reflection; and, if any person shall abuse "or deride any other for his or her different persuasion and practice, in matter of religion, "such shall be looked upon as a disturber of the "peace, and be punished accordingly."*

It is creditable to both of these noble men —living at the time they did—when religious persecution seemed to be the very essence of orthodoxy in most Churches, that although entrusted, in the organization of their Colonies, with vast powers, they incorporated in their Charters the doctrine of Religious Freedom, and never permitted any of their fellow-colonists to suffer for their religious tenets.

This principle, for which Williams, in New England, and Penn, in Great Britain and Pennsylvania, contended so nobly, has at last become universal in this country, and one of its features is incorporated in the Constitution of the United States.

Let the names of these men, who were once

---

* Janney's *Life of Penn*, 211.

3

despised as heretics and fanatics, be written in letters of gold, for their noble advocacy of a doctrine which is now so dear to every citizen of our great Republic.

The first Baptist clergyman in Pennsylvania of whom there is any account was the Rev. Thomas Dungan, who settled at a place called Cold Spring, between Bristol and Trenton, in Bucks County. The Rev. Morgan Edwards says,* ' Of this venerable father I can learn "no more than that he came from Rhode "Island about the year 1684; that he and his fa- " mily settled at Cold Spring, where he gathered " a Church, of which nothing remains [*in 1770*] " but a grave-yard and the names of the families " which belonged to it, viz, the *Dungans*, *Gard-* "*ners*, *Woods*, *Doyls*, &c; that he died in " 1688, and was buried in said grave-yard."

This small Church disbanded in the year 1702; and its members either moved to other places or became connected with the Church whose history is now to be sketched.

The Lower Dublin, or *Pennepek*, Baptist Church —the first permanent Church of that faith in Pennsylvania, is situate in what was formerly the Township of Lower Dublin, now forming part of the Twenty-third Ward of the City of Philadelphia, about eleven miles North-westwardly from Independence Hall. At first it was called the *Pemmepeka*,† *Pennepek*, or *Pennypack* Church, from a small stream of water bearing that name, which runs near the Meeting-house; and it was so designated in the *Min-*

---

* *History of American Baptists*, i, 10, Note.

† This is an Indian word, and, according to Heckewelder, in the language of the Lenni Lenape, or Delawares, signifies "*A pond, lake or bay; water not having a current.*" *Bulletin Historical Society of Pennsylvania.* Vol. i. No. II, p. 122.

utes of the Philadelphia Baptist Association, until the year 1794.

This Church may be regarded as the mother Church of the Baptists in Pennsylvania, New Jersey, New York, Delaware and Maryland, as its early Pastors were accustomed to preach the Gospel in all of these Colonies; and hence its early history is of more than ordinary interest. The Records have been carefully preserved, and are contained in a large folio volume, which is still used for the purpose of keeping the Minutes of the Church-meetings. The Records state that "By the good Providence of " God, there came certain persons out of Rad- " norshire in Wales, over into this Province of " Pennsilvania, and settled in the Township of " Dublin, in the County of Philadelphia, viz: " *John Eatton*, *George Eatton* and *Jane*, his " wife, *Samuel Jones*, and *Sarah Eatton*, who " had all been Baptized upon Confession " of Faith and Received into the Commun- " ion of the Church of Christ meeting in " the Parishes of Llandewi and Nantmel, in " Radnorshire, Henry Gregory being Chief pas- " tor. Also *John Baker* who had been Baptized " and a member of a congregation of Baptized " believers in Kilkenny, in Ireland, Christopher " Blackwell, pastor, was by the providence of " God settled in the Township aforesaid.

"In the year 1687 there came one *Samuel* " *Vaus* out of England, and settled near the " aforesaid Township and went under the De- " nomination of a Baptist and was so taken to " be."

These parties were settled in Lower Dublin, as early as 1687. The previous year, Elias Keach, a son of the famous London divine, the Rev. Benjamin Keach, an eminent author among the

English Baptists, came to America. He was a gay, wild, thoughtless young man; and was converted in a most extraordinary manner.

Morgan Edwards gives the following account of Mr. Keach: " On his landing he dressed in " black, and wore a band in order to pass for a " Minister. The project succeeded to his wishes, " and many people resorted to hear the young " London divine. He performed well enough " till he had advanced pretty far in the sermon. " Then, stopping short, he looked like a man as- " tonished. The audience concluded he had " been seized with a sudden disorder; but, on " asking what the matter was, received from him " a confession of the imposture with tears in his " eyes, and much trembling. Great was his dis- " tress, though it ended happily; for from this " time he dated his conversion. He heard there " was a Baptist Minister at Cold Spring, in " Bucks County, to whom he repaired to seek " counsel and comfort, and by him was bap- " tized."*

Mr. Keach at once devoted himself to preaching the Gospel; and, in 1687, visited the region of Pennepek, and preached as opportunity offered. His labors were greatly blessed; and on the twenty-first of November, 1687, he baptized four persons, viz: Joseph Ashton and Jane Ashton, his wife, William Fisher, and John Watts. These, so far as is known, were the first persons ever baptized in Lower Dublin Township.

In the month of January, $168\frac{7}{8}$, the following persons organized themselves into the Pennepek Baptist Church, viz: Rev. Elias Keach, John Eaton, George Eaton and Jane, his wife, Sarah

---

* Edwards's *History of American Baptists.* i, 9–10.

6

Eaton, Samuel Jones, John Baker, Samuel Vaus, Joseph Ashton and Jane, his wife, William Fisher, and John Watts.

The church book gives the following account of its constitution:

"Sometime after, about the 11th month, "[*January, 168$\frac{7}{8}$*], by the advice of Elias "Keach and with the aforesaid Baptized per-"sons consent, a day was set apart to seek God "by fasting and prayer, in order to form our-"selves into a Church state. Whereupon Elias "Keach was accepted and received for our Pas-"tor and we sat down in communion at the "Lord's table. Also at the same time Samuel "Vaus was chosen and by Elias Keach with "laying on of hands, ordained to be a Dea-"con."

Such was the founding of what may properly be regarded as the first Baptist Church in Pennsylvania. There was no pomp or ceremony; there were no white-robed priests; no letters permissory from Archbishop or other prelate. There was only the plain apostolic giving of themselves to each other and the Lord. And the little band of disciples, thus organized as a Christian Church, has continued to prosper and increase, and for a period of one hundred and eighty-one years has maintained an active and visible existence.

Mr. Keach, with that earnest zeal which characterized most of the early Baptist Ministers, travelled extensively and preached at the Falls of the Delaware, (Trenton), Philadelphia, Chester, Burlington, Middletown, Cohansey, Salem and other places, baptizing such as gave evidence of true piety. These, with such other Baptists as he found among the new emigrants, joined the Pennepek Church, so that, at one time, all the Baptists of Pennsylvania and New Jersey, were regarded as general members of this Church.

For the convenience of the brethren residing in the places named, the Church appointed "General Meetings," so that opportunity was offered for closer acquaintance, communion, and fellowship. In regard to this practice, the Records state, as follows: "But however when "Elias Keach was with us, we commonly acted "as a particular Church, and at the general "meetings all the Brethren from all parts of the "Provinces, were desired generally to come to-"gether to hear the word &c and to commu-"nicate at the Lord's Table. These general "meetings were appointed twice in the year; "once in the spring, about the 3d month, "[*May*], and one time in the fall, about the "8th month. [*October*]. In the Spring at Sa-"lem and in the fall at Dublin or Burlington. "But it is to be noted that in these times of be-"ginning, we had not opportunity to be formed "into particular Churches, for want of persons "fitly qualified to oversee a Church or to carry "on the work of the ministry."

It would seem that at these General Meetings, even when held out of Pennsylvania, ordinary Church business was transacted, for, at Salem, New Jersey, in May, 1688, Joseph Ashton was chosen a Deacon of the Church at Pennepek, and was ordained there, by Elias Keach, with laying on of hands.

Mr. Edwards remarks, "They were all one "Church and Pennepek the centre of union, "where as many as could, met to celebrate the "memorials of Christ's death; and for the sake "of distant members, they administered the or-"dinance quarterly at Burlington, Cohansey,

"Salem and Philadelphia; which quarterly "meetings have since transformed into three "yearly meetings and an Association."*

As the number of baptized believers increased in places at a distance from Pennepek, it was considered best to form separate Churches; and, hence, in New Jersey, the following were constituted, viz: Middletown, in the Winter of 1688; Piscataqua, in the Spring of 1689; and Cohansey, in the Spring of 1690; while, in the City of Philadelphia, no attempt was made by the few Baptists there, to form a Church until the second Sunday in December, in 1698, when four persons who had been baptized, in 1697, by John Watts, and five others—among them the famous John Holme, Esq.—who had been baptized in Great Britain, met in a house on *Barbadoes Lot*, at the North-west corner of Second and Chestnut-streets, and, in the words of Edwards, "did coalesce into a Church for the communion of Saints, having Rev. John Watts to their "assistance."

It seems, however, from the Pennepek Church Book, that in the Spring of 1688, Elias Keach held several meetings and preached several sermons in Philadelphia; but as no mention is made of his having baptized, it is reasonable to suppose that the first baptism was by John Watts.

As Elias Keach was at first the only Baptist Minister in Pennsylvania, the brethren at Pennepek were often left without any preacher, as Mr. Keach was compelled to visit the numerous branches of the Church, in Pennsylvania and New Jersey. In such emergencies, the Church held meetings for prayer and exhortation, then,

* History of American Baptists, i, 8.

as now, called "meetings for conference." Originating as they did in Pennsylvania with the Church at Pennepek, it may not be uninteresting to give the following account of their commencement, as detailed in the Church Records, viz:—"About the same time, that every Brother "might have opportunity to exercise what Gifts "God had been pleased to bestow upon them, "for the edification of one another, with the ad- "vice and consent of our said pastor, we ap- "pointed meetings for Conference, to be held "on the fifth days of the week in which this or- "der was observed. *First*, That at one meeting, "sometimes one Brother and then another and "so round, used to make choice of some place "of holy scripture as they pleased, to be con- "ferred upon the next time, which in the mean- "while was left to consideration. *Secondly*, "When the appointed time came, the Brethren "being assembled, the usual custom observed "was, for one Brother and then another to be- "gin with prayer and then to deliver their "judgment on the text appointed and our Pas- "tor concluded. The Brethren who used most "commonly and constantly to speak at these "meetings were Samuel Jones and John "Watts."

These exercises had the effect to bring forward such brethren as possessed gifts for prayer and exhortation, and to them the Church was accustomed to look for assistance, when Mr. Keach was absent, which, as stated, was often the case. On one occasion during his absence, the Church formally agreed that John Watts should administer the ordinance of baptism, which he accordingly did; but the candidate was not received into the Church, and soon after she became a Quaker. The administration of the

Lord's Supper was however left to Mr. Keach, as his proper work.

In the year 1689, difficulties having occurred about Laying on of hands in the reception of members after baptism, Predestination, and other matters, the pastorate of Mr. Keach was brought to a close; and John Watts was chosen in his stead, being assisted by Samuel Jones, Evan Morgan and Thomas Wood, thus following, as will be observed, the custom which obtained in the apostolic times.

It seemed to be a common event, in those days of primitive simplicity, to have in the Pennepek Church, a number of gifted brethren on trial, so that the Church was seldom at a loss for a Pastor. Meetings in the week were also regularly kept up; and these "gifted brethren" were accustomed to officiate on such occasions.

Thus this little band of disciples continued to prosper; and, in the year 1700, their number, had increased to forty-six.

Among them, as in Churches at the present day, were some troublesome and perverse spirits, tinctured with peculiar views about Gospel truth. The chief one at Pennepek, was a certain *William Davis*, who at first was a Quaker preacher, then a Keithian, and finally a Baptist. He held *Sabellian* views, which he endeavored to inculcate; but the Church, after several admonitions, were compelled to exclude him. He afterwards became a Seventh-day Baptist. To counteract the errors of Davis, and also other heresies, and to instruct the children of the members in the true Faith, John Watts was requested by the Church to prepare a Catechism, "such a one as might "also be of use for a Confession of our faith." This he did, and it was published in the year 1700.

11

The Church, at first, was wont to meet at the houses of different members; but, about the year 1707, a house of worship was erected on a lot near the Burial-ground, the gift of Samuel Jones, one of the early Pastors. In subsequent years, additional land was presented to the Church, and some was bought, so that now there is a fine glebe attached to the building, on which sheds are erected for the accommodation of those driving to Church. There is also a grove of noble oak-trees, affording delightful shade in Summer. The Meeting-house is situated in the enclosure devoted to the Burial-ground; and is separated from the grove by a public road.

The first Meeting-house was twenty-five feet square; but, in 1760, it was repaired, and, in 1770, there was a neat stone building erected, thirty-three feet by thirty, with pews, galleries, and a stove, which latter accommodation was not to be found in all the early Meeting-houses. The present edifice was built in 1805.

The Faith of this ancient Church has always been that of the New Testament, as set forth in the "Philadelphia Confession," which was adopted by the Association, in 1742.

For some years, the ancient rite of Confirmation, or the Laying on of hands on newly baptized members, on being received into the Church, was practised; but it was afterwards regarded as a matter of indifference, and hence was discontinued. This question of "Laying on of "hands" occasioned sharp disputes between them and a Welsh emigrant Church, which came from Wales, in 1701, and settled near Pennepek. The Welshmen insisted on the rite as of great importance; but finding they were opposed, in 1703, the major part of them purchased

12

a tract of land in Newcastle-county, Delaware, whither they removed and settled—and named the place "Welsh Tract." The Church assumed the name, and is still known as "The Welsh "Tract Baptist Church."

Pennepek Church also had, for many years, *Ruling Elders*—a species of officers which most of the early Baptist Churches of Pennsylvania, New Jersey, and Delaware had among them, as the early records show.

The Minutes of the Church contain the following action on the subject of Ruling Elders:

"1715. June 19th. A proposal was made for "having Ruling Elders in ye Church; left to "consideration till next Quarterly Meeting."

"1726. June 17th. At same time ye Church "called forth brother John Holme to take upon "him the office of a ruling elder, to which he "answered he thought himself not fitly qualified "for a place of charge and weight y^t y^t place "did require."

"1747. June 18. Bro. Vansandt was called "to the office of Ruling Elder by prayer and "laying on of hands."

When this office was discontinued does not appear; but it is certain that it was not used in 1770. The latest mention of such is in a manuscript List of Members, for 1763, when William Marshall is named as the Ruling Elder.

As a mother Church, numerous branches have sprung from Pennepek, and maintain, even to the present day, in their ecclesiastical relations, an active and prominent position. Among these were those of Middletown, Piscataqua, Cohansey, Burlington, and Salem, in New Jersey; and Philadelphia, Montgomery, Southampton, Brandywine, Frankford, and Holmesburg, in Pennsylvania.

13

As is well-known, *The Philadelphia Baptist Association* originated under the auspices of this Church; and to its Records we are chiefly indebted for a knowledge of the date of the organization of the Association. The "Yearly "Meetings," which were held with the different Churches, were chiefly for preaching—answering to the "protracted meetings" or "convoca-"tions" of the present day. They did not consist of Delegates or Messengers from particular Churches, but all who had leisure and were so inclined gathered together and spent several days in acts of religious worship. The brethren were thus made acquainted with each other; the spirit of piety was increased; the ungodly were often converted; and fraternal intercourse was greatly promoted. As the Churches increased in number, and also in membership, various questions arose both as to matters of Faith and Discipline. It was of course desirable for all the Churches to have the same Rules and to act in unity; and yet each Baptist Church being independent of all others, it was apparent to the Pastors and Brethren, that some general meeting was necessary where such questions could be freely and amicably discussed, and where counsel and advice could be given. Hence, it was proposed to *associate*, once a year, for this purpose, by representatives from the several Churches. This annual meeting was therefore designated by the name of an "Association;" but it had no power or authority to bind the Churches composing it, and from the very first was regarded as an *Advisory Council*—and such is the character of all the Baptist Associations in America, as well as in all other parts of the world.

The Church Records of Pennepek contain

14

the following items concerning the formation of the Philadelphia Association, which are deemed of sufficient importance to form part of this sketch.

"1706. At our yearly meeting held at Phila-"delphia the 21, 22 and 23d days of September, "it was agreed by our brethren from Middleton, "in East Jersey and us, that there should be a "meeting held yearly for as many of us as could "meet those with them at Middleton, with them "that could come there from other parts, to be "held on the third Lord's day in May."

"1707. Before our generall meeting held at "Philadelphia in the 7th month [*September*] "1707, it was concluded by the severall congre-"gations of our Judgment, to make choyse of "some particular Brethren such as they thought "most capable in every congregation & those "to meet at the yearly Meeting, to consult about "such things as were wanting in the Church "and set them in order, and those brethren met "at the said yearly meeting which begun the "27th of the 7th month, on the 7th day of the "week, agreed that the said meeting should "be continued till the third day of the week, "in the work of the publick ministry and by "whom the publick ministry of the word should "be carried on."

The Churches thus uniting in an Association —the first formed in America—were the *Pennepek*, in Pennsylvania, the *Welsh Tract*, in Delaware, the *Middletown*, *Piscataqua* and *Cohansey* in New Jersey.

From that day until the present time, the Pennepek, or Lower Dublin, Church has been a member of the Philadelphia Association, except during a period of fourteen years. After a connection of one hundred and twenty years, on

15

the twenty-ninth of October, 1827, she withdrew from the Association, and for five years remained unassociated; but, in 1832, she formed one of the constituents of The "Central Union Association," which was organized in the First Baptist Chnrch of Philadelphia, on the thirty-first of July, in that year. On the fourth of October, 1841, she withdrew from that body and united again with the Philadelphia Association, and is at the present time, the only one of the original Churches connected with the Association.

The increase in membership by baptism was at first very gradual. Prior to the year 1800, the highest number baptized in one year, judging from the records, was six.

From 1798 to 1804—a period of six years—there were no baptisms, but the services of the sanctuary were faithfully kept up under the pastoral care of Dr. Samuel Jones. In the latter year, a glorious work of grace manifested itself and a revival commenced, continuing until the venerable man of God was removed from the Church militant to the Church triumphant. In 1804, twenty-two were baptized; in 1805, twenty-four; in 1806, ten; in 1807, seventeen; in 1808, twenty-five; and in 1812, seventeen. This precious ingathering of souls seemed a fitting close to the faithful and laborious pastorate of over half a century.

The whole number baptized from 1762, when the Minutes begin to give the numbers, to 1800, a period of thirty-eight years, was sixty-three; and the membership had increased from fifty to seventy-five; while during the next thirteen years, the number baptized was one hundred and twenty-eight, and the membership had increased to one hundred and twenty-eight. The largest number baptized in any one year was ninety, in 1850, during the pastorate of Rev. Richard Lewis; and the next largest number was seventy-eight, during the pastorate of Rev. Alfred Harris. The greatest number received during any one pastorate was one hundred and fifty-six, during the seven years' pastorate of the Rev. James M. Challiss.

The total number baptized into the fellowship of this Church cannot be ascertained, but it must be over eleven hundred. Of these, seventeen were baptized by Elias Keach; twenty-seven by John Watts; twenty-nine by Abel Morgan; ninety-two by Jenkin Jones; one hundred and thirty-eight by Dr. Samuel Jones; twenty-eight by Jacob Gregg; one hundred and twenty-eight by David Jones, Jr.; one hundred and fifty-six by James M. Challiss; one hundred and twelve by Richard Lewis; and eighty-nine by Alfred Harris.

The present Pastor (Rev. William E. Cornwell) has baptized about seventy persons.

It will thus be seen that this ancient Church, during the present century, has experienced an almost continuous experience of the Divine favor.

During her long existence as a visible Church, she has had but nineteen Pastors, and in her earlier history, she had two or three Ministers at the same time, who labored together in word and doctrine as occasion offered. This arose from the fact that the "gifted brethren" were brought forward at the "Conference meetings." John Watts, Evan Morgan, Samuel Jones and Joseph Wood, were four brethren whose "gifts" were thus exercised, and who were ordained to the work of the ministry, and in turn were the Pastors of the Church. Eight of her Pastors were native-born Welshmen; and, for many years, Pennepek was the point to which the Welsh emigrants were accustomed to direct their steps, on their arrival in America.

As a Church, she has done much for the cause of Education; and one of her Pastors, the Rev. Samuel Jones, D.D., for many years kept a private school where young men were taught Theology. The name of Pennepek, or Lower Dublin, was known throughout the length and breadth of the land as the focus of Baptist influence. Twenty-two persons have been sent forth by this Church to preach the Gospel. The present membership of the Church is over two hundred and fifty. There are now in Philadelphia, forty Baptist Churches, with about fourteen thousand members, and in the entire State of Pennsylvania there are four hundred and fifty Churches, with fifty thousand, four hundred, and ninety-seven communicant members.

18

II.—BIOGRAPHICAL SKETCHES OF THE PASTORS OF THE LOWER DUBLIN BAPTIST CHURCH.

I.—The founder and first Pastor was the REV. ELIAS KEACH. He was born in Southwark, London, in the year 1666; and was the son of the famous BENJAMIN KEACH, Pastor of the Baptist Church, in *Horsely-down.* Of his early education we have no information, but it was no doubt liberal, as his father was a learned man. Like many young men of that day, Elias started off to see the world; and, in 1686, he arrived at Philadelphia, which had been founded four years. He was a wild, giddy fellow, and passed himself off for a Minister, dressing in black and wearing a band. Morgan Edwards, who relates the story, says that the project succeeded; and many people resorted to hear the young London Divine. In the middle of his sermon he suddenly stopped, as if attacked with illness; and, upon inquiry by the audience, he burst into tears and confessed with trembling that he was an imposter. From that hour he dated his conversion; and learning that there was a Baptist Minister at Cold Spring, in Bucks-county, named Thomas Dungan, he at once repaired to him for counsel and advice, and in due time was baptized by him.

The following year, we find him at Pennepek; and, in January, 1688, he was one of the constituents of the Pennepek Church, becoming its Pastor, and continuing in that relation until 1689, when the pastoral relation was dissolved. He travelled extensively in Jersey and Pennsylvania, preaching the Gospel, until 1692, when he returned to England, and was not only a popular, but a very useful, Minister. He became Pastor of a Church, which he was instrumental in gathering, in Ayles-street, Goodman's-fields, London, in April, 1693 ; and so successful was he, that in February, 1694, he wrote to Rev. John Watts, that in nine months he had baptized about one hundred and thirty persons. He remained the Pastor of that Church until the twenty-seventh of October, 1699, when he died, after a brief illness, in the thirty-fourth year of his age. His funeral sermon was preached by Rev. Nathaniel Wyles, and is entitled, *Death's Arrest, the Saint's Release.*

Mr. Keach wrote and published several works. First: Four Sermons preached prior to 1694, in Pinner's Hall. Second: A Confession of Faith, Church Covenant, Discipline, &c. Third: Two Sermons on *The Nature and Excellency of the Grace of Patience.*

While in Pennsylvania, Mr. Keach married Mary Moore, a daughter of the Hon. Nicholas Moore, who was Chief-justice of Pennsylvania, and after whom the Manor of Moreland was named, he being the owner of that tract of land. They had an only daughter, Hannah, who married Revitt Harrison, of England, and had a son, John Elias Keach Harrison, who came to America about the year 1734, and lived at Hatborough, and was a member of the Baptist Church of Southampton, in Bucks-county, Pennsylvania.

The widow of Judge Moore subsequently became the wife of John Holme, Esq., then of Philadelphia, but afterwards of Salem, N. J.

II.—REV. JOHN WATTS, the second Pastor, was born on the third of November, 1661, at Lydd or Leeds, in the County of Kent, England, and came to America about the year 1686. He was baptized at Pennepek, on the twenty-first of November, 1687, by Mr. Keach; and was one of the first four converts at that place, and a constituent of the Church. He early gave evidence of decided talents; and the same year the Church was organized, he was called to the ministry. His labors proved so acceptable, that when Mr. Keach resigned, Mr. Watts was chosen Pastor. He was assisted in his duties by Messrs. Evan Morgan, Samuel Jones, and Joseph Wood—the latter brethren officiating when Mr. Watts was called to other places.

Mr. Watts was a sound Divine, and a man of some learning. He wrote a book, called *Davis Disabled*, in reply to the heresies of a person named William Davis, who had been a member of Pennepek. This work was never printed. He also wrote a Catechism and Confession of Faith, which was printed in 1700.

The pastorate of Mr. Watts continued from the tenth of December, 1690, to the twenty-seventh of August, 1702, when he died, in the forty-first year of his age. He was buried in the grave-yard in the rear of the Meeting-house; and his tombstone has on it the following acrostical inscription:

"Intered here I be
"O that you could now see,
"How unto Jesus for to flee
"Not in sin still to be.
"Warning in time pray take
"And peace by Jesus make
"Then at the last when you awake
"Sure on his right hand you'l partake."

III.—The Rev. EVAN MORGAN, the third Pastor, was born in Wales, and came to America at an early period. He was a Quaker, but left with George Keith's party, in 1691. He was baptized, in 1697, by Thomas Rutter, a Keithian

Baptist Minister, at Southampton, Bucks-county; and, the same year, renouncing his Quakerism, he was received into Pennepek. He was called to the ministry in 1702, and was ordained, on the twenty-third of October, 1706, by Rev. Thomas Killingworth and Rev. Thomas Griffiths.

Mr. Morgan died on the sixteenth of February, 1709, and was buried at Pennepek. He was a smart, intelligent man.

IV.—The Rev. SAMUEL JONES, the fourth Pastor, was born on the ninth of July, 1657, in the parish of Llanddwi, and County of Radnor, Wales, and came to America about 1686. He was baptized, in Wales, in the year 1683, by Henry Gregory, of Radnorshire; and was a constituent of the Pennepek Church. He was called to the ministry in 1697; and was ordained on the twenty-third of October, 1706, at the same time Evan Morgan was, with whom he had joint charge of the Church.

Mr. Jones died on the third of February, 1722; and is buried at Pennepek.

The ground on which the Meeting-house stands was given by him; and he also gave to the Church a number of valuable books.

V.—The Rev. JOSEPH WOOD, the fifth Pastor, was born in 1659, near Hull, in Yorkshire, England, and came to America about the year 1684. He was baptized by Mr. Keach, at Burlington, New Jersey, on the twenty-fourth of June, 1691, and was ordained on the twenty-fifth of September, 1708, at which time he assisted Messrs. Morgan and Jones in the ministry. He died on the fifteenth of September, 1747, and was buried at Cold Spring, Bucks-county.

VI.—The Rev. ABEL MORGAN, the sixth Pastor, was born in the year 1673, at Alltgoch, in the parish of Llanwenog, Cardiganshire, South Wales, and entered on the ministry in the year 1692. He commenced preaching at the age of nineteen; and was ordained at Blaenegwent, in Monmouthshire. Enoch Morgan, the third Pastor of the Welch Tract Church, was his younger brother; and Benjamin Griffith, of Montgomery, was his half brother. They were all descended from Morgan Ap Ryddarch.

He came to America in 1711, reaching Philadelpia on the fourteenth of February, and was called to the care of Pennepek Church, preaching alternately there and at Philadelphia, with great acceptance.

In addition to his duties as a Minister, he gave himself to the work of an author; and prepared, in the Welch language, *A Concordance of the Holy Scriptures.* He did not, however, live to see it published; but it was printed in 1730, and contains an Introduction by his brother, Enoch. Mr. Morgan also prepared a Welsh *Confession of Faith*, which was published. He died on the sixteenth of December, 1722, at the age of forty-nine years. His remains are interred now in the lot of the First Baptist Church of Philadelphia, in Mount Moriah Cemetery.

VII.—The Rev. JENKIN JONES, the seventh Pastor, was born about the year 1686, in the Parish of Llandydoch, Pembrokeshire, Wales, and came to America in 1710. He became Pastor of the Pennepek Church, on the seventeenth of June 1726; but resided in Philadelphia, and officiated for the Church there, which was styled a branch of Pennepek. He had William Kinnersley as one of his assistants, and also Joseph Wood, who aided as well as he could. Mr. Kinnersley was born near Leominster, in Herefordshire, England, in 1669; and came to America, on the twelfth of September, 1714. He was never ordained. He died on the thirteenth of February, 1734; and is buried at Pennepek. His son, EBENEZER KINNERSLEY, was baptized at Pennepek, and became a Minister; but was more distinguished as a Professor in the College of Philadelphia, and for his attainments as a philosopher, having made, in connection with Dr. Franklin, many important discoveries in Electricity.

Mr. Jones continued to be Pastor until the third of May, 1746, when he was dismissed to become one of the constituents of the Philadelphia Church, which was organized on the fifteenth of May, 1746. He became their first Pastor after their separate organization, and continued such until the sixteenth of July 1760, when he died at the age of [74] years. His remains now repose in the Mount Moriah Cemetery. He was a man of considerable abilities, and was the chief cause of having the law of Pennsylvania altered so as to enable dissenting Ministers to perform the marriage ceremony. He was, besides, a generous man, leaving to the Church a legacy towards buying a silver cup for the Lord's table; and having also, partly at his own cost, built a Parsonage-house.

VIII.—The Rev. PETER PETERSON VANHORNE, the eighth Pastor, was born on the twenty-fourth of August, 1719, at Middletown, Bucks-county, Pennsylvania; and was bred a Lutheran. Having embraced the principles of the Baptists, he was baptized on the sixth of September, 1741; and having been called to the ministry, he was ordained, on the eighteenth of June, 1747. He became Pastor, on the thirty-first of October, 1747; and continued to labor with acceptance until the seventh of February, 1762, when he resgned; and on the twenty-third of June, 1764, he formed one of the constituent members of the Baptist Church at New Mills, now Pemberton, in Burlington-county, New Jersey; and became its first Pastor. He continued such until the second of April, 1768, when he resigned, and returned to Lower Dublin, Pennsylvania. On the seventh of April, 1770, he was chosen Pastor of the Cape May-church, but resigned in 1775.

In the year 1785, he became Pastor of the Salem Church, Salem-county, New Jersey; and continued in the pastorate until the tenth of September, 1789, when he died in the seventy-first year of his age.

IX.—The Rev. SAMUEL JONES, D.D., the ninth Pastor, was born at Cefen y Gelli, Bettus Parish, Glamorganshire, South Wales, on the fourteenth of January, 1735, and was brought to America by his parents, in 1737.

His father, Rev. Thomas Jones, was ordained, in 1740, as Pastor of the Church at Tulpehocken, Pennsylvania. Samuel received a liberal education at the College of Philadelphia; and obtained the Master's Degree, on the eighteenth of May, 1762. He at once gave himself to the work of the ministry; and on the eighth of January, 1763, he was ordained at the College Hall, at the instance of the First Baptist Church of Philadelphia, of which he was a member. The same year, he became Pastor of the united Churches of Pennepek and Southampton; but, in 1770, he resigned the care of the latter and devoted himself entirely to Pennepek; and continued to occupy that position until his death—a period altogether of fifty-one years.

Dr. Jones was deservedly honored and esteemed by all the Churches of our faith in the country. His learning gave him a prominent position; and his counsel was sought, not only in the Association, but elsewhere. When Rhode Island College was projected, he repaired to Newport and aided in the preparation of the Charter; and when Dr. Manning died, the Presidency of the College was offered to him; but he declined it. With the work of the ministry he connected that of a teacher of young men in Theology; and was equally distinguished in both capacities. His Academy was located on his farm, near the Church; and he sent forth many young men who became distinguished preachers of the Gospel.

Dr. Jones was the author of several small works; but, besides his Circular Letters, none were printed, except a Sermon, called *The Doctrine of the Covenant*, preached in 1783; *A Century Sermon*, preached in October, 1807, before the Association; and a small handbill, on *Laying on of hands*, which was replied to by Rev. David Jones, of the Great Valley Church.

Dr. Jones was honored with degrees from several Colleges. In 1769, Rhode Island College conferred upon him the degree of Master ot Arts; and, in 1788, the University of Pennsylvania that of Doctor of Divinity.

He died at Lower Dublin, on the seventh of February, 1814, in the eightieth year of his age, and was buried in the rear of the Church.

X.—Jacob Grigg, the tenth Pastor, was born in England, and came to America in the early part of the present century. When very young, he professed religion, united with a Baptist Church in England, and commenced to preach. Soon after, he entered the Bristol Academy and there prosecuted a limited course of study; and left to accept an appointment, as a Missionary to Sierra Leone, Africa; but soon afterwards resigned and settled in America.

He first preached at Norfolk, Virginia, and at Portsmouth, and Upper Bridge. In a few years, he removed to Kentucky and became Pastor of a Church; but he soon left and went to Ohio. In 1808 or 1809, he returned to Virginia and opened a school in Richmond; and preached either in the vicinity of that city or for the First Church.

In December, 1815, he became Pastor of the Lower Dublin Church, and continued such until the first of September, 1817. He then, for about eighteen months, was Pastor of the new Market-street Church, in Philadelphia. Subsequently, he returned to Virginia; and was employed either in teaching or preaching as an itinerant. He died in Sussex-county, Virginia, after a few days' illness, in 1836. He possessed extraordinary powers of mind, and a most tenacious memory. As an evidence of the retentiveness of his memory, it is said that while on the ocean, after leaving his native land, he committed to memory the Old and New Testaments and the whole of Watts' Psalms.

XI.—The Rev. Joshua P. Slack, the eleventh Pastor, became such, on the first of September, 1817, and remained until October, 1821. He was a student at Dr. Staughton's Theological School, in Philadelphia. He died at Cincinnati, Ohio, on the nineteenth of August, 1822. Nothing of his early history is known.

In the private Diary of Rev. David Jones, his successor, there is the following reference to his death, under date of the first of September, 1822: "This morning, after service, I announced to "the people the unwelcome intelligence of

27

" the decease of Brother Joshua P. Slack, my " predecessor in the ministry here. It was a " great stroke to them generally, as they had not heard anything of his sickness. He died at Cincinnati, Ohio, on the nineteenth of Au- " gust."

XII.—The Rev. DAVID JONES, JR., the twelfth Pastor, was born at Brachodnant, in the Parish of Llanbrynmair, Montgomeryshire, North Wales, April, 1785; and, in 1803, came to America. In early life, he lost both parents, and was placed under the care of aunts, whose indulgence had well nigh proved his ruin. He first settled on the Big Miami River, Ohio, being in the employ of a Mr. Hughes, who had brought him to America. He was then a Pædo-baptist; but removing to Columbus, where there was a Baptist Church under the care of Rev. William Jones, he became an attendant there. Thinking that he might be called upon to defend his views, he studied Dr. Lewis's *Body of Divinity*, in Welsh; but was soon convinced that his sprinkling was not Baptism; and, ere long, he was baptized by the Pastor of the Columbia Church. Having exercised his gifts, he was soon licensed by the Duck-creek Church; and then he became Pastor of the Beaver-creek Church, and at the same time taught a small school. In 1810, he resigned his pastorate; traveled extensively through several States; and, in October, attended the Philadelphia Association and visited Lower Dublin, the residence of Dr. Samuel Jones, under whom he studied Theology; and at the same time united with his Church. He then supplied the Church at Frankford; and, in 1812, became its Pastor, and so continued until 1814.

In January, 1814, he was called to the First Church, at Newark, New Jersey; and he remained there eight years. On the first of January, 1822, he became Pastor of the Lower Dublin Church, and sustained that position until his death, which took place on the ninth of April, 1833, at the age of forty-eight years.

Mr. Jones was the "*David*" in a small work on Baptism, entitled *Letters of David and John.* "John" was the Rev. John L. Dagg, D.D., then of Philadelphia, but now of Hopkinsville, Kentucky.

Mr. Jones was much beloved wherever known.

XIII.—The Rev. JAMES MILBANK CHALLISS, the thirteenth Pastor, was born in Philadelphia, on the fourth of January, 1799; was baptized in Salem, New Jersey, on the nineteenth of October, 1817, by Rev. Joseph Sheppard; and was licenced on the twenty-fourth of June, 1821, by the Salem Church.

Mr. Challiss was ordained by the Church at Upper Freehold, Monmouth county, New Jersey, on the seventh of December, 1822; but he had been preaching for that Church since June of that year. He remained as Pastor until March, 1838,—a period of about sixteen years.

Mr. Challiss became Pastor of Lower Dublin, on the thirty-first of March, 1838; and continued there until the first of April, 1845. He was subsequently Pastor at Moorestown, New Jersey, from April, 1845, to March, 1852; and at Cohansey—one of the constituent Churches of the Philadelphia Association—from April, 1852, to March, 1860.

He retired from pastoral duties; and after residing for some years at Bridgeton, New Jersey, he died there on the fifteenth of April, 1868, aged sixty-nine years.

XIV.—The Rev. THOMAS ROBERTS, the fourteenth Pastor, was born in Denbighshire, North Wales, on the tenth of June, 1783; came to America in October, 1803; and settled in the State of New York. He was baptized by Rev. John Stevens, on the ninth of March, 1806; and by invitation of Rev. Dr. David Jones, Pastor of the Great Valley Church, Mr. Roberts became co-pastor with him, and was there ordained, in 1815, by Rev. Dr. Staughton and Rev. Messrs. David and Horatio G. Jones.

When the Mission to the Cherokee Indians was founded, Mr. Roberts went out as a Missionary with Rev. Evan Jones; and upon his return, he became Pastor at Lower Dublin, on the third of August, 1845, and so continued until the first of April, 1847. Although in the Minutes he is styled "a supply," yet he was in effect their Pastor; and was so returned on the Minutes of the Association.

Mr. Roberts was also Pastor of the ancient Church at Middletown, New Jersey. He published a small treatise on Baptism.

He died at Middletown, on the twenty-fourth of September, 1865, aged eighty-two years.

XV.—The Rev. Richard Lewis, M.D., the fifteenth Pastor, was born on the twenty-fifth of July, 1817, at Llanidoles, North Wales, but left that place when very young. He was baptized in the year 1833, when sixteen years of age, by Rev. Cornelius Morrell, Pastor of the Baptist Church at Stalybridge. The following year he was called to exercise his gifts, and was licensed to preach; and, at the same time, he became Principal of a flourishing Seminary. Meanwhile he prosecuted his studies under Mr. Morrell.

In June, 1841, Mr. Lewis embarked for America; and, on his arrival, spent some time in New York, but eventually made Philadelphia his abode. In 1842, he became Pastor of the Mount Tabor Church, in Philadelphia, where he remained until 1847. On the twenty-seventh of April, 1847, he commenced his pastorate at Lower Dublin, but resigned in 1852, and left on the twenty-fifth of April, in that year. He then labored as Pastor of the Church at Holmesburg, until 1860, when he resigned.

Mr. Lewis afterwards studied medicine at the Pennsylvania, Jefferson, and Homeopathic Medical Colleges, and graduated at the latter as M. D. He now resides at Frankford and practices medicine.

XVI.—The Rev. WILLIAM HUTCHINSON, the sixteenth Pastor, was born in the town of Drumlample, County of Londonderry, Ireland, in 1794; and came to America in the year 1819.

He was baptized at Cazenovia, New York, in 1820, by Rev. John Peck, and was licensed, by the Cazenovia Church, in June, 1821. He entered Hamilton Institution, and graduated in 1824, and was ordained that year at Cazenovia. He returned to Ireland, and preached to his countrymen under the Patronge of "The London Baptist Irish Society." In 1827, he again came to America; and, in 1828, became Pastor of the Church at Brandon, Vermont, where he labored for three years. While at Brandon, he established *The Vermont Telegraph*, a weekly religious newspaper, of which he became its first Editor. In 1831, he became Pastor of the Church at Amenia, Duchess-county, New York, and continued there until 1833, when he removed to Fayetteville, Onondaga-county, and officiated for about three years as Pastor of the Church in that place. In 1836, he went to Oswego, and labored as Pastor of that Church, until the fifteenth of December, 1852, when he was chosen

31

Pastor of the Lower Dublin Church, and remained such until December, 1856, when he resigned.

XVII.—The Rev. ALFRED HARRIS, the seventeenth Pastor, was born in 1829, at Bulchmawr, Pembrokeshire, South Wales; and came to America in 1841. He was baptized by his father at Remsen, Oneida-county, New York, in the Winter of 1842. He was licensed by the Remsen Church, of which his father was Pastor. He was educated at a Free Will Baptist Institution at Whitesboro', New York; and was ordained at the Berean Baptist Church, in the town of Marcy, New York, for which Church he preached about six years. Mr. Harris was afterwards called to the charge of the Beakleyville and Upper Mount Bethel Churches in Pennsylvania, and remained with them one year, when he became Pastor of the Willistown Church. After serving that Church for two years, he became Pastor of Lower Dublin, on the sixteenth of March, 1857; and labored with much success until March, 1860, when he resigned, and took charge of the Church of Hoboken, New Jersey.

Mr. Harris has contributed numerous articles to the *Welch Magazines*, and is able to preach in that language.

XVIII.—The Rev. GEORGE KEMPTON, D. D., the eighteenth Pastor, was born on the twenty-ninth of August, 1810, in the Parish of St. Thomas, South Carolina.

He was baptized in February, 1832, and joined the Robertsville Church, by which he was licensed, on the twenty-second of December, in that same year.

In January, 1833, he entered Furman Theological Institution; where he remained two years. In October, 1835, he entered the Freshman Class, of Madison University, then called Hamilton Institution, and graduated there in the Arts, in August, 1839. In 1840, he was called as a supply by the Church at Smyrna, South Carolina, and while there was ordained; and the following year he became Pastor of the Robertsville Church, where he remained until 1844, when he was called to the Spruce-street Church, Philadelphia. In 1852, he removed to New Brunswick, and became Pastor of the Church at that place; and continued there until 1857, when he was called to the Pastorate of the Church at North-east, Duchess-county, New York.

In 1852, the Honorary Degree of Master of Arts was conferred upon Mr. Kempton, by the University at Lewisburg, Pennsylvania; and in 1857, he received the Degree of Doctor of Divinity from Madison University, at Hamilton, New York. In October, 1860, he became Pastor of the Lower Dublin Church.

Dr. Kempton has preached several sermons which have been printed. He resigned the charge of the Church in 1865; and now resides at Hammonton, New Jersey.

XIX.—The Rev. WILLIAM E. CORNWELL, the nineteenth Pastor, was born in Philadelphia, Pennsylvania, on the twenty-fourth of October, 1836. He was baptized at Bridgeton, New Jersey, on the thirteenth of February, 1853; and commenced to study for the ministry in the Spring of 1854; and on the twenty-eighth of July, 1859, he was graduated at the Theological Department of the University at Lewisburg, Pennsylvania.

He was ordained on the twenty-sixth of Octo-

33

ber, 1859, at Woodstown, New Jersey; and was subsequently Pastor of the Church at Canton, Salem-county, New Jersey.

On the eighteenth of March, 1866, he commenced his labors as Pastor of the Lower Dublin Church, and still continues to hold that honorable position. During his pastorate he has baptized a large number; and a Mission Chapel has been built and dedicated, at Fox Chase, a few miles from the parent Church.

The following tabular statement will give a brief summary of the various Pastors, and the length of each pastorate:

ELIAS KEACH served the Church from January, 1688, to 1689.

JOHN WATTS, from December 10, 1690, to August 27, 1702.

EVAN MORGAN, from October 23, 1706, to February 16, 1709.

SAMUEL JONES, from October 23, 1706, to February 3, 1722.

JOSEPH WOOD, from September 25, 1708, to September 15, 1747.

ABEL MORGAN, from February 14, 1711, to December 16, 1722.

JENKIN JONES, from June 17, 1726, to May 3, 1746.

PETER PETERSON VANHORNE, from October 31, 1747, to February 7, 1762.

SAMUEL JONES, D.D., from January 1, 1763, to February 7, 1814.

JACOB GRIGG, from December, 1815, to September 1, 1817.

JOSHUA P. SLACK, from September 1, 1817, to October, 1821.

DAVID JONES, JR., from January 1, 1822, to April 9, 1833.

34

James M. Challiss, from March 31, 1838, to April 1, 1845.

Thomas Roberts, from August 3, 1845, to April 1, 1847.

Richard Lewis, from April 27, 1847, to April 25, 1852.

William Hutchinson, from December 15, 1852, to December, 1856.

Alfred Harris, from March 16, 1857, to March, 1860.

George Kempton, D.D., from October 7, 1860, to April 1, 1865.

William E. Cornwell, from March 18, 1866.

Charles Warwick from Feb 1. 1881.

III.—LICENTIATES.

The Church, during its long existence, has granted liberty or license to preach to the following persons, many of whom subsequently became eminent Ministers of the Gospel, viz:

JOHN WATTS,	EVAN MORGAN,
SAMUEL JONES,	JOHN HART,
JOHN SWIFT,	WILLIAM KINNERSLEY,
GEORGE EAGLESFIELD,	GEORGE EATON,
EBENEZER KINNERSLEY,	JOSEPH BULL,
PETER EATON,	WILLIAM VANHORNE,
PETER SMITH,	JOHN PITMAN,
BURGISS ALLISON,	JOHN STANCLIFF,
GEORGE GUTHRIE,	CHARLES BARTOLETTE,
JOHN BOOZER,	DAVID BATEMAN,
JOSEPH WRIGHT,	CHARLES E. WILSON.

36

IV.—RULING ELDERS.

Messrs. John Holme, John Vansandt, and William Marshall were the only persons who were chosen to act as Ruling Elders.

37

V.—DEACONS.

The following persons have been elected as Deacons:

SAMUEL VAUS, January, 1687.

JOSEPH ASHTON, May, 1688.

SAMUEL JONES and JOSEPH WOOD, October, 9, 1699.

GRIFFITH MILES, October 23, 1706.

JOHN HART, June 16, 1721.

DANIEL DAVIES, December, 1721.

GEORGE EATON, June 17, 1726.

ALEXANDER EDWARDS, August 2, 1746.

CRISPIN COLLETT, May 2, 1747.

THOMAS WEBSTER, June 6, 1758.

JAMES DUNGAN, and JOSEPH ENGLES, March 30, 1775.

JOHN WRIGHT, February 3, 1776.

BENJAMIN DUNGAN, March 30, 1782.

THOMAS HOLME, August 2, 1806.

JOSEPH WRIGHT, October 1, 1814.

THOMAS MILES, 1814.

JOHN FOSTER, April 10, 1817.

MORGAN HOLME and THOMAS SCATTERGOOD, October 10, 1831.

JOHN NEVILLE and JACOB W. OTT, August 5, 1839.

JOHN BLAKE and BENJAMIN M. DUNGAN, February 5, 1844.

GEORGE SNYDER and SHADRACH MILES, December 25, 1849.

FRANKLIN JOHNSON and SAMUEL HERITAGE, April 6, 1867.

38

VI.—ADDITIONS TO THE CHURCH BY BAPTISM; AND TOTAL MEMBERSHIP IN EACH YEAR.

Year.	Bap.	Total.	Year.	Bap.	Total.	Year.	Bap.	Total.
1687	4		1729	1		1783	5	64
1688	3		1730	3		1784	4	67
1691	4		1731	4		1785	4	69
1696	2		1732	5		1788	2	69
1697	8		1733	1		1789	1	68
1698	2		1734	6		1790	1	67
1699	4		1735	5		1794	1	62
1700	3	46	1736	1		1795	1	64
1701	2		1737	8		1796	3	70
1702	13		1738	9		1797	1	70
1704	8		1740	17		1800		74
1705	4		1741	4		1801		75
1706	6		1742	5		1802		73
1707	9		1743	4		1803		72
1708	11		1746	3		1804	22	95
1709	12		1748	6		1805	24	116
1710	24		1750	2		1806	10	124
1711	1		1753	2		1807	17	138
1712	1		1755	4		1808	25	155
1713	11		1761	3	50	1809	6	158
1714	13	137	1763	6	58	1810	3	160
1715	3		1764	2	54	1811	4	162
1719	1		1770	1	50	1812	17	178
1720	5		1771	1	47	1813	3	178
1722	4		1772	5	54	1814		170
1723	4		1773	6	63	1815	3	163
1724	2		1774	1	63	1816	11	157
1725	1		1776	5	69	1817	14	169
1726	2		1778	4	73	1818	5	172
1727	7		1781	2	58	1819	10	175
1728	7		1782	3	59	1820	1	174

39

Year.	Bap.	Total.	Year.	Bap.	Total.	Year.	Bap.	Total.
1821	11	183	1838	23	223	1854	4	296
1822	10	193	1839	21	219	1855		283
1823	5	192	1840	47	255	1856	13	277
1824	3	191	1841	18	273	1857		267
1825	2	188	1842	3	260	1858	78	341
1826	2	140	1843	42	302	1859	8	352
1827	5	143	1844	2	299	1860	3	340
1828	8		1845		281	1861	9	339
1829	4		1846	9	278	1862	1	316
1830	9		1847		254	1863		311
1831	52		1848	4	240	1864	1	295
1832	28	176	1849	2	235	1865		262
1833	34	206	1850	90	321	1866	2	220
1834	8	204	1851	16	325	1867	52	252
1835	10	205	1852		305	1868	8	250
1836	17	210	1853	5	299			

David Jones (1736-1820, third pastor of the Baptist Church at Great Valley, Pennsylvania. Jones made two visits to the Ohio territory as a missionary under the auspices of the Philadelphia Association. He also served as a chaplain during the Revolutionary War. As a prominent member of the Philadelphia Association, he was chosen moderator in 1798. Portrait from Richard B. Cook. *The Early and Later Delaware Baptists* (Philadelphia: A. B. P. S., 1880) p. 54.

"...TO SET THEM IN ORDER :"

HISTORY

OF THE

BAPTIST CHURCH IN THE GREAT VALLEY.

TREDYFFRIN TOWNSHIP, CHESTER CO., PA.

BY

HORATIO GATES JONES, D. C. L.

Vice-President of the Historical Society of Pennsylvania

PHILADELPHIA:

PRESS OF WILLIAM SYCKELMOORE, NO. 1420 CHESTNUT STREET

1883

PREFATORY NOTE

The following History of the Great Valley Baptist Church was prepared at the special request of the church, by our brother Horatio Gates Jones, Esq., who is a member of the Lower Merion Baptist Church, and who has been President of the Board of Trustees of the Philadelphia Baptist Association since the year 1867. We knew that he had peculiar qualifications for such a historical labor, and that he had a special regard for our church. His grandfather, Rev. David Jones, A. M., had been its third pastor, and his father, the late Rev. Horatio Gates Jones D. D., was baptized into its fellowship, was one of its first Trustees, had been licensed by it to preach the gospel, and when he left Salem, N. J., which was his first settlement as pastor, he again became a member with us, and so continued for several years, and was dismissed in 1808, to form one of the constituents of the Lower Merion Church.

This brief notice is all that we presume to offer Brother Jones as a testimonial for his labor of love in writing the "History of the Great Valley Baptist Church."

JAMES M. GUTHRIE, *Pastor*

ISAAC A. CLEAVER, *Clerk*

Berwyn, Pa., Nov., 1883.

"...TO SET THEM IN ORDER :"

HISTORY

OF THE

GREAT VALLEY BAPTIST CHURCH

BY

HORATIO GATES JONES

VICE PRESIDENT OF THE HISTORICAL SOCIETY OF PENNSYLVANIA

The Great Valley Baptist Church, the second oldest in Pennsylvania, is situated in Tredyffrin Township, Chester County. Its history takes us back to the early settlement of the Province, when large numbers of emigrants fled from England and Wales, as well as from the Continent, to secure for themselves and their children what, to them, was the greatest boon of their lives - liberty to worship God according to the dictates of their consciences.

Among the early settlers of the eastern part of Chester county were the Welsh emigrants, who, to show their love for their native land, gave names to many townships - names which belonged to the places they had left., Tredyffrin, Caernarvon, Brecknock, and Cymry (these last three now in Berks county), Radnor, Haverford, Gwynedd, Uwchlan, Merion, and others are Welsh names full of interest to the historian and reveal the nativity of the early settlers. Indeed, the number of Welsh settlers was so great that among the Quakers, in several places, services were held in the Welsh tongue, and, in 1707, the citizens of Radnor, to the number of one hundred, petitioned the Bishop of London to send them a minister of the Church of England who could preach to them in the ancient British language.*

In his "Materials towards a History of the American Baptists."** Morgan Edwards says, "In 1701-2 several families from Wales arrived and settled in the east end of said valley, one of whom was James Davis, a member of the Baptist Church of Rhydwillim, in Carmarthenshire. Near to

---

* See Bishop W. S. Perry's "Papers relating to History of the Church in Pa.," p. 35.

** Edwards' *Materials*, Vol. I., [Pennsylvania] p. 26.

his plantation in Radnor Township lived one Richard Miles, who, with his wife, had been baptized a little before by William Beckingham, in Upper Providence. These two families consorted together and invited ministers from other parts to preach at their houses, by which means several were baptized." In 1710, Rev. Hugh Davis and several other Baptists arrived from Wales, so that their number had increased to sixteen persons, and they then resolved to form a church. This important event took place April 22, 1711, with the approval of the Welsh Tract Church, in Delaware, whose pastor, Rev. Elisha Thomas, was present and conducted the services. *The Century Minutes*, p. 16, state that on this occasion they had the assistance of "Mr. Elisha Thomas and others from the Welsh Tract Church, and after solemn prayers to God for his blessing, they gave themselves to God, and to one another in the Lord, according to 2 Cor. viii.5, and had a right hand of fellowship as a sister church." The names of the constituents were *Rev. Hugh Davis, William Thomas Hugh, Arthur Edwards, William Davis, Margaret Davis, Joan Miles, Jane Miles, Margaret Phillips, Margaret Evans, William Rees, Alexander Owen, John Evans, Margaret Evans, James Davis, Richard Miles and wife.*

Being now fully organized, the church sought admission to the Philadelphia Association, and at its session, in 1711, it was formally received being the first new body to join that now venerable sanhedrim of American Baptists. For many years, the church met for worship chiefly at the dwelling of Mr. Richard Miles, in Radnor, but in 1722 they built a meeting-house twenty-eight feet square, "with seats, galleries, and a *stove*," which latter article was not found at that early day in every meeting-house. The house stood in what is now known as the northern part of the graveyard.

Mr. Edwards says "The situation is pleasant, being rising ground, by the highway, and bordering on a small brook called *Nant yr Ewig*."* Since that time the church has become the owner of a plantation or farm of about fifty acres, with numerous out-buildings, the gift of Mr. Henry Davis, and which is now usually occupied by the pastor.

---

* *Materials*, Vol. I., p. 25. *Nant yr Ewig* is Welsh and means in English, "The brook of the deer."

As this was the only Baptist church in Chester County, its membership became very scattered by removals, until, in 1737, so many had settled at the Yellow Springs, in Vincent Township, and among them a Welsh minister named William Davis, that the Valley Church joined with them in the erection of a meeting-house, and in 1748 they were granted church privileges as regarded the observance of the ordinances and the exercise of discipline. At this time, the Rev. Owen Thomas, who had been pastor of Welsh Tract Church, removed to Vincent and preached for this branch of the Valley Church until his death, in November, 1760. He too was a Welshman and an able preacher of the Gospel. But, on the 12th of October, 1771, the members at the Yellow Springs were duly constituted a regular independent church and joined the Association that same year, under the name of the Vincent Baptist Church.*

The only difficulty which disturbed the harmony of the church occurred in the year 1726, when several brethren, with their families withdrew because they believed in the continued obligation of the Fourth Commandment, and the observance therefore of Saturday as the Sabbath. The same trouble occurred in several other churches of our faith, but in all cases little harm was done, for these conscientious brethren withdrew, as they had a right to do, and removing from the Valley to French Creek, in East Nantmeal Township, they there organized a Seventh-Day Baptist Church. A meeting-house was built, but in 1770 they had no stated preaching, and Mr. Edwards says they were for some time as sheep without a shepherd.**

As in most of the early Baptist churches, the Valley had a co-pastor with Mr. Hugh Davis; his name was John Davis, who, in 1724, was chosen Ruling Elder, then was licensed, and in 1732 was ordained and assisted the pastor. When David Jones was pastor, he had associated with him during both of his pastorates, John Boggs, Jenkin David and Thomas Roberts. In Mr. Jones' case this was rendered necessary, as he was chaplain in the army, and afterwards traveled very extensively in the Western country.

---

* The Association met that year, October 15th. - *Century Minutes*, p. 118.

** Edwards' *Materials*, Vol. I., p. 27.

When the American Revolution took place, the Church was on the side of right and truth. Its pastor entered the service of his country as chaplain, and so continued during the whole war. As Mr. Whitehead truthfully remarks in his sketch of the Church,* "The membership and clergy were yet largely Welsh, and were as stern and rugged and fixed as the mountains of their fathers' land, the pure air of which had caused the hearts of their sires to bound with the most noble impulses for the right in both Church and State. The thrill of these impulses was not lost in their children. And when the oppression of royalty became too burdensome for the colonists, they arose in their manhood and might, to cast themselves upon the protection of a just God and their own true hearts and arms, the Baptists, led by their love of both civil and religious liberty, sprang into the ranks. And this too, notwithstanding they were even then being persecuted as a people in some of the colonies. Their preachers and private members were being imprisoned and fined and whipped, and their farms, in some cases, and even as in Ashfield, Mass., their *burial ground*, were sold to pay the expenses of settling ministers and building meeting-houses for another religious denomination."**

So severe were the oppressions that our Association, in October, 1774, appointed a committee of nineteen, who were called a *Committee of Grievances*, to consider and consult upon the best measures to relieve their persecuted brethren and the churches were urged to contribute for their relief. It was at this time that Isaac Backus, James Manning, D. D., and many of the members of the Association, met, in Carpenters' Hall, the delegates from Massachusetts to the Continental Congress, and laid before them their grievances and besought them to change the laws in New England, where our brethren were suffering from the ecclesiastical oppression of what was termed "The Standing Order" [the Congregational churches].

"This application." as Mr. Whitehead remarks, "met with no sympathetic responses; yet, when afterwards the government appealed for pecuniary help, we find this Association investing all their funds in Cont-

---

* Whitehead's *Sketch of the Valley Church*, p. 9.
** [the Presbyterians - Editor]

inental bonds or scrip." No doubt, Gen. Howe knew of the devoted patriotism of the Valley Church, and so, when marching to Philadelphia, "let loose the dogs of war" and broke into the meeting-house and did the church all the damage he could.

Dr. George Smith, in his *History of Delaware County*, has preserved a valuable document, which is now given to show the rapacity of the British during the Revolution. It is as follows: *

"*An Account of a Sacrilege committed in the Baptist Meeting-house in Tredyffrin, in the County of Chester, Pa., by some of the British Army under General Howe, in their march from the head of Elk to Philadelphia, the 18th, 19th, and 20th days of September, when said Meeting-house was broke open and was stole from thence the Sacramental Dishes! Viz.:*

2 pewter dishes, - - - - - - - - - - - -	£0 15 0
2 " pints, - - - - - - - - - - - - - -	-0 8 0
1 diaper table cloth, - - - - - - - - - - -	-0 12 0
1 Bible of the English language - - - -	-0 15 0
A change of raiment for the administration of Baptism, viz.: -	
2 linen shirts, - - - - - - - - - - - - - -	-0 16 0
1 pair linen drawers, - - - - - - - - - - -	-0 10 0
The lock of the chest the goods were in,	0 5 0
The sexton's tools for burials, viz.: -	
1 grubbing hoe, 8s., 1 spade, 7s. 6d.,	
They destroyed and burnt the parsonage farm, viz.: - 135 panels of fence, equal to 810 rails,	
at 4s. per hundred, - - - - - - - - - - -	1 12 4
	£6 8 10

Attested by JAMES DAVIS, Elder."

---

* Dr. Smith's *History*, p. 549.

But none of these things influenced the patriotism of pastor or people, only it made them more determined to fight for liberty. This same spirit actuated them in the late war for the Union, when many of their brave and noble youth left their homes, and, as their sires did in 1776, so in 1861, they too followed their pastor, the brave and patriotic WILLIAM M. WHITEHEAD, who, in these latter days which tried men's souls, became Chaplain of the 97th Regiment, P.[ennsylvania]V.[olunteers].

The Valley Church, in its early history, was noted for the long service of its pastors. Its first three pastors were Hugh Davis, James Davis, and David Jones, who, together, served one hundred and seventeen years.

It has also been a missionary church, and its pastors were wont to visit remote places, preaching the blessed gospel wherever opportunity offered. Such was the case in later years with David Jones and Thomas Roberts and Evan Jones, the latter two going, in 1821, as missionaries to the Cherokee Indians in Tennessee. At the same time, Isaac Cleaver, John Farrier, Elizabeth Roberts, Elizabeth Jones, and Rachel Cleaver were also dismissed for the same purpose; and when the great question of foreign missions was presented to the Baptists of America, the sisters of the Valley Church formed a society for mission purposes and were able to contribute about $130 each year.

The total number of baptisms into its fellowship is not accurately known, as many of its early records are lost; but in a paper written in 1859, Mr. Whitehead says that the number from 1711 to 1831, a period of 120 years, was 408, while from 1831 to 1859, a period of 28 years, the number was 561. Since then, up to 1883, a period of 23 years, 74 baptisms are reported, making a grand total of 1,043. There is no doubt that Mr. Fletcher, who was the pastor from 1832 to 1840, baptized more than any other one. Mr. Whitehead says Mr. F. baptized more than 400. His settlement and career are so graphically described by Mr. Whitehead, in his History of the Church, that respect for his memory and his services will justify its reproduction here: "We cannot close this sketch without particularly noting, with profound gratitude to the head of the Church, the abundant outpouring of His Spirit during the pastorate of the Rev. Leonard Fletcher. The church was without a pastor, yet their desire for the salvation of souls led them to appoint a four-days' meeting. Ministering brethren came, and among them the one whose pastorate was, in succeeding years, so graciously blessed. The opening sermon was preached by one of the Church's own sons, Rev. Horatio G. Jones, of the Lower Merion Church. As in the days of Pentecost, the Spirit was poured out, and sinners, as then, anxiously asked what they should do. Day after day the house was thronged with rejoicing worshippers and weeping penitents. Hundreds were brought to Christ in that revival, for we may say that it continued with but little cessation during Bro. Fletcher's entire stay. During the eight years of his labors here, he baptized more than 400. The missionary spirit again filled the church. Norristown had no Baptist church. The pastor, deacons, and brethren went there to preach the gospel as their hearts earnestly received it. Although at first they were denied a place in which to meet, yet they were not discouraged, but made the Court-house their pulpit and God's unfettered firmament their canopy. Then West Chester called for their prayers and efforts. Again the little band went forth, and as Paul stood in the Areopagus on Mars Hill to proclaim Christ and the resurrection, so did the pastor of the Valley Church stand in the court-house with the same message. At length his work seemed done; with a weary heart he went to tread a pilgrimage of twenty years. He labored among the sunny fruitfulness of the South, yet, as year after year passed away, his heart was ever returning to the people here, whom he loved so well. And, as God heard the prayer of Jacob and brought him back to his father's home in peace, so He brought Brother Fletcher back in the evening of his life, that his flesh might repose in the midst of those whom he had led to Jesus, awaiting with them the resurrection of the just."*

The Valley may, with great truth, be termed a *mother* church, for from her membership and labors of her pastors, eight churches have been formed, viz: -

1. The French Creek, Seventh-Day Baptist Church, 1726
2. The Vincent Church, Chester County, 1771
3. The Lower Merion Church, Montgomery County, 1808
4. The Phoenixville Church, Chester County, 1830
5. The Norristown Church, Montgomery County, 1832

* Whiteheads's *Sketch*, p. 20-21.

6. The Willistown Church, Chester County, 1833
7. The West Chester Church, Chester County, 1834
8. The Radnor Church, Delaware County, 1841

For many years the Valley Church had what was a quite general thing among the early churches, ruling elders, but now that officer is not chosen by any of the regular Baptist Churches. The ruling elders of the Valley were -

ALEXANDER OWEN,	chosen	April 22, 1711
WILLIAM REES,	"	" 22, 1711
JOHN DAVIS,	"	" 22, 1724
JAMES DAVIS,	"	October 23, 1760
ISAAC ABRAHAM,	"	January 22, 1803

DEACONS

Dr. Whitehead, in his "Historical Sketch," has given a list of all the Deacons of the Church up to the year 1872, when his book was published. Only two have since been chosen. Their names, with the times of their appointments, are as follows: -

ALEXANDER OWEN, April 22, 1711.
GRIFFITH JOHN, February, 1712.
THOMAS JOHN,
SAMUEL JOHN, October 23, 1760.
ENOCH JONES, June 27, 1789.
JONATHAN PHILLIPS, June 27, 1789.
ISAAC ABRAHAM, June 27, 1789.
JOHN EASTBURN, July 27, 1793.
JOHN GWIN, August, 1820.
JOHN PUGH, JR., August, 1820.
EDWARD SITER, February 22, 1823.
DANIEL ABRAHAM, November 23, 1832.
PHINEAS PHILLIPS, November 23, 1832.
SAMUEL KING, November 23, 1832.
SAMUEL D. PHILLIPS, November 23, 1832.

JOHN GARBER, March 27, 1841.
JONATHAN JONES, March 27, 1841.
HENRY KAUFFMAN, SR., March 27, 1841.
THOMAS JONES, March 27, 1841.
ISAAC RICHARDS, January 14, 1847.
HIRAM CLEAVER, January 14, 1847.
CHARLES BEAVER, September 24, 1863.
SAMUEL P. ABRAHAM, September 24, 1863.
MORDECAI D. CORNOG, December 24, 1863.
SAMUEL PRIEST, August 19, 1869.
HENRY KAUFFMAN, JR., August 19, 1869.
JAMES J. DEWEES, November 7, 1881.
DANIEL C. ABRAHAM, November 7, 1881.

In this connection, it may be of some interest to give a fact related by Morgan Edwards, in his sketch of this church.* The Apostle James, in his Epistle, says: "Is any sick among you? Let him call for the *elders* of the church; and let them pray over him, anointing him with oil in the name of the Lord: And the prayer of faith shall save the sick and the Lord shall raise him up."

Mr. Edwards says of Rev. Hugh Davis, the first pastor, that

> " some years before his death he had a severe pain in his arm, which gradually wasted the limb and made life a burden. After trying many remedies, he sent for the elders of the church to anoint him with oil, according to James v.14-17. The effect was a perfect cure, so far that the pain never returned. One of the elders concerned,

* Edwards' *Materials*, Vol. I., p. 28.

from whom I had this relation, is yet alive, [in 1770] and succeeds Mr. Davis in the ministry."*

The church was chartered March 27th, 1799, under the corporate name of "The Baptist Church in the Great Valley."

LICENTIATES,

There have been fifteen persons licensed by the Valley Church, viz.:

John Davis, November 16, 1732.
Horatio Gates Jones, 1800.
Thomas G. Jones, 1801.
Isaac Eaton, 1801.
Richard Gardner, M.D., April 24, 1824.
Thomas B. Brown, April 2, 1832.
William B. Bingham, January 5, 1835.
John L. Clinger, January 5, 1835.
Manassah McClees, January 5, 1835.
Edward D. Fendall, January 5, 1835.
Thomas T. Kutchin, January 5, 1835.
Nathan Stetson, January 5, 1835
Thomas G. Keen, January 5, 1835.
Charles Barrie, March 22, 1839.
David Phillips, October 25, 1840.

---

* He refers to Rev. John Davis, who was chosen a ruling elder in 1724. On p. 23 of *Materials*, Vol. I., Mr. Edwards relates the cure of Rynallt Howell, of Welsh Tract by the anointing of oil. On page 111, Rev. Elias Keach, in letter to Rev. John Watts, dated February 20, 1694, tells of a wonderful cure, and on pages 115-121 he gives an account of a cure at Colchester, England, obtained from papers which were given him by the celebrated Prof. Ebenezer Kinnersley. In the *History of the New Jersey Baptists*, pages 63-4, he relates the remarkable cure of a certain Hannah Carman

PASTORS

During its existence of 172 years, the Valley Church has had only 20 pastors. It is true that the *Century Minutes* give the name of Thomas Jones as Pastor from 1776 to 1783; but it appears that, although requested by the church, to assume the pastoral care, he refused to do so. His membership, however, was with the Valley, and as Chaplain Jones, their regular pastor, was in the Continental Army, Thomas Jones often supplied the pulpit during his absence. He had been for many years pastor of the Tulpehoken Church in Berks County. He was born in Glamorganshire, South Wales, in 1708, came to America in 1737, was ordained at Tulpehoken, and remained until the church disbanded, owing to the great influx of Germans. About this time, he removed to Willistown, where his son, Griffith, had a farm. He died in 1788. He was the father of the learned and famous Rev. Samuel Jones, D. D. of Lower Dublin.

The following statement gives the names of all the regular Pastors and the length of their several pastorates:

1. HUGH DAVIS, the first pastor, from April 22, 1711, to Oct. 13, 1753.
2. JOHN DAVIS, from November 16, 1732, to 1778.
3. DAVID JONES, A.M., from 1775 to 1786, and from 1792 to 1820.
4. NICHOLAS COX, for 1783.
5. JOHN BOGGS, from 1799 to 1801.
6. JENKIN DAVID, from 1795 to 1798.
7. THOMAS ROBERTS, from 1815 to 1822.
8. THOMAS J. KITTS, from 1822 to 1823.
9. JOHN SHIVE JENKINS, from 1823 to 1827.
10. THOMAS BROWN, from 1828 to 1831.
11. LEONARD FLETCHER, from 1832 to 1840.
12. CHARLES BRIGHT KEYES, from July, 1840, to March, 1845.
13. JAMES FULLER BROWN, D.D. from 1846 to 1854.
14. GEORGE SPRATT, M. D., from 1854 to 1858.
15. WILLIAM MANLOVE WHITEHEAD, A.M., M.D., from 1858 to 1861.
16. JAMES ELY WILSON, from 1863 to 1865
17. BUCKLEY CARLL MORSE, from 1867 to 1870.
18. JAMES HENRY HYATT, from Sept. 28, 1870, to Sept. 28, 1873.
19. GEORGE PIERCE, from April, 1873 to 1883.
20. JAMES MEMINGER GUTHRIE, from August 12, 1883.

"...TO SET THEM IN ORDER :"

BIOGRAPHICAL SKETCHES OF THE PASTORS

1. The first Pastor, HUGH DAVIS, was born in Cardiganshire, South Wales, in 1665, and was ordained at Rhydwillim. He came to America, April 26, 1711, and settled in the Valley, was one of its constituents, and remained as its chief pastor until his death, which took place October 13, 1753. Mr. Whitehead, in his sketch, gives his last name as *David*, but Mr. Edwards calls him *Davis*, and I find both names given him Thomas' *History of the Welsh Association*,* and also in the *Century Minutes*. Mr. Edwards, however, was very careful in all his sketches, and hence I prefer to follow him.

2. The second Pastor, JOHN DAVIS, was born November 1, 1702, in Llanfernach, Pembrokeshire, Wales. He came to America, July 27, 1713, was called to the ministry in 1722, but was not ordained until November 16, 1732, at which time he assisted Mr. HUGH DAVIS. When the latter died, in 1753, John Davis had sole care of the church, until 1775, when David Jones was associated with him. He, however, remained as one of the pastors until his death, in 1778.

3. The third Pastor, DAVID JONES, A. M., was born May 12, 1736, in White Clay Creek Hundred, near Newark, in New Castle County, Delaware. His parents were Morgan and Eleanor Evans Jones, and his great-grandfather was Morgan ap Rhyddarch, of Alltgoch, Cardiganshire, South Wales. He was baptized, May 6, 1758, into the fellowship of Welsh Tract Church; was educated at Hopewell Academy, N.J.; studied theology under Abel Morgan, of Middletown, and was ordained, December 12, 1766, as pastor of the church of Freehold, Monmouth County, N. J. In 1772-3 he made two visits to the Indians in Ohio, as a missionary. In April, 1775, he

---

[* Joshua Thomas, *A History of the Baptist Association in Wales, From the Year 1650, to the Year 1790* (Philadelphia, 1795). Thomas (1719-1797) wrote another work, *A History of the Welsh Baptists*, which formed the basis for the later work by Jonathan Davis in 1835 by the same title - Editor]

became pastor of the Valley Church, and the next year became a chaplain in the army, and so continued until the war closed. In 1786 he became pastor of Southampton Church, but in 1792 returned to the Valley, and remained as its chief pastor until his death. In 1798 he was Moderator of the Association, and, in 1811, preached the introductory sermon. In 1794-96, he was Chaplain of Gen. Wayne, in the Indian wars, and again, in 1812-14, he was also a Chaplain. He died February 5, 1820, in his 84th year.

4. The fourth Pastor, NICHOLAS COX, was born March 24, 1742, in New Castle County, Del. He was licensed at Philadelphia, in 1771; was ordained at Wantage, N. J., April 15, 1772, remained there until 1783, when he was called to the Valley. He afterwards became Pastor of Kingwood, N. J., November 4, 1784. It was at this time that great excitement existed among the Baptists, on account of the defection of the popular and eloquent Elhanan Winchester, who, while pastor of the Philadelphia church, became a Universalist. Mr. Cox, having become a believer in Universalism, was disowned by the Baptists on account of his heresy, and we find, in Rev. Abel C. Thomas' *Century of Universalism*, p. 34, that when the Universalist Convention met in Philadelphia, May 25, 1790, Mr. Cox is named as one of the ministers present. Mr. Thomas says he never became the pastor of any church, but preached as an Evangelist in New Jersey, Maryland and Virginia. He died at Mansfield, Warren County, N. J., March 20, 1826, aged 84.

5. The fifth Pastor, JOHN BOGGS, was born in East Nottingham, Pa., April 9, 1741, was bred a Presbyterian, and so continued for many years. He became a Baptist, and was baptized at the Welsh Tract Baptist Church, Delaware, November 3, 1771. He was ordained December 5, 1781, and took charge of the Welsh Tract Church. *The Century Minutes* show that he was greatly blessed in his labors, for, from 1784, to 1794 he baptized 114 persons into the fellowship of that church. In 1799, he was called to the Great Valley as co-pastor with Rev. David Jones and, in 1800, he was appointed by the Philadelphia Association as the alternate of Dr. Staughton, to preach the Introductory Sermon before the Association. The Minutes for 1801 contain the following record, "Brother Boggs being about to remove

from the precincts of this Association, Brother Smalley is appointed to preach the sermon next year." He died in the year 1803, and the Minutes state that "The Rev. John Boggs, Sen., late of our Association, finished his course, in the 63rd year of his age, and in the 27th of his ministry." He had a son, John Boggs, Jr., who was a pastor in Delaware and also in New Jersey. The latter died at Hopewell, N. J., October 4, 1846, at the age of 76 years.*

6. The sixth Pastor, JENKIN DAVID, was born in 1753, in Pembrokeshire, Wales. In 1778 he was set apart for the ministry, studied at Bristol Academy, was a missionary to the Island of Anglesea, and there gathered a church. He came to America in 1794, and, in 1795 settled at the Valley and remained until 1798. In June, 1808, he became Pastor at Cape May, N. J., where he remained until 1822. He then went to South River, Middlesex County, N. J., where he died, June 23, 1834, in his 81st year.

7. The seventh Pastor, THOMAS ROBERTS, was born in Denbighshire, North Wales, Jun 10, 1783, came to America in 1803, and was co-pastor of the Valley Church with David Jones, from 1815 until Mr. Jones death, in 1820, and there remained until 1822, when he resigned and went as a missionary to Cherokee Indians, with Evan Jones and several other members of the Valley Church. He was Moderator of the Philadelphia Association in 1819, and wrote the Circular Letter in 1818. He afterwards was Pastor of the Middletown Church, in New Jersey. In August, 1845, he settled with the Lower Dublin Church, and remained until April, 1847. He died at Middletown, September 24, 1865, aged 84 years.

8. The eighth Pastor, THOMAS J. KITTS, was born in 1789, and in 1818, he appears as a licentiate of the First Church of Wilmington, Del. The same year he was chosen Clerk of Delaware Baptist Association. He began his pastoral labors at Canton, N. J., and also preached at Camden, N. J. In 1822 he became Pastor of the Valley and in 1823, was called to the Second Church of Philadelphia, which he served for fifteen years. He had few early advantages, but by steady and earnest application, he became tolerably versed in Latin, Greek and Hebrew. He was Clerk of the Association in

1827, and Moderator in 1828, and wrote the Circular Letter for 1833. He died at Philadelphia, January 24, 1838, aged 49 years.

9. The ninth Pastor, JOHN SHIVE JENKINS, was born February 11, 1789, in Gwynedd, Montomery County, Pa. He was baptized, in 1816, by Dr. Hough, of the Montgomery Church, and, in 1818, was licensed by that church. On the twenty-second of September, 1819, he was ordained as Pastor of the Lower Providence Church, to which he was called, March 20th, of that year. He remained 6 years and 6 months, and then took charge of the Valley Church, where he labored until 1828, when he returned to Lower Providence. He subsequently was Pastor of Hephzibah, West Caln and Piqua churches. In 1855, he took his letter to the Spring Garden Church. Mr. Jenkins was Clerk of the Association in 1824, and Moderator in 1836. He died in Philadelphia, October 31, 1865, in his 76th year. By his will, he left his residuary estate to the Association, and directed that it should be invested and income devoted to pay the incidental expenses of the Association. He also left generous legacies to the Home Mission, Grand Ligne Mission, Missionary Union, Bible Union, Pennsylvania Baptist State Convention, and the Spring Garden and Montgomery churches. Though dead, Bro. Jenkins yet speaks to us, for every year, we are reminded of his noble gift to the Association, the income of which pays all our incidental expenses.

10. The tenth Pastor, THOMAS BROWN, was born in Newark, N. J., November 1, 1779. He was a member of the Presbyterian Church, but after attaining his majority, his views on baptism changed, and he became a member of the Newark Baptist Church. On the 26th of March, 1803, he was licensed, and then entered the Academy of Dr. Samuel Jones at Pennepek, where he remained until 1805, when he was called to Salem, N. J. Early in 1806, he was ordained as pastor of the church there, and so continued until 1808, when he was called to Scotch Plains, one of the oldest churches in the State, and remained for about twenty years. In 1828, he became pastor of the Valley Church, and he entered on this field of labor with every prospect of success. But, after a pastorate of a little more than two years, he was laid aside from his beloved work, and died, January 17, 1831, in his fifty-second

year, honored and renowned as a sound and earnest divine.

11. The eleventh Pastor, LEONARD FLETCHER, was born in Lancaster, Worcester Co., Mass., in December, 1796. In 1810, his parents went to Washington County, N. Y. When twenty-three years of age, he began the study of law, in Philadelphia; but, after two years of study, his health failed, and he went to the South. While at a hotel, he took from a mantel-piece, a tract called "The Dairyman's Daughter," the reading of which led to his conversion, and he was baptized by the pastor of the Baptist Church at Newbern, N. C. Feeling called to preach the gospel, he placed himself under the Rev. William Staughton, D. D. , and entered Columbian College, D. C. His health again failed, and he left college and was ordained as pastor of the church at Salisbury, Md., where he labored successfully for three years. Then he settled in Sussex County, N. J., where his labors were greatly blessed. In 1832, he became pastor of the Great Valley, and remained for eight years. He was pastor at Hamilton, N. Y. for two years and then devoted himself to evangelistic work in the South. His last pastorate was at Penningtonville (now Atglen), Chester County, Pa. He died, August 16, 1859, in his sixty-third year, and his remains are interred in the Great Valley Baptist Cemetery.

12. The twelfth Pastor, CHARLES BRIGHT KEYES, was born, September 26, 1802, at Bennington, Vt., and was baptized November 7, 1819, at Portland, N. Y. Having, in his youth, lost his father, he did not receive any collegiate education; but, possessing more than ordinary talents, he felt called to preach the gospel, and he was duly licensed, May 26, 1827, and was ordained at North Adams, Mass., November 27, 1828. In the year 1837, he became pastor of the Third Church of Philadelphia, remained until 1839; in July, 1840, was called to the Valley to succeed Mr. Fletcher, and resigned, in March, 1845. He preached the Introductory Sermon of the Association, in October, 1840. He afterwards was pastor at Carmel, Putnam County, and North East, Dutchess County, N. Y. In 1852, he settled at Westfield, Chatauqua County, N. Y., which was his last pastorate. During the late civil war, Mr. Keyes was appointed Chaplain of the Ninth New York Cavalry, and proved himself to be a brave, fearless patriot. He was taken prisoner by

Moseby's* troops, in August, 1864, carried to Richmond, and sent to Libby Prison. While in prison, he preached as occasion offered. After his release, he returned to Westfield, and died there, March 6, 1869.

13. The thirteenth Pastor, JAMES FULLER BROWN, D. D., was born, July 4, 1819, at Scotch Plains, N. J., where his father, Rev. Thomas Brown, was pastor. In June, 1833, he was baptized, and united with the Fifth Church of Philadelphia. He afterwards united with the First Church, by which he was licensed, November 18, 1841. In July, 1841, he graduated at the University of Pennsylvania. In 1843, he was ordained as pastor of the church at Gainesville, Ala., and remained there until 1846, when he became pastor at the Great Valley. He remained at the Valley until 1854. He was Clerk of the Philadelphia Association for 1851 and 1852, and Moderator in 1853. He then became pastor at Scotch Plains, where his father also had been settled, and in the fall of 1860, he was called to the First Church of Bridgeton, N. J. Failing health, compelled him to resign, in 1878.

14. The fourteenth Pastor, GEORGE SPRATT, M. D., was born in Winchester, England, July 8, 1787. In 1811, he sailed for the East Indies as a medical missionary, but he was led to Quebec, Canada, where he labored as pastor of an "Independent" Church. Removing to Philadelphia, he then became a Baptist, and he was duly licensed and ordained. His first charge as a Baptist was the Church at Bridgeton, N. J. He then removed to Pennsylvania, and labored faithfully at Shamokin and with several churches in the northwestern part of the State of Pennsylvania, In 1854, he was called to the Valley, as successor to Dr. J. Fuller Brown, and he remained such until 1858, when growing infirmities compelled him to resign. In 1858, he preached the Introductory Sermon at the Philadelphia Association. Dr. Spratt died, January 28, 1863, in his seventy-sixth year and the fifty-third of his ministry.

[*John S. Mosby (1833-1916) - Editor]

15. The fifteenth Pastor, WILLIAM MANLOVE WHITEHEAD, A. M., M. D., was born in Philadelphia, December 12, 1823, and was baptized at the age of sixteen years. In 1844, he entered Madison University, N. Y., and went partly through the senior Collegiate year. He was ordained in 1850, and became pastor of the Beulah Church, Chester County. In 1852, he was called to the Frankford Church, where he labored with great success, and, in 1858, he was called to the Great Valley, as successor to the venerable Dr. Spratt. He found a large field to cultivate and worked with all his energy. But when the civil war began, he resigned his pastorate and entered the army as Chaplain of the 97th Reg. P. V., of which Col. Guss was the commander. He was commissioned November 19, 1861, and performed his duty with patriotic zeal. Exposure incident to army life injured his health, and he was reluctantly compelled to resign. He was honorably discharged, August 20, 1862. In April, 1863, he settled at McKeesport, Pa., and in 1866, at New Britain. Having studied medicine and graduated as a physician., in 1871, he settled as pastor at Woodbury, N. J., where, after months of suffering, he died, January 30, 1873.

16. The sixteenth Pastor, JAMES ELY WILSON, was born in Philadelphia, March 17, 1830; was baptized at Marlton, N. J., January 12, 1846; was licensed March 6, 1852, and pursued a regular course of study at the University at Lewisburg. He was then ordained as pastor of the Cape May Church, June 11, 1853, and remained there until 1858. He has also served as pastor of the churches at Milestown and Blockley, Pa., Haddonfield, N.J., and South Abington, Mass. In 1863, he became pastor at the Great Valley, and remained until 1865. During the late war, Mr. Wilson was a Chaplain in the Union Army. He is now settled at Woodstown, N. J.

17. The seventeenth Pastor, BUCKLEY CARLL MORSE, was born in Rahway, N. J., April 2, 1811. In February, 1826, he united with the First Presbyterian Church of that place, but, in 1833, his views about the mode of baptism having changed, he was baptized and united with the Rahway Baptist Church, by which he was licensed to preach. In 1838, he graduated at Madison University, and, on February 20, 1839, he was ordained and settled at Lyons Farms Church, in New Jersey. He afterwards served as

pastor of the following churches: Sing Sing, N. Y.; New Albany and Franklin, Indiana; Piqua, O.; Philadelphia and Montrose, Pa.; Somerville and Croton, N. J. He became pastor of the Great Valley Church in 1867 and remained until 1870. He died at Marlboro, N. J., April 29, 1876.

18. The eighteenth Pastor, JAMES HENRY HYATT, was born at Warwick, Orange County, N. Y., November 15, 1843; was partly educated at the Warwick Institute, N. Y. His parents were "Old-School Baptists." He was baptized March 19, 1865, and joined the Herbertsville Church. In 1865, he removed to Hightstown N. J., entered Peddie Institue, and graduated, in 1869, with the highest honors of his class. He was licensed by the Hightstown Church that year, settled with the Dividing Creek Church (N. J.) and was there ordained October 20, 1869. He became pastor of the Great Valley, September 28, 1870, and continued until September 2, 1873. He afterwards was pastor at Hephzibah, and is now at the Pequa Church, Lancaster County.

19. The nineteenth Pastor, GEORGE PIERCE, was born July 18, 1820, at Salem, Mass.; baptized by Dr. Banvard, in 1843, and joined the Second Church of Salem; was ordained at Salisbury, Mass., in 1846, and was pastor at Pawtuxet, R. I., from 1851 to 1857, and of the First Church in Manchester, N. H., from 1857 to 1865. Then he removed to Warren, Ohio, and was there until 1869, when he settled at Harrisburg, Pa., and remained until 1873. While at Harrisburg, he was appointed Chaplain of the House of Representatives. He served the Great Valley Church from April, 1873, until the fall of 1883, when he removed to Faribault, Minnesota.

20. The twentieth Pastor, JAMES MEMINGER GUTHRIE, was born April 10, 1845, in Shippenburg, Pa. He was educated at the Ohio Wesleyan University. During the late war, he served, in 1864-5, in the U. S. Navy, in the Mississippi Squadron. He was baptized, in 1870, by Rev. J. B. Tombes, D. D., at Delaware, O., and, in 1872, was licensed by the Chesterville Church. In 1876, he was graduated at Crozer Theological Seminary, and became Pastor of the Windsor Church. In 1881, he settled with the Berean Church at West Chester, and on the 5th of August, 1883, he accepted the call

of the Great Valley Church, and began his pastoral on August 12, 1883. In addition to his duties as pastor, Mr. Guthrie edits and publishes a monthly paper called "The Baptist Treasury."

"...TO SET THEM IN ORDER :"

SELECTED BIBLIOGRAPHY

A. BIBLIOGRAPHICAL SOURCES

A Baptist Bibliography. Being a Register of Printed Material By and About Baptists; Including Works Written Against the Baptists. Edited by Edward C. Starr. Vol. 1, Section A. Philadelphia: The Judson Press, 1947.

A Bibliographical Guide to the History of Christianity. Edited by S. J. Case, Chicago: The University of Chicago Press, 1931.

McGlothlin, J. W., *A Guide to the Study of Church History.* Louisville, Kentucky: Baptist World Publishing Co., 1908.

Mode, Peter G., *Source Book and Bibliographical Guide for American Church History.* Menasha, Wisconsin: George Banta Publishing Company, 1921.

B. PRIMARY SOURCES

A Compendium of the Minutes of the Warren Baptist Association From Its Formation in 1767 to the Year 1825, Inclusive.

A Confession of Faith Put Forth by the Elders and Brethren of Many Congregations of Christians (Baptized upon Profession of Their Faith) In London and the Country. Sixth Philadelphia edition. Philadelphia: Benjamin Franklin, 1743. (See Appendix I.)

A Confession of Faith Put Forth By the Elders and Brethren of Many Congregations of Christians, (Baptized upon Profession of Their Faith) In London and the Country. Second Charleston edition. Charleston, South Carolina: J. Hoff, 1813.

Allen, I. M., *The United States Baptist Annual Register for 1832.* Philadelphia: Printed by T. W. Ustick, 1833.

______, *The Triennial Baptist Register.* Philadelphia: Baptist General Tract Society, 1836.

Asplund, John, *The Annual Register of the Baptist Denomination in North America; To the First of November, 1790.* Southampton County, Virginia: 1791. [Facsimile Reprint by Church History Research and Archives, Gallatin, Tennessee, 1979.]

Biographical Memoirs of the Late Rev. John Gano of Frankfort (Kentucky) Formerly of the City of New York Written Principally by Himself. New York: Printed by Southwick and Hardcastle, 1806.

Edwards, Morgan, *Materials For a History of the Baptists in Rhode Island,* Vol. VI of *Collections of the Rhode Island Historical Society.* Edited by C. Edwin Barrows and James W. Willmarth. 10 vols. Providence, Rhode Island: Hammond, Angell & Co., 1867-93.

________, *Materials Towards a History of the Baptist in [New] Jersey.* Vol. II. of *Materials Towards a History of the American Baptists.* Philadelphia: Thomas Dobson, 1792. [Facsimile reprint by Regular Baptist Publishing, 1998.]

_________, *Materials Towards a History of the Baptists in Pennsylvania Both British and German.* Vol. I. of *Materials Towards a History of the American Baptists.* Philadelphia: Joseph Crukshank and Isaac Collins, 1770. [Facsimile reprint by Regular Baptist Publishing, 1998.]

Jones, Samuel, *A Treatise of Church Discipline, and a Directory.* Lexington: Printed by T. Anderson, 1805. (Photostatic Copy).

Minutes of the Late Meetings of the Baptist Education Society of the Middle States of America. Philadelphia; No Publisher, 1813.

Minutes of the Philadelphia Baptist Association, from A. D. 1707 to A. D. 1807; Being the First One Hundred years of Its Existence. Edited by A. D. Gillette. Philadelphia: American Baptist Publication Society, 1851. [Tricentennial Edition facsimile reprint with added material by Particular Baptist Press. Springfield, Missouri, 2001.]

Minutes of the Philadelphia Baptist Association 1788-1819.

Minutes of the Warren Association 26th-71st Annual Meetings 1795-1838.

Historical Collections Relating to the American Colonial Church. Edited by William Stevens Perry. 5 Vols. Hartford, Connecticut: The Church Press.

Semple, Robert B., *A History of the Rise and Progress of the Baptists in Virginia.* Richmond, Virginia: John O'Lynch, 1810.

Sweet, William Warren, *Religion on the Frontier: The Baptists.* Chicago: The University of Chicago Press, 1931.

The Baptist Annual Register. Edited by John Rippon. 4 vols. London: 1790-1802.

The Diary of John Comer, Vol. VIII of *Collections of the Rhode Island Historical Society.* Edited by C. Edwin Barrows and James W. Willmarth. 10 vols. Providence, Rhode Island: Hammond, Angell & Co., 1867-93. [Reprinted in *An Anthology of Early Baptists in Rhode Island* by Particular Baptist Press, Springfield, Missouri, 2001 .]

The First Annual Report of the Baptist Board of Foreign Missions for the United States. Philadelphia: William Fry, 1815.

The Journals of Henry Melchoir Muhlenberg. Translated by Theodore G. Tappert and John W. Doberstein. 2 vols. Philadelphia: The Muhlenberg Press, 1942, 1945.

The Writings of the Late Elder John Leland, Including Some Events in His Life, Written by Himself with Additional Sketches. Edited by Miss L. F. Greene. New York: G. W. Wood, 1845. [Facsimile reprint by Church History Research and Archives, Gallatin, Tennessee, 1986.]

Winchester, Elhanan, *The Universal Restoration Exhibited in Four Dialogues Between a Minister and His Friend.* Bellows Falls, Vermont: Bill Blake & Co., 1819.

C. WORKS WITH PRIMARY SOURCES

Backus, Isaac, *A History of New England With Particular Reference to the Denomination of Christians Called Baptists.* 2 vols. Newton, Massachusetts: Published by the Backus Historical Society, 1871.

Benedict, David, *A General History of the Baptist Denomination in America, and Other Parts of the World.* 2 vols. Boston: Manning & Loring, 1813. [Facsimile reprint with added index by Church History Research and Archives, Gallatin, Tennessee, 1985.]

____________, *A General History of the Baptist Denomination in America, and Other Parts of the World.* Abridged and revised. New York: Lewis Colby and Company, 1848.

__________, *Fifty Years Among the Baptists.* New York: Sheldon & Company, 1860. [Facsimile Reprint by the Baptist Republication Society, Nappanee, Indiana, n.d.]

Burkitt, Lemuel and Read, Jesse, *A Concise History of the Kehukee Baptist Association, From its Original Rise to the Present Time.* Halifax, North Carolina: A. Hodge, 1803.

_____________, *A Concise History of the Kehukee Association From Its Original Rise to the Present Time.* Revised and Improved by Henry L. Burkitt (Philadelphia: Lippincott, Grambo and Co., 1850). [Facsimile reprint by Arno Press, New York, 1980.]

Cox, F. A. and Hoby, J., *The Baptists in America; A Narrative of the Deputation from the Baptist Union in England, to the United States and Canada.* New York: Leavitt, Lord & Co., 1836.

Cutting, Sewell S., *Historical Vindications: A Discourse on the Province and Uses of Baptist History, with Appendixes. Containing Historical Notes and Confessions of Faith.* Boston: Gould and Lincoln, 1859.

Extracts from the Itineraries and Other Miscellanies of Ezra Stiles 1755-1794 with a Selection from His Correspondence. Edited by Franklin Bowditch Dexter. New Haven, Yale University Press, 1916.

Fristoe, William, *A Concise History of the Ketocton Baptist Association.* Staunton, Virginia: William Gilman Lyford, 1808. [Facsimile reprint in *An Anthology of the Early Baptists in Virginia,* Particular Baptist Press, Springfield, Missouri, 2001.]

Furman, Wood, *A History of the Charleston Association of Baptist Churches in the State of South Carolina.* Charleston, South Carolina: J. Hoff, 1811.

Guild, Reuben A., *Chaplain Smith and the Baptists, or Life, Journals, Letters, and Addresses of the Rev. Hezekiah Smith, D. D. of Haverhill, Massachusetts.* Philadelphia: American Baptist Publication Society, 1885.

Guild, Reuben Aldridge, *History of Brown University with Illustrative Documents.* Providence, Rhode Island: Providence Press Company, 1867.

__________, *Life, Times, and Correspondence of James Manning and the Early History of Brown University.* Boston: Gould and Lincoln, 1864. [Facsimile reprint by Arno Press, 1980, of the 1897 edition retitled, *Early History of Brown University, Including the Life, Times, and Correspondence of President Manning, 1756-1791.*]

McGlothlin, W. J., *Baptist Confessions of Faith.* Philadelphia: American Baptist Publication Society, 1911.

Mercer, Jesse, *History of the Georgia Baptist Association.* Washington, Georgia: No Publisher, 1838. [Facsimile reprint by the Georgia Baptist Association, Washington, Georgia, 1980.]

Purefoy, George W., *A History of the Sandy Creek Baptist Association from Its Organization in A. D. 1758 to A. D. 1858.* New York: Sheldon & Co., Publishers, 1859. [Facsimile reprint by Arno Press, New York, 1980.]

Semple, Robert B., *History of the Rise and Progress of the Baptists in Virginia.* Edited by G. W. Beale. Richmond, Virginia: Pitt & Dickinson, 1894. [Facsimile reprint by Church History Research and Archives, Gallatin, Tennessee, 1976.]

Sheppard, Daniel, *Baptist Confession of Faith: and a Summary of Church Discipline.* Charleston, South Carolina: Printed by W. Riley, 1831.

Spencer, David, *The Early Baptists of Philadelphia.* Philadelphia: William Syckelmoore, 1877. [Facsimile reprint by New Philadelphia Baptist Historical Preservation Society, n.p.n.d.; printed in Benton, Arkansas.]

Sprague, William B., *Annals of the American Pulpit.* Vol. VI. Baptists. 9 vols. New York: Robert Carter & Brothers, 1860. [Facsimile reprint by Arno Press, New York, 1969.]

Staples, William R., *Annals of the Town of Providence, from Its First Settlement, to the Organization of the City Government, in June, 1832.* Providence, Rhode Island: printed by Knowles and Vose, 1843.

The Life of the Rev. James Ireland, Who was, for Many years Pastor of the Baptist Church at Buck Marsh, Waterlick and Happy Creek, in Frederick and Shenandoah Counties, Virginia. Winchester, Virginia: J. Foster, 1819.

Wright, Stephen, *History of the Shaftsbury Baptist Association From 1781 to 1853.* Troy, New York: A. G. Johnson, Steam Press Printer, 1853.

D. SECONDARY SOURCES

Alexander, Archibald, *Biographical Sketches of the Founder, and Principal Alumni of the Log College.* Princeton, New Jersey: J. T. Robinson, 1845. [Facsimile reprint by Banner of Truth Trust, London; Billing & Sons, 1968.]

Armitage, Thomas, *A History of the Baptists.* New York: Bryan, Taylor & Co., 1887. [Reprinted by James and Klock Christian Publishing Co., Minneapolis, Minnesota, 1977; and others.]

Backus, Isaac, *Church History of New England, from 1620 to 1804.* Philadelphia: Baptist Tract Depository, 1830.

Christian, John T., *A History of the Baptists of the United States.* Vol. II. Nashville, Tennessee: Broadman Press, 1945.

Cone, Edward W. and Spencer W., *Some Account of the Life of Spencer Houghton Cone; A Baptist Preacher in America.* New York: Livermore & Rudd, 1856.

Cook, Richard B., *The Early and Later Delaware Baptists.* Philadelphia: American Baptist Publication Society, 1860.

Davis, Jonathan, *History of the Welsh Baptists From the Year Sixty-Three to the Year One Thousand Seven Hundred and Seventy.* Pittsburgh: D. M. Hogan, 1835.

Gewehr, Wesley, M., *The Great Awakening in Virginia, 1740-1790.* Durham, North Carolina: Duke University Press, 1930.

Hovey, Alvah, *A Memoir of the Life and Times of the Rev. Issac Backus.* A. M. Boston: Gould and Lincoln, 1859. [Facsimile reprint by Gano Books, Harrisonburg, Virginia, 1991.]

Howell, Robert Boyle C., *The Early Baptists of Virginia.* Philadelphia: The Bible and Publication Society, 1857. [An adaptation taken from chapters 2, 3 and 4 of Howell's work was also printed in *The Baptists and the National Centenary. A Record of Christian Work, 1776-1876,* edited by Lemuel Moss. (Philadelphia: A.B.P.S., 1876), pp. 27-48.]

Kirtley, J. A., *History of Bullittsburg Church, with Biographies of Elders Absalom Graves, Chichester Matthews, James Dicken and Robert Kirtley.* Covington, Kentucky: Printed by Davis, 1872.

Little, Lewis Payton, *Imprisoned Preacher and Religious Liberty in Virginia.* Lynchburg, Virginia: J. R. Bell Co., Inc., 1938. [Reprinted by Church History Research and Archives, Gallatin, Tennessee, 1987.]

Morison, Samuel Eliot, *Three Centuries of Harvard 1636-1936.* Cambridge, Massachusetts: Harvard University Press, 1936.

Newman, Albert Henry, *A History of the Baptists in the United States.* Sixth edition. Philadelphia: American Baptist Publication Society, 1915.

Riley, B. F., *A History of the Baptists in the Southern States East of the Mississippi.* Philadelphia: American Baptists Publication Society, 1898.

Sweet, William Warren, *Religion in Colonial America.* New York: Charles Scribner's Sons, 1942.

__________, *The Story of Religion in America.* New York: Harper & Brothers, Publishers, 1939.

Taylor, James B., *Lives of Virginia Baptist Ministers.* Richmond, Virginia: Yale & Wyatt, 1837.

Torbet, Robert G., *A Social History of the Philadelphia Baptist Association: 1707-1940.* Philadelphia: Westbrook Publishing Company, 1944.

Tupper, H. A., editor, *Two Centuries of the First Baptist Church of South Carolina, 1683-1883.* Baltimore: R. H. Woodward and company, 1889. [See also the more recent work by Robert A. Baker and Paul J. Craven, Jr., *Adventure in Faith: The First 300 Years of First Baptist Church, Charleston, South Carolina.* (Nashville, Tennessee: Broadman Press, 1982.]

Tustin, Josiah P., *A Discourse Delivered at the Dedication of the New Church Edifice of the Baptist Church and Society in Warren, R. I.* Providence, Rhode Island: H. H. Brown, 1845.

Vedder, Henry C., *A History of the Baptists in the Middle States.* Philadelphia: American Baptist Publication Society, 1898.

________, *A Short History of the Baptists.* Philadelphia: The American Baptist Publication Society, 1941.

Williams, Charles B., *A History of the Baptists in North Carolina.* Raleigh, North Carolina: Edwards & Broughton, 1901.

E. MAGAZINE ARTICLES

"American Baptists," *The Baptist Magazine* (London), 1809.

Broadus, John A., "American Baptist Ministry 100 Years Ago," *The Baptist Quarterly,* IX (January, 1875).

Guild, Reuben A., "Charter of Brown University," *The Baptist Quarterly,* IX (April, 1875).

___________, "The Denominational Work of President Manning," *The Baptist Review,* III (January, 1881).

King, Henry M., "Education Among the Baptists of This Country During the Last Hundred Years, *The Baptist Quarterly,* X (October, 1876).

Knowles, James D., editor, "Ministerial Education," *The Christian Review,* II (June, 1837).

Paschal, G. W., "Shubal Stearns," *The Review and Expositor,* XXXVI (January, 1939).

Ulyst, W. C., "The Orators of the Baptist—William Staughton," *Ford's Christian Repository,* XXXVII (May, 1884).

Index

A

B

C

Index

D

Index

F

G

Index

H

Index

I

Index

J

K

L

N

O

P

Q

R

Index

S

Index

Y

Actual citations of works listed in the text by Horatio Gates Jones:

Other Publications

The Life and Works of Joseph Kinghorn
edited by Mr. Terry Wolever
(in four volumes)

The Life and Ministry of John Gano
by Terry Wolever

The Annual Register of Indian Affairs
by Isaac McCoy

The British Particular Baptists
edited by Dr. Michael Haykin
(in three volumes)

Early Indian Missions:
as Reflected in the Unpublished
Manuscripts of Isaac McCoy
by Dr. Edward Roustio

The Three Mrs. Judsons
(second revised and expanded edition)
Arabella Stuart

A Noble Company:
Biographical Sketches of Notable
Particular-Regular Baptists in America
edited by Terry Wolever
(a multi-volume set)

Minutes of the Philadelphia Baptist Association 1707 - 1807
edited by A. D. Gillette, in a new and expanded *Tricentennial Edition, 1707 - 2007*. Includes a complete index of persons and complete index of churches. Illustrated

An Anthology of Early Baptists in New Hampshire

An Anthology of Early Baptists in Rhode Island

Forthcoming Publications

An Anthology of Early Baptists in Virginia

An Anthology of Early Baptists in South Carolina

The Life and Ministry of Hezekiah Smith
(two volumes)
by John David Broome